Sharing a Glass

Inspirational Memoirs & Memories
of the Women Who Shaped Ontario's
Grape & Wine Industry

Jennifer Wilhelm

 FriesenPress

One Printers Way
Altona, MB R0G 0B0
Canada

www.friesenpress.com

Copyright © 2024 by Jennifer Wilhelm
First Edition — 2024

Elena Galey-Pride – Editor

Cover Photography by Nataschia Wielink

All rights reserved.

No part of this publication may be reproduced in any form, or by any means, electronic or mechanical, including photocopying, recording, or any information browsing, storage, or retrieval system, without permission in writing from FriesenPress.

ISBN
978-1-03-919388-8 (Hardcover)
978-1-03-919387-1 (Paperback)
978-1-03-919389-5 (eBook)

Social Science, Women's Studies

Distributed to the trade by The Ingram Book Company

*Dedicated to the women.
To those who appear in these pages,
to those who don't but should,
and to those who continue to fill our cups
as we move through life.
We raise our glasses to you with gratitude.*

Table of Contents

Foreword 7
The Importance of Storytelling 9
Setting the Scene: The Magic Begins for the Author 11
Debi Pratt 23
Tributes to Debi Pratt 56
Dr. Helen Fisher 63
Tributes to Dr. Helen Fisher 80
Donna Lailey 87
Tributes to Donna Lailey 113
Dr. Linda Bramble 117
Tributes to Linda Bramble 128
Debbie Zimmerman 137
Tributes to Debbie Zimmerman 151
Ann Sperling 161
Tributes to Ann Sperling 178
Barbara Leslie 185
Tributes to Barbara Leslie 195
Nicolette Novak 203
Tributes to Nicolette Novak 225
Madame Andrée Bosc 233
Tributes to Madame Bosc 236
Afterword 241
PostScript by Author 251

Note: Tributes have been edited for brevity and clarity

Foreword

It is an immense honour that the first words you read in this important book should be mine. When Jenn first hatched the idea to put together a book about the women who blazed the trail in the Ontario wine industry, I was excited for her and the path ahead of her to get this book off the ground. I listened, I counselled, I clarified, and I even cajoled a little as the plans for the book took shape. I feel that I've been with Jenn throughout this endeavour, albeit sometimes only in spirit, but always with spirit! When Jenn came up for air after compiling the main elements of this manuscript, my involvement became much more corporeal. I took on the task of reading and reviewing the drafts to shape and structure them for your reading enjoyment and to best honour the subjects.

What I learned along the way was astonishing. I thought I already knew most of these women. But Jenn's conversations and research have revealed a fascinating, deeper level of understanding about their lives and their drives. There is so much here to inspire, to sustain, to inform, and even to caution those of us working in this industry today. And my hope is that it will be especially thought-provoking for women entering the industry now.

By the time you are reading this, I'll be completing my twenty-fifth year in the wine industry. And that's a second career after starting out in public relations and marketing. OK, so maybe not exactly a career change, but it definitely was a new career focus. It was wine and wine growing that attracted me, but it was the people who kept me here. I very quickly learned that wine people are fascinating—and philosophical, driven, quirky and above all, generous. (I'm with Clifton Fadiman, who said, "I've never met a miserly wine lover.")

At one time, my fascination with the people of wine led me to think I would like to write a column about all manner of personalities in this business. I thought to call it "Purple People"—people whose lives were stained, whether by grape juice, wine, or ink. And while that project has not manifested for me (yet), it is very apt and gratifying to have played a role in manifesting this book of Jenn's.

To the women of this book, thank you. I've learned something from each of you. I even see a little bit of each of you in me.

To the women who are not in the book, I see you, too. Some of you declined to be profiled, some of you choose to keep a low profile, and some of you are newer to the stage. Your contributions have no less value.

And to the women who are just starting out in our industry, regardless of your role in it, please consider that the while the trail has been blazed, there are still miles and miles to go and so much left for you to achieve. Raise a glass to those who came before and embrace your sisters who travel with you.

Elena Galey-Pride
Winestains.ca

The Importance of Storytelling

The sharing of stories has always been an important part of evolution within societies. Storytelling is a means of passing down lessons, wisdom, values, and knowledge. Well-told stories incite passion, excitement, motivation, and courage. Storytelling reveals to us what can be done and provides us with role models who demonstrate exceptional character traits that listeners can aspire to cultivate. Storytelling celebrates and fosters leadership, conscientiousness, and the value and power of working together in pursuit of a common goal. In the most inspiring stories, a hero or heroine faces challenges and setbacks, wrestles with their emotions, and ultimately succeeds in their quest. We cheer for them, we celebrate them, we see parallels in our own lives and feel inspired to follow our dreams, to be more, to do more, to contribute more, to strive to be our best and to never settle for less. The significance of the lesson is found in the journey. Consequently, we are stronger and wiser for knowing these stories.

There are books that tell the stories of the men who forged the Ontario wine industry, remarkable men who absolutely warrant our respect, admiration, and eternal gratitude for their tireless efforts. Too little has been written, however, about the incredible women who worked and still work in this realm. Unsung heroines juggling families, children, homes, farms, and the endless daily tasks that make life and communities sustainable—all while planting and tending vineyards, affecting change through politics, lobbying for new laws and government assistance for growers, developing brilliant business plans, pouring their passions into winemaking, keenly marketing our wines, and strategically building world-class experiences in Ontario wine country.

These women entered the grape and wine industry at a time when it was not seen as the glamourous, trendy business often depicted today. Rather, it was a hardscrabble agricultural industry with complex barriers. These extraordinary women were up against challenges and obstacles that many would have seen as insurmountable. They were undeterred. They had a vision for what could be, and they were committed to making that vision a reality. They dug in their heels and did not stop until that vision was achieved, and then they continued to raise the bar and push for constant excellence and progress. They built alliances and communities and made it a point to mentor others. The Ontario wine industry is full of these remarkable women and their inspiring stories of strength, courage, resilience, and grace under pressure. Their fiery determination has ignited sparks in us, and we must fan those flames and honour their legacy by keeping their blazing visions a reality.

These are women our young people can and should look to as role models. Women who show us that we can scale mountains and should indeed aspire to achieve anything we dream possible. Those who have made it a personal practice to lead by example and lift up the people around them as they rise. The women who teach us to find growth in the journey and who share with us their experiences so that we may be inspired to be resilient, innovative, and live to our fullest potential.

This is a compilation of some of their powerful stories, insights, and words of wisdom. The narratives that exist between the better-known facts, dates, and awards; it's an attempt to gather the intricate pieces of their lives, complete with dreams, doubts, triumphs, and tribulations. A glimpse into their minds and hearts to understand what fuelled their fires through life's storms and forged them into difference makers.

Setting the Scene: The Magic Begins for the Author

It was 1999 when I first felt the magic of being a part of a community so powerful and awe-inspiring that it profoundly changed the way I looked at life and my hometown. I was working in hospitality in Niagara, Ontario, at a time when the farm-to-table movement and focus on local food and wine were making the exciting and long overdue shift away from stuffy, starched linen dining rooms with British and French-inspired cuisine. Passionate chefs were connecting with dedicated farmers and grape growers. They were collectively and unapologetically announcing that this piece of the world we were so blessed to live and work in had its own unique and wondrous gifts to offer. It was a time of discovery, of getting back to our roots, and celebrating the bounty of our own harvest.

We were (and still are) surrounded by abundance: sweet cherries, pears, and peaches so ripe that the juice ran between our fingers and down our arms when we bit into them. People were foraging for local treasures like paw paw fruit from the nearby band of Carolinian forest (with the request from growers to please save and return the seeds!). Small-scale farmers were seeing demand for their produce and joining the ranks of rock-star chef status with their names on the best restaurant menus. Something big was happening here; you could feel it. Everyone was excited and wanted to be a part of it.

Sipping wine, dining out, and indulging in posh meals were not part of my childhood or teenage years, and hospitality was certainly not an industry I expected to build my profession around. The women in my family were nurses, accountants, or teachers. None of those careers appealed to me. In my final years of high school, I struggled to find a post-secondary program that genuinely caught my interest. I took advantage of an intensive four-day personality and skills assessment that was meant to align me with a university program and career best suited to me. All results pointed to a service industry: hospitality, tourism, restaurants, or food nutrition.

I enrolled in the Hotel and Restaurant Management program at Niagara College, thinking that it would give me a taste of each. As I had hoped, we students were exposed to many facets of the business. I donned the apron, white coat, and hat with one hundred folds—to represent the one hundred ways in which an accomplished chef should be able to prepare an egg. Upon learning that fact, I remember standing in the culinary lab, silently counting on my fingers the limited ways I knew how to prepare an egg... fried, boiled, scrambled, poached. Four. I could prepare an egg in four ways. I had a lot to learn. In the meantime, I was full of awe and admiration and intoxicated by the endless aromas and flavours swirling around me.

In my years, ambitious students like me clamoured for the attention of visiting chefs and many of us were happy to work unpaid stages. To us, it was a valuable opportunity to learn by proximity to their greatness. These chefs were akin to rock stars, holding status in our circle long before the Food Network glorified the profession. We were encouraged to purchase subscriptions to the best food magazines of the time, and while famous and upcoming chefs were highlighted in these glossy pages, it was made unequivocally clear that quality ingredients were key and to be sought out and purchased at all costs whenever possible. One of these ingredients was wine, not only to be used in the preparation of the dish, but also as a carefully chosen accompaniment. As foreign to me then as truffles and saffron, I was nonetheless expected to be knowledgeable about all components of a fine meal—and that included wine.

SHARING A GLASS

In addition to culinary labs and theory classes, students in this hospitality program were required to work shifts in the college restaurant, both in preparation of food and service. We welcomed guests, spoke with them about our program, and the Niagara Region, and guided them through the daily menu and beverage options. Patrons knew we were students, and they were patient, tolerant with our wobbly service, and usually genuinely interested in what we were learning. It was the perfect environment for us to practise our new skills and build confidence. I discovered that I enjoyed service: I loved talking about food and the exciting things happening in Niagara. I signed up for as many shifts as I could and was soon promoted to dining room supervisor, a coveted role given to students showing professional promise and leadership.

Until this point, neither science nor geography had ever been my strong suit. So, when I entered my first wine class, I was immediately intimidated by the map covered walls. Our teacher was Albert Cipryk, a talented and dedicated chef professor, and knowledgeable wine connoisseur. He was well travelled, regularly following his appetite and thirst around the globe. always returning to pour those passions into his students, through stories, recounted experiences, thoughtfully prepared dishes, and his liquid love—wine.

I anxiously approached Albert at the end of the first class and shared my concerns: I hadn't travelled, my family didn't drink much wine, and I struggled with science and geography, never mind foreign languages. Did I have even a remote chance of succeeding in this class and industry? I asked with furrowed brow. He kindly put my concerns to rest and suggested that I throw myself into every opportunity available to taste wine, and wine with food, to meet chefs, winemakers, growers, and sommeliers. Sommeliers? Another term new to me. I couldn't have imagined then the depth and breadth of what I would need to know in the very near future.

I was attending college on an academic scholarship, generously awarded to me by the Branscombe Family Foundation. This privilege came with a fair expectation of academic achievement. Thus far, I had met those expectations. Consequently, it was quite alarming to me that I should be so challenged by what I had naively thought of, until that point, as fermented grape juice. Once again, I had a lot to learn!

JENNIFER WILHELM

I took my professor's wise advice and volunteered for every Showcase of Chefs event he organized. I followed the brigade of white-coated chefs and fell in line with the other servers standing at attention awaiting the order to "pick up." I was introduced to the magic that occurs when food and wine elevate one another, to passionate winemakers and the excitement of the burgeoning Niagara wine industry. The pride with which each course was prepared and presented was tangible. I looked on as guests relished each bite and sip, exclaiming to one another about the pairing. At the end of each service, front and back of house came together to jubilantly celebrate the joint triumph, each recognizing that such a success is not possible without the other and understanding that respect is an essential part of the most effective teams. Night after night, backs were clapped, glasses were raised, and toasts were made to a well-executed event. We students were high on this small taste of success, and full of optimism for our future in an industry and a region to which we were, from that point on, fully and enthusiastically committed.

The summer after graduation, I worked three jobs, not just because I needed to make ends meet but also because each job was so different, and I wasn't yet sure where my place in this industry would lie. A posh, upscale hotel in Niagara-on-the-Lake was my bread and butter. As a young server, I was learning a lot there about etiquette and technique. I was also exposed to a lifestyle far beyond my means and egos beyond my imagination. This was a realm in which chefs were near gods, revered and never questioned, no matter how tyrannically they behaved. This was a world of "work hard, play hard."

Fine wine and fabulous food were an expected part of every gathering. Everything was accessible and in excess. Guests spent considerable money and the most professional servers had the opportunity to earn what, to me as a young single parent, was life-sustaining income. I was surrounded by extensive and lavish buffets, exotic fruit, tiered dessert carts, and free-flowing libations, while in my personal life, I was frugally shopping clearance racks and clipping grocery coupons. The dichotomy was mind-boggling and not lost on me. I often felt like Alice in Wonderland, having stumbled into an alternative and foreign reality, complete with fine porcelain and outlandish characters dressed in elegant attire.

To sell these exquisite dishes and wines, it was imperative that we servers were able to speak knowledgeably and genuinely about them. We were privileged to work in an establishment and with chefs and sommeliers who understood that to do this well, we had to taste and experience each offering, from amuse bouche to dessert. How else could we upsell a menu or wine, or answer the many questions of guests? A privilege yes, but one that required diligence and unflinching deference. We would stand at the pass before picking up the piping-hot plates (we used to joke that we had all had our fingerprints burnt off!). Prior to leaving the kitchen, we would recite back to the chefs exactly what each component was in exactly the way it was to be presented to guest. The plate itself was more than just for transportation, it was a canvas for their creative genius and to be treated as such. We were to think of this canvas as a clock and if instructed to place the plate in front of the diner with the meat at six o'clock, it would be presented so. Yes, Chef!

The world of wine itself was still quite new to me. I found the seasoned servers and sommeliers intimidating. I lived in fear of setting in the wrong varietal stemware or, heaven forbid, breaking the delicate crystal. I recall standing tableside and being asked to recommend wine to match specific courses. I would break out in a cold sweat, trying desperately to remember "the rules" I had been taught about wine pairing. I signed out very heavy books from the library and would will the pages to come to mind whenever I was asked for "my" opinion. If the sauce has mint... Oh but if the poultry is dark meat, rather than white... Ah, the stakes seemed so high when guest expectations (and my tips!) were on the line!

Some people view their time in hospitality as a transition period, a means to an end between school and entering their chosen career. But for those of us who caught the fire and felt the passion, we knew that we were hooked.

Of the restaurant industry at that time, I think often of the parallels my young self drew to Alice in Wonderland, specifically of a quote by the Mad Hatter in the Tim Burton movie version: "There is a place, like no place on earth. A land full of wonder, mystery, and danger. Some say, to survive it, you need to be mad as a hatter." At another point, he asks Alice

"Have I gone mad?" to which she replies, "I'm afraid so. You're entirely bonkers. But I'll tell you a secret. All the best people are."

Those who challenge the norm and refuse to accept status quo are often seen as bonkers by others. However, without these visionaries, inventors, and change makers, we would still be living in the dark. Quite literally. The restaurant, hospitality, tourism, and grape and wine industry are full of creative, innovative people who can see a different perspective, a new way forward. Despite the naysayers, these extraordinary individuals continually forge a new path for the rest of us to follow and our industry to thrive.

Summer in Niagara's hospitality industry was, and is, a time to work, and jobs were plentiful for those willing to work hard. In the summer of 1998, in between shifts at the Niagara-on-the-Lake hotel, I worked in the restaurant at Walter's Estates. At that time, it was a small family owned winery perched at the end of a bucolic drive down Locust Lane in Beamsville. It was peaceful there in the vineyards and the view from the restaurant windows encouraged one to just breathe, relax, and soak up the moment. A tiny cottage was nestled into the side of a large pond and the sunlight reflected back onto the vines. It was common to see hawks soaring above, coasting on the air currents, and the occasional deer or fox would make an appearance to dip its head for a drink at the pond's edge. It was a world away from the black tie, celebrity-studded, Champagne-flowing galas at the fancy hotel. I fell under the spell of this beautiful place.

In this unpretentious setting, I was able to begin to explore the world of wine in an unhurried manner with no intimidating sommeliers sniffing that I had set in the wrong wine glasses. Rather than coming from far off places with names and producers I couldn't pronounce, these wines had a connection to the land we stood on and were made by the people who were standing on that very land, here in front of me, and happy to talk with me about what they had created. In addition to small-batch wines, the winery sold juice to home winemakers. It wasn't uncommon for these customers to congregate in the winery or on the veranda to exchange fermentation tips or winemaking techniques. I began to develop the knowledge and confidence to speak with guests about wine, the story behind it, and even to suggest appropriate food pairings.

SHARING A GLASS

In the year I was there, the winery changed ownership and became the newly named EastDell Estate, after its owners Michael East and Susan O'Dell. They had big plans to take the business to the next level. As much as I loved the winery, it was a long drive to work a lunch shift there between a breakfast-dinner split at the hotel, so when an offer came to join a new restaurant in St. Catharines, I said goodbye to the tiny winery. But not to my newfound love of wine.

In 1998, fine dining in downtown St. Catharines consisted of either the established, formal, and old school Blue Mermaid Seafood & Steak House or the tastefully upscale and regionally focused Wellington Court Café. Newcomer Kristin Tupper wanted to bring a third option to the area. A talented young chef from Nova Scotia, Kristin had a vison to offer fine cuisine from a chalk-board menu in a bright Provençal inspired setting.

Like the other chefs I had worked with, Kristin was imposing, driven, and passionate. She was also kind and personable and, oftentimes, a one-woman show, very different from the brigades of chefs with assigned stations and roles that I was used to. Kristin could and literally did do it all. She had studied business in university before completing culinary school and managed her company herself—when she wasn't planning and preparing delectable dishes for her guests and lucky staff members.

I was in awe of this woman. As word of the talented female chef spread, the restaurant, simply named Kristin's, garnered much attention and many regulars. As the new kid on the block, it wasn't uncommon to see diners lined up down the street. I loved the personal atmosphere, small team, and excitement of being part of something new. I was only working part-time shifts at Kristin's, scheduling around my full-time job in Niagara-on-the-Lake. But living in St. Catharines, I appreciated the proximity to her restaurant.

Kristin and I worked well together. After six months, she offered me the position of dining room manager and I happily accepted. Task one she said, was to update the wine list. Although I had been eagerly exploring the world of wine, I was unprepared for this challenge; I certainly didn't know enough to create an impressive list! Ever supportive, Kristin offered me what would later become known in my mind as The Golden Ticket, the opportunity to take a wine class for which she would pay half if I passed. Putting my past uncertainties aside, I immediately jumped at this chance to study what I had since learned was more than just fermented juice. Back to Niagara College I went to immerse myself in the world of wine.

This was one of the first formal night classes offered in wine education at that time. Well-appointed sensory labs were just being built. In the meantime, I found myself in the greenhouse at Niagara College with other knowledge-thirsty industry professionals, learning about the renowned wine regions of the world and their respective grape varieties. Far off regions with names and grapes I could barely pronounce. Compared to those well established and regulated countries, our little Niagara was just a fledgling! What I was realizing however, was that while it may still have been in its infancy, there were people here with a powerful vision, loads of talent, and iron-clad determination and tenacity. The class was small, and my fellow students consisted of Liquor Control Board of Ontario (LCBO) product consultants and local winery owners and managers. I was intimidated, but we were all there with a common goal, to learn about wine and to help put the Niagara Region on the world wine map.

Back at the restaurant, I began to tentatively stretch my wings and craft the small wine list. Fortunately for me, this timing coincided with a new magazine publication called *VINES*. Co-founder, editor, and contributing writer Christopher Waters poured his passion and knowledge into those pages with a focus on local producers and happenings. Through these articles, I began to feel like I knew the people behind the wineries. I followed their stories and celebrated their progress and successes. Christopher included in the magazine a section in which both local and international wines were reviewed and recommended. I felt like I had found a pot of gold! Excitedly, I began purchasing and tasting the top-scoring wines and visiting the wineries. I got to know the sales reps and to hear firsthand what was happening in the industry.

Although we were still years away from a full Vintners Quality Alliance (VQA) wine list, a few leading-edge restaurants were beginning to proudly replace some international wines with premium home-grown selections and enthusiastically urging guests to try them. In fact, the *Vintners Quality Alliance Act* was passed that very year, in June 1999, with the purpose to establish and maintain an appellation of origin system for VQA wine that would allow consumers to identify these wines on the basis of the areas where the grapes are grown, and to feel assured that wines bearing the VQA designation met high standards with regard to winemaking and the methods used in making the wine. It was exciting to present these wines to visitors and diners, to point out the grape-growing appellation on the labels, explaining that VQA was a guarantee that the wine was made from 100 per cent Ontario-grown grapes. I loved sharing with diners the stories of the passionate people behind the formation of the VQA, and how it was modelled after the world's most respected wine-producing countries.

While opening the bottle, I would personalize the wine to receptive guests by telling them about the producer and encouraging them to visit and meet the growers and winemakers themselves, (Thanks to *VINES* magazine for having done just that for its readers in every issue). Many folks hadn't been exposed to very much Ontario wine and some didn't even know we made it! So, it was exciting to share bits of history with them: "Did you know that in 1974 Inniskillin was granted the first new winery licence since 1916 Prohibition? Yes, you can visit the winery and taste the wines! They love welcoming visitors. Make sure to taste the Icewine if you go. It was named best wine in the world at Vinexpo!" That always got their attention and opened up opportunities for further conversation.

There were skeptics, of course, who were shocked that we could grow grapes to produce fine wine here. To my own great surprise, I suddenly found geography interesting! At least as it pertained to grape growing in the Niagara Peninsula. I loved to share details of our unique terroir, of the effects of the escarpment and Lake Ontario in protecting the grape vines in the spring by delaying budbreak with cool breezes from the lake which moved over the vineyards and blew back after meeting the escarpment. In the fall, those same breezes, now full of warm air, lengthen our season, allowing our grapes to reach optimal ripeness. Our soils are diverse and provide a range of conditions suited to a wide variety of grapes. The more I learned about grape growing, winemaking, and the people behind both, the more I wanted to learn and share.

It was a transformative feeling to be bursting with pride for my hometown, and the passionate people (farmers, grape growers, winemakers, chefs alike!) who were changing the narrative of Niagara and putting us on the map as a special place to seek out. "Local" was the buzzword and Niagara felt like the land of opportunity and talent.

Another happy shift that was happening here at that time was the emergence and rise of spectacular female chefs. In 1999, the culinary industry was largely dominated by men, and Niagara was no different. Yet. As the best women do, these female chefs gravitated to one another and formed strong supportive bonds to empower and inspire each other. Kristin's talent and reputation for excellence landed her smack dab in the middle of this fabulous group. These incredible women had the fantastic idea to host an event showcasing the combined culinary artistry of the group paired with top local wine. And they had just the place to host it.

Nicolette Novak had recently converted her family farm into a cooking school, aptly named The Good Earth Cooking School & Food Co. It was a stunning property and a culinary mecca of gardens and fruit trees, the perfect backdrop for the very first Blossom Brunch, which was set to take place outdoors under the blooming fruit trees on Mother's Day weekend 1999, a celebration of local food and wine with a unique focus on innovative female chefs.

The menu was planned, the wines were chosen, and the event quickly sold out. Nicolette's attention to detail was meticulous, and she and her mother Betty graciously welcomed the guests to their beautiful property. The energy of the group was contagious. The birdsong was joined by twinkling laughter. The atmosphere was festive. Mothers, daughters, sisters, and friends gathered together to share, honour, and celebrate one another. This was a powerful celebration of love: love of life, and the savouring of beautiful food prepared thoughtfully by and for women; love of the gifts of the earth in this special place; love of being a part of a sisterhood so ancient and timeless. The toasts were heartfelt, smiles were genuine, hands were clasped, hugs were long, and spirits and bodies were nourished. It was pure magic.

Being there, turning in circles and taking in with awe what these incredible women had accomplished by working together, shifted something inside of me. The way I saw the industry and what was truly possible when women join forces and support and inspire one another literally took my breath away. I looked around me and realized that I had the incredible fortune to be even just a small part of something so much bigger than I could ever have imagined. These women, their circle, their dreams, their determination, and tenacity—they rose higher together by lifting one another. Together, they could and would achieve their dreams and help others achieve theirs.

Women like this are magnets for other like-minded game changers and, as the years passed, their ranks began to swell. Obstacles were tackled, alliances were forged, and an industry was built. The Niagara Region became a well-reputed destination. This is not to say that this happened without the involvement of talented visionary men; for an industry to flourish, it needs input and collaboration from diverse persons. In order to become a premiere destination, many organizations and individuals must work together with a common goal to create a clear regional image with a strong underpinning of hospitality. We each have a role to play in that success and must find and develop our own unique strengths to add to the community. Along the way, we decide what kind of person we want to be and how we will impact others.

Although it was that first spectacular group of female chefs, facilitated by Nicolette, who opened the portal for me into this sisterhood and to whom I am forever grateful, my journey has led me not into the chef world but rather into the wineries and to the equally brilliant, hardworking, women without whom this industry would certainly not exist as it does today. I have also had the great privilege of meeting, working with, and learning from many truly exceptional men who have themselves been game changers and difference makers, and I am grateful to know them. Still, I want to shine a light on the often-unapplauded women and keep them alive in our archives, and our hearts, for their distinctive contributions.

It is my hope that as you read of their journeys you, too, will come to feel the magic that each of them brought to life and continue to breathe into this world. I hope that you will gain inspiration from their strength and determination, that you will choose to keep their legacy alive, and pay it forward by inspiring and supporting others along your way. These are our foremothers, and we owe them a lifetime of gratitude.

JENNIFER WILHELM

In the following pages, you will meet a grape grower, a farmer, a scientist, a winemaker, a public relations specialist, an entrepreneur, politician, educator, and author, to list just some of the multiple roles each woman held, often simultaneously. While they are all leaders, their journeys are as unique as the women are diverse. Without this diversity of people and skills, the Ontario grape and wine industry would not have evolved as it did. The chapters do not read the same. Though the women were presented with the same interview questions, their experiences and voices are distinct; what each has chosen to share or not share is their personal decision and one that has been respected. This is not a tell-all book. Each woman has been asked to reflect upon her life to date and, with the advantage of 20/20 hindsight, to share what she has learned. In the wise words of Debi Pratt, "As time goes on, we gain so much through our experiences that we can pass on to others so that they can be more successful. It is amazing that you can share—in fifteen minutes or less, what has taken a lifetime to learn."

Thank you, each of you, for your contributions and your generosity in sharing your stories.

Thank you also to those who shared their memories of and tributes to these remarkable women.

Thank you, Elena, for your care of these women throughout the editing process. You kept their voices clear, distinct, and true to who they are. From the start, you were unwavering in your commitment to them, to this project, and to our industry and the chronicling of its inception and protagonists. You have left your indelible wine stains upon each.

Debi Pratt

"Pride, passion, and professionalism. All three should show from the first greeting to the last 'thanks for visiting' comment. Show your passion and enthusiasm. Present yourself, your company, and your product in the best possible way. Treat people how you would like to be treated."

Deborah Pratt's interest in the Ontario grape and wine industry was stolen fast in the 1970s, a time when the words "Ontario" and "premium wine industry" were not being strung together by many people. She was instrumental in changing that perception over the following decades.

The tourist draws of the Niagara Region in the 1970s were Niagara Falls, Fort George, Brock's Monument, and the popular Sunday drive down the Niagara Parkway. While Niagara may have been known to some as The Fruit Belt, that list of fruit did not include *Vitis vinifera* grapes (the European grapes that premium wines are made from). Yet, early plantings of vinifera had been started by growers like Bill and Helen Lenko, John and Adriana Marynissen, to name a few, as well as experimental vineyards planted by Chateau Gai and Brights Wines.

It is a brisk but bright February day in 2019 when I arrive at Inniskillin Winery to interview Debi Pratt. The sun is glinting off the sleeping grape vines, and a hawk is circling in the clear blue sky above. It is impossible not to feel the power of this historic winery, the first to have been established in the Niagara Peninsula. Although she is retired now, Debi suggested meeting here, saying she has always felt at home on this property. She greets me at the door, elegant and smiling, with her hallmark welcome and warmth. Then we head upstairs to the Founders Hall, where she begins her story.

Deborah (Debi as she is known), was born in Toronto, Ontario, on July 29, 1948, the second child and only daughter of Catherine Mary and William LeRoy Pratt, fondly known to all as Kitty and Leroy. They met and married in the Canadian Armed Forces and served in England in World War II. Debi paints a picture of a very happy childhood, growing up in the Niagara lakefront community of Port Weller West (Weller Park), with loving and supportive parents. She and her older brother Mike, whom she idolized as only a little sister does, spent summers swimming in the lake, hiking in the nearby woods, and watching the ships move through the Welland Canal. Winters saw them skating on the frozen water and building snow forts with neighbourhood kids. In retrospect, Debi likens this group to a merry gang of adventurers. There was a freedom in that band in the 1950s and early 1960s; they looked out for one another and, provided they were home before the streetlights came on, parents had no need to worry.

As a child, Debi was active in ballet, Sunday school, church concerts, Brownies, local parades, assisting elderly neighbours, and helping in the family garden. She spent a great deal of time with her maternal grandmother, Alice Maude MacKellar, whom she remembers as cheerful, positive, and creative. Alice was full of stories about her life in England and Scotland, keeping Debi connected to her heritage. Debi recalls appreciatively that her grandmother played a significant role in her life saying, "She was deeply interested in all I did from childhood to the early days at Inniskillin. She loved that I became a teacher but also thought my second career in the wine industry was very exciting and encouraged me to pursue it."

Debi feels grateful for her fortunate upbringing, saying that when one is raised with wonderful parents, extended family, and a strong community, it provides a solid base to continue to build on. She is proud of her parents' serving in the Canadian Armed Forces. "My parents are at the core of who I am. I am so privileged to be their daughter. I learned from them the elements of how to be the best person I could be. My brother Mike also passed on lessons of working hard and professionalism through his successful career as a marine pilot."

In addition to orchestrating the family's daily life, Debi's mother Kitty organized a team of about eight women who would tie and pick labrusca grapes together. Debi recollects, "They had a ball. They would take their own lunches, and I'm sure there was 'a little something extra' in their lemonade, and off they'd go. It wasn't always nice weather either, but they still showed up and did their work."

Looking back, Debi finds it interesting that her mother picked and tied grapes, though it seemed inconsequential at the time. Fast forward a few decades, and Debi recounts a story of Albrecht Seeger, a premium grape grower for Inniskillin, calling her and saying "Debi, I really need some pickers for tomorrow." She recalls his surprise when she replied with "Let me call my mother." Debi says it's key to keep in mind that her mother's experience was with *Vitis labrusca* grapes (a species of grape native to eastern North America, well suited for juice and jam but considered inferior to *vinifera* when it comes to premium winemaking). Many of Debi's early years with Inniskillin were spent impressing upon folks the importance of using *vinifera* grapes for premium wine production. For all her hours explaining this to her mother, Debi says, like most Canadians at the time, her mother didn't believe that there could be so much difference between the type of the grapes used and the quality of the wine.

"Well," says Debi, "at the end of that day of picking for the Seegers, my mother called me and said 'Debi, I get it. I thought a grape was a grape. Now I get it. The Seegers showed me how to hand select and harvest premium grape varieties with the key standard of quality over quantity.'"

Debi surmises that her environment may have indirectly led her to her eventual career of choice. Growing up in a fruit belt, picking fruit was usually one of the first jobs young people could obtain, and many residents continued to pick fruit seasonally—both for extra income and at many area "pick your own fruit" farms for their own households. This helped Debi, at an early age, to understand just how fickle agriculture can be. She knew firsthand that a crop could be lost swiftly due to hail, frost, or hungry birds. She watched local farming families work hard all year, just to have capricious nature steal it all away in minutes. This gave her a greater appreciation, years later, for the gamble that Donald Ziraldo and Karl Kaiser were prepared to take in pursuit of their dream of making premium wine from premium grapes grown in the Niagara Peninsula.

After completing high school, Debi took a summer job teaching nursery school with St. Catharines Parks and Recreation. While she found the enthusiasm of the little ones rewarding, the experience made her realize that she needed to be challenged more. While two- to five-year-old children are admittedly challenging, after the tasks of engaging them in activity centres and teaching them to share, what Debi found intriguing was their curiosity and inquisitive minds. This planted the seed in her own mind that she might like to teach primary classes in the elementary school system. In 1967, she returned to school, this time to St. Catharines Teachers' College, a collaboration between Brock University and the Ontario Ministry of Education.

Fond memories of her own school days may have subconsciously played a role in her decision to become a teacher. Debi credits her time at Lakeport Secondary School as fundamental to her strong character, personal strength, and confidence, along with learning the value of being a team player. She appreciates having had the guidance and support of many coaches, one of whom nominated her for the Ontario Athletic Leadership Camp, at Lake Couchiching. Debi remembers being surprised that she was chosen, having previously shied away from leadership roles. In retrospect, she feels grateful that her coach saw her potential, ultimately shifting her own perception of herself. She loved that two-week camp. She came away changed and ready for new leadership roles. Debi realized later that this camp was pivotal for her future endeavours. In paying it forward, she has made a point of noticing and encouraging strengths in the young people around her.

She began her sixteen-year teaching career in 1969 with primary grades at Brockview School on Line 3, in Niagara-on-the-Lake, and then at Laura Secord Public School, in the village of Queenston. In her words, she then proceeded to "jam pack" her life. She taught school during the week and went to Brock University in the evening to earn a BA in psychology and education (in those days you didn't need a degree to teach if you had a certificate from teachers' college). During this time, she met and became friends with Donald Ziraldo and Karl Kaiser. She listened with interest as the two told her about the wines they had been making from French hybrid grapes (Maréchal Foch, Chelois, De Chaunac). With his strong agricultural experience and education, Donald fervently believed that vinifera grapes could be grown in certain areas in Niagara, despite being told otherwise from just about everyone. He began propagating the vines at his nursery. Local growers, however, weren't as convinced as he, leaving him in 1974 with some 30,000 vinifera vines. Donald decided to plant these Chardonnay, Riesling, and Gamay vines himself at the newly purchased farm on Line 3 across from the current Inniskillin Winery. This vineyard was later purchased by the Seeger Family in 1978.

This same year, Donald met personally with Major General George Kitching, CEO of the Liquor Control Board of Ontario (LCBO) and applied for a winery licence. Kitching was impressed with the vision that Donald and Karl had and granted them a provisional licence for one year, allowing them to produce 2,000 cases of wine. Kitching stipulated that this wine be sold through the LCBO's Rare Wine and Spirits Store, known today as Vintages, as well as at the winery base in Niagara-on-the-Lake. The wine sold so successfully that in 1975 Donald and Karl were granted the first Ontario winery licence since Prohibition. Debi recalls the triumphant excitement of the announcement. Already a strong supporter of the quality of Karl's wines and of Inniskillin's vision of making premium wine from premium Ontario grapes, Debi says Kitching's confidence in the plan's success further cemented her own.

Debi felt that the well-travelled CEO of the LCBO clearly comprehended where the Canadian wine industry was and was not at that time. Kitching also recognized that it was changing. The LCBO had been selling high volumes of imported wine due to its customers' long-standing confidence in European winemaking. Many patrons were of European decent. The French bought French, the Italian bought Italian, the Portuguese bought Portuguese. The Canadian-born next generations, however, were evolving from these traditions and were open to premium wine from other places. This opened a new segment of the market known as New World wines, well timed with Inniskillin's marketing strategy. Kitching knew that the path to the future had to relate directly to the type, origin, and quality of the grapes. Donald, a farmer himself, concurred, adding the importance of naming the wine after the grape variety. Kitching came to Niagara to meet Karl, returning to Toronto even more confident in the vision for premium wine from premium grapes grown in the Niagara Peninsula.

Debi, too, became confident in this vision and began helping Donald and Karl part-time on the weekends and during summer months. Picture, if you will, this ignited trio of twenty-somethings, running on adrenalin, dreams, and faith.

Debi recounts the first days of being open for business: "The Winery" as it was simply called, being the only estate winery in Ontario at the time, was a packing shed on the property of Donald's existing family business, Ziraldo Nurseries. The name "Inniskillin" came from that original site where Colonel Cooper had fought in the wars in the 1800s and was granted Crown land. Three years later, the small team opened the doors of Inniskillin Winery on Line 3 at the Niagara Parkway on the Brae Burn Estate. "Brae burn" is old English for "hill stream," an indication of its proximity to the Niagara Escarpment and the Niagara River. The names of both the winery and the new estate reflected the strong sense of place and history of Inniskillin. This connected well with consumers and media as it reinforced the authenticity and origin of the grapes/vineyards. Debi asserts, "This was extremely important to dispel early misconceptions about where the grapes came from and that we were and are a cool climate grape growing region. Most believed that premium grapes could not grow in Niagara."

Debi loved the challenge of learning something new and found that her teaching skills could be applied to educating customers and fellow colleagues about Inniskillin's wine and history. Her knowledge, enthusiasm, and welcoming nature were instrumental in creating a faithful, loyal group of patrons. What began as 'helping out' part-time soon turned into a full-blown passion. This led to Debi taking a Teacher Financed Leave (TFL), and then extending her time away from teaching in 1986 by taking a Leave of Absence (LOA). In 1988, she joined Inniskillin full-time, resigning completely from the school board.

For many, leaving behind job security, pension, benefits, and summers off seems unfathomable, but Debi says she planned it carefully to retain the security of her teaching position until officially resigning. Though she felt confident in her decision, she admits that her father, while supportive as always of her dreams, was concerned about her leaving such a good, secure profession for the "unknown." With a reflective smile, she reveals that she asked her father to build her a wooden wine rack for Christmas one year. She says that his hobby blossomed from there, and that in his retirement he made wooden wine racks that became very popular with both friends and Inniskillin customers throughout Niagara Region and Canada. "It's fun when I visit others and see one of his wine racks in their home. Written on the bottom of each is, 'Royal Inniskillin by LeRoy.'"

Debi confides that a few things led to her decision to leave teaching. She was burning the candle at both ends and beginning to feel the effects. She astutely realized that one can only run full steam on passion and adrenalin for so long. When her mother died suddenly in 1982, Debi realized that the precarious balance of her own life was no longer sustainable. She confesses, "I absolutely loved teaching. I loved everything about it, and I loved the kids. But I was hooked, I was totally hooked, on the feeling I had when I was at the winery and working towards that shared vision with Donald and Karl." She continues in a passionate voice, "When you are curious about something you know nothing about, and it interests you, it totally, totally becomes fun. The four of us would sit together, Donald, Karl, and Silvia [Karl's wife], and they would start to talk. Their energy inspired me, and I just became hooked. This kept me wanting to stay and learn more."

She continues, "There is something about entrepreneurs that fascinates me. An entrepreneur is a rare breed of person who takes amazing risks. I like entrepreneurs because they are confident and ambitious, they do their homework, they are smart, and they work smart. Watching Donald and Karl mesmerized me because it was against all odds; it didn't make any sense. They took something that was so negatively viewed in the wine and business world [Canadian wine] and thought they could be successful. They thought they could do it and so that was it. When you tell people they can't, an entrepreneur wants to prove they can.

"I admired the logic in how they worked together, and their synergy. Karl was the winemaker, he had technical skills, and I do believe he had a photographic memory. Donald was business savvy and understood public relations and sales and marketing. The two were so opposite and yet they had overlapping concentric circles: the love of wine, their confidence, and the belief that they could accomplish something together was what they had in common.

"When I considered my role in the trio, I looked at my skills, and it was simple. I knew how to create a comfort zone for people to loosen up, learn about and enjoy wine without being intimated. I could see them relax when I took it down to the basics of explaining grape varieties, putting two glasses of wine in front of them and letting them compare. If they said they liked white wine, I poured them two different kinds of white wine and asked which they preferred. Then I told them about the grapes that they were made from. You could not take for granted that people understood that the name of the grape could be the name of the wine. In the early years, there were many Ontario wines with European names or cutesy animals. It was confusing. Once people understood that the characteristics of the wine related to the grape name, it became easier to build upon what they liked and why.

"During harvest time, I would have folks taste the actual grape with the matching wine to continue to reinforce the connection. I enjoyed providing experiences that gave them the opportunity to compare wines side by side to learn the differences for themselves. Simple but impactful methods during harvest of having them taste an actual Chardonnay grape with a Chardonnay wine. WHY? Raw product linked to [the] end product. One day early in my wine career, a customer said to me, 'I love your white Chardonnay; could I now try your red Chardonnay?' Why should I have ever assumed that they even knew that a Chardonnay was a type of grape no less a white grape that only made a white wine. DON'T ASSUME ANYTHING!"

Educating was always Debi's directive; she believed that to effectively teach, one must first start with what the pupil doesn't know. Debi is adamant about eliminating the distracting fluff. That began with showing people where the wine regions of Ontario were located. To do this, she presented a map illustrating where the world's famous wine regions were located—between thirty and fifty degrees latitude. Ontario's regions are between forty-one- and forty-four-degrees north latitude, with Niagara at forty-three, right in the middle. Once people realized the similar latitude and climate to the famous wine regions of Burgundy and Bordeaux, they started to change their mindset.

"Our mission was always 'premium wine from premium grapes grown in the Niagara Peninsula,' and that is the unwavering message we strove to deliver every day. Guests had to drive past the vineyards and then walk past them to enter the winery, which was key. When they asked the question, 'Where do you get your grapes from?' we could turn their attention right back to our estate where they could touch the grapes, vines, and soils if they wanted to, and everyone wanted to have their picture taken in the vineyards. Sometimes people forget to keep it simple.

"These were my transferable skills. It was all about educating and creating a comfort zone. Anytime I have learned anything or progressed, it was because people created a comfort zone for me, or I created my own by doing my homework. Karl and Donald were patient with me as I learned more about wine and agriculture. Donald was a visionary who understood the short-term strategies to reach the long-term goals, both with Inniskillin and with the industry. This fit for my role with Inniskillin but also for my role in the growth of the Ontario wine industry. When you realize that you are turning a corner and a whole new leaf, it's about critical mass and credibility for an industry to be successful."

Debi says she drew confidence from the two, and from their unshakeable confidence in Karl's wine. "You can't have a winery business unless you know your product is good and your winemaker is skilled, creative, and confident." She remembers people asking her how she mustered up the courage to go into the LCBO to sell wine, to which she would reply, "It's quite simple. I'm confident because Karl is confident, and Donald has already set the scene. The LCBO knew who Inniskillin was and how good the wines were because of the media coverage, and they were all rooting for the underdog. It was exciting and it was pivotal."

Little did they know how successful they would become and the impact they would have. Inniskillin paved the way for other wineries and soon there were two more in Niagara-on-the-Lake: Château des Charmes (1978), and Hillebrand (established in 1979 as Newark before being sold and renamed in 1982). Debi led a meeting in The Loft at Inniskillin with these two wineries. She had a clear vision of Niagara as a wine and culinary destination. She wisely knew that the key lay in concentrating the efforts of early producers while personalizing each winery based on their individual strengths and wines. They all recognized the power of working together with a clear vision to be a unique wine and culinary destination, making and showcasing premium Ontario wines. They formed the first joint marketing efforts of Niagara wineries.

A true leader, Debi rallied the others to explore and develop year-round tourism through festivals, passport programs, and the ever-increasing interest in wine and food pairings, linking local foods within the destination of Niagara. By the mid 1990s, there were seven wineries in Niagara-on-the-Lake, aptly called The Group of Seven. As the numbers grew, Debi led them with great foresight as they expanded into the Wineries of Niagara-on-the-Lake (which still exists with approximately twenty-seven wineries involved.)

Continuing to build credibility was the ongoing challenge. Making great quality from key hybrid and cool climate vinifera grapes, as well as educating the consumer and media, needed the next step of international exposure and recognition. Key wine competitions were important, but none as important as France's Vinexpo.

Vinexpo, then considered the world's most significant wine trade show, was established in 1981 to bring together exhibitors and buyers from around the globe. Held every two years in Bordeaux, France, it included a competition in which wines were tasted blind by the globe's most revered wine judges. Donald Ziraldo had attended the event as a visitor in 1987 and left determined to return to introduce premium Canadian wine alongside the then mostly European exhibitors. When he and Debi returned in 1989, she astutely set up a map of the world's most renowned wine regions at Inniskillin's booth. Not only did the map capture attention, but it also built credibility by clearly displaying the forty-third-latitude connection, leaving no room for argument or disbelief. It was clear. Ontario wasn't just warmer than Bordeaux and Burgundy, it also had the moderating factors of the Great Lakes and the Niagara Escarpment to mitigate spring cold and extend the autumn growing season.

Debi and Donald had brought a selection of Inniskillin wine: Chardonnay, Pinot Noir, and an Icewine made from Vidal. It's important to note that in 1989, Canadian Icewine was essentially unknown to the world; its only peer in the naturally frozen grape wine category would have been German and Austrian Eiswein, where ice wines originated from. Also to note is that this style of winemaking was being tried then not just in Niagara, but also in Pelee Island, Ontario, and in British Columbia. Over the course of Vinexpo, Donald observed that, of the three Inniskillin wines, guests were most interested in tasting the sweet, concentrated style. Consequently, when he registered as the only Canadian exhibitor at the next Vinexpo in 1991, he submitted Inniskillin's 1989 Vidal Icewine. This now legendary wine beat out 4,000 other entries to emerge triumphantly as the world's best wine, receiving the Grand Prix d'Honneur. Incredulous attendees swarmed the Canadian booth. The wine industry, and Canada, were forever changed.

As Inniskillin's public relations director, Debi and her team excitedly spread the news. Sommeliers around the globe were hustling to secure bottles, collectors were eagerly calling, and media was rushing to report on the little winery from Niagara-on-the-Lake and its phenomenal accomplishment in France. Newspaper headlines announced the likes of "Canadian Wine Wins in France." Silvia Kaiser, Karl's wife, captured this pivotal moment with her (now) well known quote, "It is like winning an Oscar."

Always well prepared, Debi arrived at the next Vinexpo in 1993 with a plan to paint an enticing picture of Niagara, Canada, bringing pamphlets in several languages, complete with maps and pictures, and linking their proximity to the famous Niagara Falls. It was key to market with the word Canada in those days as Ontario did not have the same impact or recognition. With her trademark enthusiasm and attention to detail, she left people wanting to experience this piece of magic for themselves and gave them the necessary information to do so easily.

Furthermore, she told them warmly and genuinely that she looked forward to seeing them at Inniskillin. Many believe that the visitors came as much to see Debi again as they did to taste the wine. There is something so authentically welcoming about Debi. In every area of her life, she makes people feel like they truly matter, that they are being listened to and heard, and she draws them past any hesitancy or intimidation they may feel. Inniskillin became successful not just because of Karl's exceptional wine and Donald's exceptional business acumen but also because Debi Pratt herself is exceptional. As a teacher, as an ambassador, and as a mentor, she has a significant impact on the individuals and on the communities, she interacts with.

She says proudly, "I always enjoyed welcoming visitors to Inniskillin with the key comment and question, 'Welcome to Inniskillin. Where are you visiting us from?' They shared their origin as well as their excitement on why they had come to us, and I always thanked them for coming."

Debi innately understood the complex principals of tourism from the start and quickly became a role model and mentor for others as Ontario's hospitality and tourism industry grew. She says she learned more about wine and grew personally through customers, conferences, travelling, reading, and tasting but most of all through observing and listening. She loved sharing her passion with everyone but especially with students, in their eagerness to learn. She led many staff trainings at restaurants to equip them to serve Ontario wines proudly and with confidence.

At one such training at the Holiday Inn, St. Catharines in 1989, Debi fondly recalls meeting a young server named Maria Moessner. As Debi tells, "Maria was very enthused as she learned more about wine, wine service, and selling. She has now been with Inniskillin [Arterra Wines] for more than thirty years. She is extremely accomplished and has never lost the desire to learn more."

Debi goes on to say, "Icewine is an obvious example of Canadian weather, and it got our foot in the door, but we wanted consumers to know that we produce premium table wines as well. We did this at Inniskillin, but then we also did this as a collective as the industry grew. We all had the common goal of producing premium wine from premium grapes and we stuck to that. That was important, especially in the early years before the Vintners Quality Alliance (VQA) and as it was getting started. People were confused buying wines and not knowing completely which grapes made the wine. It could be labelled Chardonnay, but in those early days it was likely predominantly Vidal and Seyval Blanc with very little Chardonnay in it. There were no parameters yet.

"VQA was a major step in building credibility. VQA on a label is a guarantee to the consumer of standards of excellence and understanding of origin. It meant the wine was made with 100 per cent Ontario grown grapes. The standardization of VQA was important to the whole future of the wine industry and for tourism as well. That's why it was great working with people like Linda Bramble and Madame Bosc [from Château des Charmes]; we were all working hard with our own twist to elevate and maintain these standards. Tourism is so important, and these partnerships were key. I use the phrase 'partners in excellence' because you can partner with many people, but unless they have the same standards as you, it's a waste of your time and they will bring you down. We used that term originally to describe Donald and Karl but went on to include many other people and organizations." Debi uses the example of the 2006 merger with Constellation Brands, which included Robert Mondavi. "My goodness, did we ever think when we started that we would ever be in the same portfolio as Mondavi?"

Her pride in what she, Donald, and Karl were able to build is evident in every story she recounts. She says, "Whether standing in front of Inniskillin welcoming guests, or visiting other countries and hearing people speak of Inniskillin, that, THAT is always the biggest highlight, because it is the result of *everyone's* hard work. Not mine, not Donald, not Karl, but everyone collectively who has joined us and is continuing to do this work. Seeing this hard work pay off is the ultimate high for me. I love to ask guests where they are visiting from, especially international visitors. Hearing that they have come all this way to visit us is just thrilling. I never, ever take that for granted."

Inniskillin has been featured repeatedly by global wine market research company Wine Intelligence and Drinks International in their yearly release of The World's Most Admired Wine Brands. She continues, "It was also a very proud moment to be included in a book entitled, *The World's Most*

Famous Wines. Keeping scrapbooks over the years has been most rewarding when reflecting on our success. These books clearly outline the story of Inniskillin but also how we became successful in the words of a broad spectrum of writers and through the lenses of many photographers."

Her thoughts drift back in time here as she reminisces. "I asked Karl once, when he was being filmed in the back barrel cellar at Inniskillin, if he ever dreamed that Inniskillin would go so far and make such an impact in the industry. He said reflectively, 'Debi, I knew we could make good wine, but I never imagined all of this.' It stood out in his interview as a humbling, reflective moment of Inniskillin's amazing success."

These days, Debi believes that while the customer's expectations and level of knowledge have changed, they are still seeking a hospitable, non-intimidating environment in which they can taste and learn. Consumers may now be looking for heightened experiences, ultimate food pairings, and Instagram-worthy backdrops, but she impresses that we mustn't lose sight of the educational component, of sincerely welcoming people and sharing who we are as a region and what we do well. As a destination region, we must be exceptional to compete and connect in the international wine world. Debi personally made it a point to learn all she could and to keep up to date with trends, demographics, opportunities, and competition, whether dealing with LCBO managers, sommeliers, or restaurant owners. Early on, she identified and honed persistence and professionalism as essential to be a respected and credible representative of Inniskillin.

As Inniskillin continued to succeed as Canada's premier estate winery, it became involved with mergers over the years, starting in the early 1990s. The parent company became Vincor with Jackson-Triggs, Le Clos Jordanne, and wineries in British Columbia and, eventually, other cool climate wineries around the world. Debi remained with the company. She says, "The larger the company, the more layers there were. There were shareholders that now had a say. I believed always in personalizing Inniskillin. I felt I was one of the main connections to the real story of Inniskillin and wanted that to continue and have others follow that lead." She built a strong team of talented people and made sure each of them clearly understood and articulated the original key message of producing premium wine from premium grapes grown in the Niagara Peninsula.

In addition to that key message, Debi says that her actions were guided daily by her unwavering values: "Work hard, be honest, create strong working relationships where people could depend on me, and always educate while selling."

Debi tells of facilitating blind tastings for wine club members and visitors to the winery with the goal of opening their minds to wines that they may not otherwise try. In the early days, and sometimes still, people would buy within their comfort zones or be led by peer preferences. If Merlot and Cabernet Sauvignon were the wines to drink, then those were the wines they purchased without question. Debi made a point to always make these events fun, rather than intimidating, with a focus on the joy of discovery, often brilliantly tied to new releases. Attendees left pleasantly surprised and with bottles to share with friends and family. Debi adds sincerely, "It is always my hope that when these bottles are opened, they are accompanied with stories of experiences shared at Inniskillin, of memories, or maybe something they learned there that they can pass along. I want them to take away more than just bottles."

It wasn't just while selling wine that she endeavoured to educate. As Inniskillin garnered international acclaim, winemakers from around the globe came to learn from and work with Karl. Often, they came from sunny warm regions and their palates were habitually tuned to jammy fruit, high alcohol, and ripe tannins. Cool climate Cabernet Franc with its food friendly acidity and savoury, herbal notes was frequently a surprise. Debi found the best way to introduce them to and familiarize them with the Inniskillin portfolio was to present the wines blind. She did the same with the retail team. This ensured that they authentically talked about each wine and, when asked, could genuinely name their favourites, and explain why, rather than parroting the opinions of others.

Sincerity was, and is, crucial to Debi. She pulled older wines from the cellar to help both her team and guests understand how wines age and when best to enjoy them according to their own preferences. After an experience with Debi, customers often left with a case or two of wine. Debi would say, "Take this one out and enjoy it this week with dinner.

Then don't open the next one for three months. Notice how they change. When you get down to those last three bottles, you're going to be afraid to open them because you will want more and there's going to be none left."

Sometimes they would come back after six months and buy a second case because they were already impressed with the aging ability of the wines. Debi loved that so many loyal and wine savvy customers, writers, local sommeliers, and licensee buyers took notes and were genuinely interested, gradually developing a real understanding of Niagara wines. Debi felt, and still feels fervently that the key to our industry's success lies in building enthusiastic and effective wine ambassadors who then go out and spread the word of Ontario wineries to the rest of the world.

When Debi left teaching to join her friends Karl and Donald, she couldn't possibly have known what would lie ahead for the three of them, or how significant her own role would be in shaping the Ontario and Canadian wine industry. She reflects on the forty years she spent with Inniskillin and pronounces them "challenging, stimulating, and rewarding in every aspect." These three words are succinct but so powerful. Her voice is rich with pride and nostalgia as she recounts the stories. When asked, she identifies some of the accomplishments she feels most proud of: "Selling lots of wine; creating a faithful, loyal group of customers; educating staff and customers, along with students from Niagara College and Brock University; developing year-round tourism; working to manage regional tourism and founding the Wineries of Niagara-on-the-Lake."

To be clear, these are just a few of her impressive contributions. She recalls some of the highest highs: the awards and international recognition of Inniskillin and Ontario wines, educating and sharing the story with people around the world, attending wine shows, speaking engagements, and meeting famous people and being inspired by their strengths and skills. She lists the lowest low as "simply running out of energy and wanting to do too much as there was so much to do." In 2006, three major losses occurred that significantly affected her energy: Donald resigned, Karl retired, and their beloved resident chef Izabela Kalabis died.

Still, Debi feels so passionate that Inniskillin remains relevant in the new landscape today. Many wineries now wear several hats, producing not just wine but beer, cider, and spirits, as well as having restaurants, markets, and cooking schools. On one hand, she says, it was easier when there were just three wineries; now each one needs to keep competitive and offer unique, quality experiences. If one lets their quality of product and experience fall, it effects the entire industry. It is so important to her that Inniskillin remains a leader, innovative and creative. "By all means," she says passionately, "keep innovating to remain successful but DO NOT forget why and how you became successful to begin with. You will lose your footing if you are not connected to the identity and philosophy of your company."

It was vital to Debi when she was training others to take on her role, that they understood and could tie everything back to Inniskillin's original mission and story, and that guests were consistently and warmly welcomed and treated like family, whether visiting for the first or fiftieth time.

A quote from the late Don Hewitt, producer of *60 Minutes*, rang true for Debi, when she was training co-workers on how to have Inniskillin continue to be the prominent leader in the wine industry while continuing to be successful. "You need to have a foot in the past to understand the present. Past milestones inspire future milestones."

Debi Pratt has been mentored many of Ontario's successful wine professionals. Each one recounts her incredible warmth, authenticity, and genuine care. She blazed that first trail and lovingly passed the torch of her beloved winery and industry to the next generation of stewards, each of whom carries her fire within them. Debi says, "If you truly care about your company and industry and their future, and if you care about people, you must invest in mentoring. As time goes on, we gain so much through experiences that we can pass on to others so that they can be more successful. They are doing jobs that are challenging and you can possibly help make them less challenging by sharing some words of wisdom. It's amazing that you can share in fifteen minutes or less, what has taken a lifetime to learn."

In fact, at the end of every talk Debi gives to students, whether in class or at the winery, she always ends with the sincere invitation: "If you would like to meet one on one and talk about where you see your future in the wine industry and how you might best fit into that aspect, please call or email me and I would be happy to talk with you." She says she often has people reach out and ask if she will speak with a friend, a neighbour, family member, etc. who is thinking of getting into the wine industry. She goes on with a firm nod, "I always say yes. I don't do it as a job. I usually spend about an hour and half with each of them. If they are willing, I suggest they come to Inniskillin, and I take them on a tour. Often, we talk about transferable skills and what they already have to offer a winery. I really like to do that, and I love to see the results."

Debi urges that "One should never be afraid to ask for advice. If you don't know something, you can't move forward on a supposition. I believe that if you are competent, you can be confident. Therefore, my goal was to learn to be as competent as I could be in every aspect of every job that I was doing. Sometimes people get hung on what they think they can't do. I love to sit and brainstorm with them and be creative. Sometimes I will say things that are off the wall, but you must be creative to be successful. I think this comes from my teaching days. Donald would say to me, 'Debi, don't you get bored teaching the same thing year after year?' to which I would reply incredulously, 'Are you kidding me? There are twenty ways to teach anything and every year, the children change, and I need to learn their needs so I must be creative and connected to each of them. I think I would be the worst teacher in the world if I taught the same lesson in the same way every year expecting that each child learns the same way! I applied that same perspective to every person that visited the winery, year after year. As the industry changed and grew, I knew that it was critical that we remain creative in order to engage visitors and continue to retain the leading edge. Always stay creative and personally and emotionally connected to people."

Debi talks about a recent local event at which she spoke to fifteen women about other women in the wine industry. She gave them each an envelope containing the name of a woman and three of her roles: a combination of winemaker, social media manager, grape grower, farm manager, human resources, health and safety, financial business planner, estate chef, writer of press releases, author, and the list goes on. She astutely did this to brilliantly showcase the many skills needed and the propensity, and often necessity, of them overlapping. She wanted to make a point that it is crucial that we do not pigeonhole one another, or ourselves, into just one role. She goes on to say that the smaller the winery, the broader the scope of skills needed from each team member. She relates it to Inniskillin's humble beginnings when she, Donald, and Karl did everything. She said she never expected otherwise.

"Listen," she confides, "I came from a small schoolhouse across the street. We had a part-time principal, and a part-time janitor, and we all took turns doing what was needed. That's just the way it was. When I joined Inniskillin and someone asked, "Debi, can you take this wine over to The Prince of Wales Hotel,' I said, 'Of course,' and just did it. Over the years, and with the seasonality of the business, your staff may not always be as large as you would like it to be so at those times, everyone is back to making sure that they can do many things. Multilayered, transferable skills are essential to rise above challenges. As women, I think it's imperative that we have other women who we can go to with questions and for support."

Here, Debi names her Women Uncorked group. She says fondly, "It's the coolest thing. It's structured sometimes and not structured others. We can be sitting around the table and mention that we are looking for someone who could do such and such, does anyone know someone? It can be as simple as that, or it can be as complex as really needing advice and support. To this date, it is one of the greatest groups I have ever been a part of. It's fun and it's educational. We all have something in common: we like wine, and we work hard. I enjoy every woman that is in the group, some of whom I would have never gotten to know otherwise."

I interject here and ask for Debi's forgiveness. I remember her saying that she packed her life. From my own experience, it can be tricky sometimes to know what to add to our already busy schedules. As our social circle grows, we are offered so many opportunities, opportunities to do good in many cases, such as being on boards and raising funds for important causes. However, we have jobs that we truly love and want to give our best to, and we have our families and our social lives, our basic life maintenance of groceries and haircuts and oil changes and taxes…. It can be a gruelling schedule and often making time for the things that fill our cups, like Debi's Women Uncorked group, can become a last priority that falls to the wayside. I ask Debi if this was the case for her. As women, we tend to think that everyone but us has it effortlessly together. But Debi concurs, saying it was exactly like that. She admits that she was always late for family dinners on Sundays, and would arrive rushing in saying, half joking, "I could tell you that the bridge was up, but that wasn't the case."

Debi says that she would often carpool with Wilma Lowrey (co-proprietor of Five Rows Craft Winery) to the Uncorked tastings. Wilma would almost always raise her glass at the end of the evening, saying, "You women just don't know how much I enjoyed tonight. It's just so much fun to be able to talk about anything and everything with you ladies because you have all been there." Debi says that inevitably one of the women would remark, "You know, I was so tired today that I almost didn't come, but I knew when I got here that I would be glad I came."

There would be knowing nods around the table, as each of them had felt that way many times herself. In the car on the way home, Debi and Wilma would talk about how valuable the group of women had become to them. Debi says ardently, "We never take these friendships for granted. I strongly suggest that women think about starting a fun wine tasting group like Women Uncorked. It's very therapeutic."

When you have a position with so much responsibility, it can be a struggle to make time for things that aren't an immediate priority. Too often, many of us put off the dates with friends, Sunday dinners with our parents, or solitary walks in nature that we once had time for, telling ourselves, "There is so much I need to do, or I'm so tired. I'll just miss this one but will go next time for sure.' But the myth of having more time next week, or next month, is exactly that—a myth. Next week will be just as busy, and maybe even more so, because there will unavoidably be tasks on our "to-do" lists that get shuffled to the next day, week, month, leaving us more stretched for time. Before we know it, we have "next-timed" ourselves right out of the connective friendships and pleasures that add so much joy to our lives. Sometimes it is not a fire that needs to be put out but one that needs to be relit, that we must make time for.

Debi reveals, "During a long lunch one day with a friend and colleague, we both confessed that we needed to take more time for ourselves. We attributed this to the fact that the hospitality/wine industry does not run on a regular schedule but is always full of last-minute surprises and changes. Having a weekend or even two days off in a row is so very important to have a proper break both mentally and physically. Even if you managed to have two days off each week, it wasn't the same if they were not two consecutive days."

Debi admits, "It was difficult in the early years because I didn't have many women to talk to about winery business, simply because there weren't other wineries at that time with women in positions of management. Marion LeBlanc originally ran the office at Inniskillin as well as managing on the road sales at LCBO and restaurants. She taught me so much, including how to multitask and get things accomplished in a very organized and professional way. Then I met Wendy Cheropita and Jill Brewster, who were with Brights and Chateau Gai, who both faced the same challenges of women selling Canadian wine. Madame Andrée Bosc at Château des Charmes was a very strong woman and an early mentor. Madame Bosc and I both juggled two careers as she was also a teacher. She and I would teach all week and then drive to Toronto and spend the weekend at a wine show or the weekend at the winery and then be back teaching on Monday again. We each understood the hectic pace but needed to laugh about it together. We did it because we knew we had to for the success of our wineries, but we genuinely wanted to as well.

"She and I were doing similar things early on and both appreciated our loyal customers who wanted to spread the word about premium Ontario wines. I would have guests visit Inniskillin in those early years, and I would ask them where else they had been. If they said Château des Charmes, I always asked if they had been lucky enough to meet Madame. If they had, they would rave about her and their experience: 'Oh yes; she took us into the cellar, and we tried this amazing wine that isn't even released yet!'" Debi says with admiration, "Madame built an incredible and loyal clientele base. She knew how to make people feel special and also how to sell wine. I would then call her up and say, 'Andrée, I hosted the same people as you did today. They told me all about their visit with you.' And we would laugh and share stories. Really, I just used it as an excuse to call her, to laugh together." On a serious note, Debi continues, "She was absolutely amazing. The men in the Bosc family get a lot of credit, but she doesn't get nearly enough. She was so important to this groundbreaking era. Both she and then her daughter-in-law Michelle were the matriarchs of the family." Michelle Bosc was the powerhouse behind public relations and social media starting in the early 2000, and worked tirelessly and with passion until she passed away in 2019.

Debi goes on to name Linda Franklin (early Wine Council of Ontario executive director) and Linda Bramble (sommelier, wine author, and professor) as well, saying, "They were incredible women, both the epitome of leadership. Linda Franklin came from the political world, and really affected change for the wine industry before going on to run Ontario Colleges Association. Those were the early days. There is a much broader women's support system today, especially through educational institutes like Niagara College and Brock University's Cool Climate Oenology and Viticultural Institute [CCOVI], winemakers, sommeliers, grape growers, and the hospitality business. There is a high proportion of women out there selling wine and promoting our industry that can relate to each other and be there for one another.

"I was fortunate in my early years of learning about agriculture in general, along with the growing of grapes, to spend time with Derna and Irma Ziraldo [Donald's aunt and mother]. They shared many a story about the commitment needed to be involved with the growing of fruit. They had learned much through the many years of the family business, Ziraldo Nurseries, and then helped whenever possible with Inniskillin.

"In 1977, CBC filmed a piece called 'Ziraldo's Zap,' based on the challenge of producing premium Ontario wines and overcoming immense challenges. The filming coincided with the worst vintage yet. It rained continuously throughout the six weeks of harvest. Machinery was getting stuck in the vineyards and people had to hand pick the grapes in the rain. Derna helped with the picking and was interviewed for the film. She epitomized the feelings of all who were so frustrated working hard to harvest what grapes they could and getting people to pick them. When asked about the harvest, she simply shrugged and said, 'What are we gonna do?' She knew that you had to keep working and do the best you could with the weather conditions, and that you never gave up."

Debi says, "Irma Ziraldo's words of wisdom kept my spirits high when I had worked a long day or struggled to understand something. She would

SHARING A GLASS

call at 4:30 p.m. to the office and say, 'Come for pasta when you lock up.' I could never say no, and would sit for hours with her, eating, sipping wine, and learning from a pro. One Saturday, it took me three tries to get down the one-car gravel road as customers were coming the other way saying that they had travelled afar to buy our wine and had finally found us. The funny part was that Irma's house was adjacent to the laneway. She could see from her kitchen that I kept getting stopped by cars and that I would turn around and go back to the office to sell them wine. Finally, I arrived at her house feeling bad for being late but also craving her amazing pasta. As I entered, I started to apologize, but she was laughing. She just kept pointing to the lane way and saying, 'I know. I saw the cars!'

"Before we would sit at her kitchen table to enjoy a delicious pasta meal, with green salads, chicken, cheeses, and fresh vegetables, my job was to go down to the basement and select an Inniskillin wine. Imagine, I was 'Irma Ziraldo's personal sommelier.' There were many lunches and dinners full of her flavourful food, her laughter, her words of wisdom, and her warm, caring friendship. Her door was always open, and it was never long before others would join us, including her sons, of whom she was equally proud. Together, we would all be enjoying the most 'famous kitchen on the Niagara Parkway.'

"One big lesson Irma taught me was simply 'first impressions.' What do people first see when they arrive at your place of business and how are they greeted? She would often visit the winery boutique after it had closed knowing that I would still be there 'finishing up' after a busy day. She would weed the small garden in front and pick up any garbage that might have been left. The staff still jokes about me not being able to pass a piece of litter or a weed without removing it. First impressions!

"While these women were directly involved with the wine industry and tourism, I also learned from strong business professionals in other fields. In my late teens, I had the pleasure of meeting Pauline Marino, a very strong and confident woman whom I admired greatly. I was fascinated by her strong personal identity, and I observed her in an appreciative way. She balanced her careers with family commitments in a house with her husband and three sons. Pauline held several progressively responsible jobs in Niagara, including legal secretary, assistant director at the Hotel

Dieu Hospital, completing her working career as a justice of the peace for the Ministry of the Attorney General. She graduated high school at age fifteen and was an established working woman at age eighteen. She was an amazing woman well ahead of her time! I followed her many accomplishments over the years. She demonstrated to me the skills of always speaking up for yourself, working hard at all you do, and always being ready and willing to learn more.

"Another great role model was Donna Scott, OC, co-founder and publisher of *Flare* magazine, chair of Canada Council for the Arts [and many more distinguished positions]. She showed me that your strength and creativity in getting the job done was more important than worrying about 'male vs. female.' If you were good at your job, and worked hard and worked smart, you would succeed. She understood supporting excellence and how to connect people. She hosted the editors of French *Elle* and *Vogue* magazines and their teams for lunch in Toronto and at her home in Niagara-on-the-Lake. She served Inniskillin table wines and Icewine and insisted that the owner/vintner would attend. Both [Donald] Ziraldo and I attended. She wanted to profile the quality of our wines and to also personalize it at the same time. When she attended functions in Paris or other regions of France with the fashion industry, she noted that they always served French wine and had the wine owner or winemaker present. She was proud to do the same as she believed in the quality of our wines. The visitors from the French fashion industry were very impressed but also very surprised that Canada could make premium wine. Another example of Partners in Excellence."

Debi talks a bit about how events have grown as the industry has grown. When the events were small, Debi says she knew most of the guests and could easily move through the room and greet them warmly by name. Now, the events are much larger and draw new people from all over. Take, for instance, the outdoor amphitheatre concerts at Jackson-Triggs. The collection of talented and well-known Canadian performers is so magnificently curated, the concerts often sell out in hours. Rather than taking a well-earned front-row seat, Debi could always be found at the very back of the crowd, expertly scanning the gathering for anything or anyone who might need attention. The consummate PR professional, she wisely treated each event, big or small, as an opportunity to make genuine connections and create lasting and loyal relationships.

Always quick to give credit, Debi says, "Donald was a great teacher. I watched and learned. He was a connector, always collecting business cards and then having exactly the right person to call or to recommend for someone else to call. I have seen Donald write the names of five people on the back of someone's business card with whom he thinks they should be connected. He was an expert," she says with a smile of admiration.

Debi admits that if she had to name her biggest and most influential mentor, it would be Donald Ziraldo. "He was always on and as the face of the winery, he was also directly involved in the same type of things that I was doing. I remember coming back from a wine show in New York and telling Donald about the wine route signs there. I said, 'I don't know why we don't have them here.' Next thing I knew, he was making calls to the Ministry of Tourism and the Wine Council of Ontario. In the early days of developing the VQA, Donald and I would meet in the board room at Inniskillin on Sundays, as we were closed to the public then, and go through books and magazines gathering information on reputable appellation systems. There was no Google at that time, so we had to do our research and look things up. We were literally finding articles in magazines and ripping out the pages."

She shakes her head, remembering, and continues humbly, "I wasn't responsible for this accomplishment, I just assisted from the background. Witnessing how that endeavour unfolded and all the hard work and people who made that happen was just incredible. To see the amount of effort that goes into one industry initiative is mind-blowing."

Debi goes on. "In the early years, Donald would often get pulled away to do something important like the case study he was working on with Professor Nick Fry and some MBA students at the University of Western Ontario. It was a really pivotal study being done in the 1970s. I would sometimes be overwhelmed and say to him, 'Donald, I need your help here. I just can't do everything that needs to be covered at the winery by myself on a Saturday.' To which he would reply, as a strategic visionary, that the case study was critical to the success of both Inniskillin and the industry. So, we hired other people to help me at the winery. To this day, that case study is an integral part of Inniskillin's history. Donald saw the big picture."

As she was honing her own business skills, Debi was effectively putting her current proficiencies to use. Innately knowing that people learn and retain information through experiences, Debi always made a point to engage visitors in all aspects of the winemaking process. When Debi talks, people listen. She has an extraordinary ability to command an audience. Attending an event at which she is speaking is always something special. She got people thinking about wine differently, not just table wine but also Icewine. Icewine has been marketed so successfully as something very special —and rightfully so. The downside of this is that people tend to hold onto it for a special occasion, asking themselves, "Is THIS occasion special enough? Are WE special enough?" oftentimes convincing themselves that they should hold onto it for a more worthy occasion or company. Much like the best dinnerware, it might languish in people's cellars or cupboards.

Debi astutely flipped the mindset to consumers that enjoying Icewine is the celebration, rather waiting for a reason to celebrate. She would say, "Sparkling Icewine is a party waiting to happen at any time." And it's true! As soon as that bottle is open, and we lower our nose into the gorgeous, tropical aromas, we are transported, swept away by the luscious nectar as it washes over our palates.

Debi presided over dinner parties and cooking classes throughout which Icewine was the star ingredient, elevating simple vinaigrettes, marinades, glazes, and sorbets. Cocktails were made even more sophisticated by adding Icewine. She was one of the founding members of the Niagara-on-the-Lake Icewine Festival, part of her brilliant plan to develop year-round tourism in wine country. The team at Inniskillin, along with other wineries, rallied to transform the empty winter streets and the town square into a glittering and festive celebration of all things ice and snow, complete with carved sculptures, horse-drawn sleighs, Icewine luges, local chefs preparing delectable treats, Icewine cocktail competitions, and toasty outdoor fires around which guests could gather and warm themselves. This festival grew to include a ritzy black-tie gala, with world-class food served alongside the liquid treasure, and a collection of local winemakers proudly pouring their Icewine elixir to colleagues and guests.

With a smile, she says, "I enjoyed being part of an amazing and hardworking team of people at Inniskillin but also the broader industry team that included so many dynamic people. We all worked hard for a common goal."

In recognition of her outstanding contributions, Debi received countless awards before retiring. To name a few: Niagara Business Woman of the Year, 2003; Binational Star Award-Women in Tourism, 2009; Exceptional Hospitality Award (Ontario Wine Society Committee) 2009; RBC Business Citizen of the Year (Niagara Grape and Wine Festival) 2013; Gold Award, Educator (Ontario Hostelry Institute) 2014; the very first Brock University VQA Promoter Award was given to Debi in 2006 in the category of Education meant for "teachers, in formal or informal settings who educate and inspire students about Ontario VQA wines."

This award is testament to Debi's mission to keep education at the core of everything she does. In 2013, The Tourism Industry Association of Ontario honoured Debi with the Lifetime Achievement Award. In her acceptance speech, Debi simplified her philosophy into three words: pride, passion, and professionalism, stating, "Three words that can make or break you in the tourism business. All three are very evident to the tourist and should show from the first greeting to the last 'thanks for visiting' comment. Pride, passion, and professionalism will bring your customers back to you as regulars or keep them away forever. Show your passion and enthusiasm or get another career. Know how to present yourself, your company, and your product in the best possible way: service, cleanliness, fair practices. Treat people how you would like to be treated."

Debi's deep understanding and love of education drew her to become involved in both Brock University and Niagara College on many levels, from a highly respected and in-demand guest lecturer to advisor and member of the various educational boards. It was common to see her walking the corridors of both institutes, stopping to speak with students in the halls, or being warmly greeted by institutional heads. Debi mentions Dan Patterson, former president of Niagara College for twenty-five years. "His enthusiasm and commitment to leading the college and the students taught me so much. Sitting on the Board of Governors for five years at the college allowed me to experience in an even closer way the skills he had to be a successful leader."

In 2015, Debi delivered the convocation address to the graduating classes of Niagara College. Hundreds of eager faces focused on her words as she spoke to the importance of stepping out of one's comfort zone and listening to one's heart. "Generations passed tended to select one career and stick to it until retirement. While some of you might do this, I suspect that many of you will reach out and explore different career options including starting and running your own businesses. The opportunities are endless, but you must realize that you are the one in control now and you will create those opportunities and make those choices. By applying not only what you have learned through your education but what you have learned about yourself. Each step in life takes us out of our comfort zone and forces us to challenge ourselves. It may be awkward at first or considered a risk, but your inner self will keep you doing what is best for you.

"While you have spoken to many people up to this stage of your life, seeking advice, the person you really need to connect with and talk to is yourself. Over the years, I have had many conversations with many people who assisted and guided me, and I thank them for their input, but the most impactful conversations were those I had with myself. While others know a lot about you, your own perspective is what will make the decisions that 'feel right' and are right for you."

She concluded the speech by earnestly urging the graduates to "Challenge yourself. Inspire yourself. Keep strong role models but be a strong role model, too. Keep strong support systems around you, but also be a strong support to others. Do not underestimate your talents and capabilities. Recognize your own strengths and build upon them while working individually and as a team member. Keep your life balanced. Have fun. Keep your sense of self and keep your sense of humour." Following her speech, Debi was awarded an honorary post-graduate certification in winery business management, a program that owes much of its existence to Debi, as she herself forged the very first path and title of its kind in the 1970s.

As she neared her retirement date, Debi was asked by many what might be next for her after such an illustrious career. She responded often with, "As far as what is yet to come, I am looking forward to less hectic times. While I love the liveliness of what I do, I need to balance more personal time." Adding, "My ultimate quiet time is paddling up the Niagara River in my kayak."

Upon Debi's retirement in 2014, Constellation named ninety acres of vineyard in her honour. Local newspapers showed her smiling in front of Inniskillin while accepting the plaque reading:

PRATT VINEYARD
DEDICATED TO MS. DEBORAH PRATT
FOR HER 40 YEARS OF SERVICE WITH INNISKILLIN WINES

When asked how it feels to know that people will read that plaque for decades to come and work within those vines, she replies, "That was the best retirement gift I could have received as it will be around forever. If I had stayed a teacher, no matter how good a teacher that I was, I don't think they would have named a school after me!" She adds, reflectively, "I can't help but think of my mother and her years spent in vineyards. Who would have ever dreamt that one day there would be one named after her daughter?"

Debi has now officially retired, but she hasn't stopped sharing the stories, mentoring others, or being an extraordinary ambassador of Niagara, its people, and its wine industry. Always generous with her time, she has a depth of knowledge and life wisdom to impart. She feels "it's essential to give back as we should always be building for the future and paying it forward to help others." In fact, when asked what the next chapter might hold for her, Deb replies, "Simply doing what I feel like doing on my own time frame, which includes giving back but not in a structured way. I love Niagara-on-the-Lake and enjoy helping in many ways to keep our town as historic and beautiful as it is—a living heritage community, managed properly as a dynamic year-round wine tourism destination that balances the lives of residents and visitors."

JENNIFER WILHELM

In 2014, Debi was chosen by the Niagara Foundation as recipient of the Living Landmark Award. Established in 1962, the Niagara Foundation works hard to preserve the unique heritage of the town of Niagara-on-the-Lake. Each year the board chooses a resident of Niagara-on-the-Lake to receive the prestigious award, a recipient who the foundation feels has made an outstanding contribution to the quality of life in Niagara. In her acceptance speech, Debi admits to feeling speechless when learning of the nomination.

She goes on to say, of the previous recipients, "What an amazing collection of distinguished individuals, whom I have followed and admired over the years for their many contributions to 'our' unique and historic town. I do know for sure, that what I have in common with all of the former recipients is that I love Niagara-on-the-Lake and have tried in my own way to contribute as much as I can to keep it the special town, we all know it to be and want it to continue to be. When you live in Niagara-on-the-Lake, you fall in love with the town, and you want to help protect and preserve it. It becomes very personal."

Always one to readily give credit to others, Debi shares, with pride, the influence of her parents. "I know that my sense of community started early in my life through my parents, Kitty and LeRoy, just down the lake at Port Weller. My mother was the unofficial mayor of Port Weller, who was constantly at City Hall or calling them on issues to help our community be better. When they didn't listen, she would send a terse but focused message via the letters to the editor in *The Standard*. My Dad was very active in starting and being a member of the Port Weller Volunteer Fire Department. They both instilled in me that your community is what you make it, and you need to get involved to make things happen."

Her love of her community and celebrating the people within it fuels her to breathe life into their stories. In her current role as a Niagara Community Foundation Committee Member for Niagara-on-the-Lake, she not only helps to raise funds for her beloved town, but she also chronicles the stories of other exceptional citizens contributing to the town through their endowed funds. The interviews are brilliantly conducted and written; Debi's genuine care and interest in others, coupled with her ability to really listen, encourages them to relax, trust her, and truly open up. This is one of the unique gifts that she has made a practice of giving over her lifetime—in the classroom, tasting room, the board room, dining room, or simply sitting with friends. She adds, "When you believe in what you are doing, you can't help but be successful." She encourages each of us to know our strengths and be true to ourselves and where those strengths may lead us. She reiterates that this industry was built by a collection of individuals who each brought something unique and integral to the table and advises, "Don't try to fit into someone else's box or allow yourself to be pigeonholed."

Most recently, Debi was honoured at the Women in Business awards (sponsored by the Greater Niagara Chamber of Commerce) with the 2019 Lifetime Achievement Award recognizing women for their accomplishments in business, leadership. As she took the podium, she prefaced her speech by saying that the preceding introduction made her feel like she was in a time warp as the words sparked so many memories of her life. As she listened to the accolades, she thought to herself, *Oh I forgot about that! I remember doing that now. That was such fun, or, that was really challenging.*

She reveals, "I think what I forgot the most was how hard it was in those first few decades. You know, you're looking now at a very successful billion-dollar industry with a strong appellation system and a wine route. I look back on initiatives like that and recall the struggles but also the satisfaction of being a part of something so spectacular. These accomplishments affected so many people and built the foundation of what we have today." She shakes her head in remembrance. "It was really something to be a part of."

On receiving the award, she said, "I felt incredibly honoured as it allowed me to reflect on such a wonderful and fulfilling wine career. Reflecting allows one to unfold the layers of how it all happened." Always gracious, she continues, "It also put me in the company of women whom I truly admire."

When spending time with Debi Pratt, one can sense that they are in the presence of a strong and wise woman at peace with herself, her decisions, and the way in which she has lived her life. When asked if, in retrospect, she would offer her teenage self any words of advice, she replies sagely, "Let life unfold. Don't push it. Follow your instincts. Follow your curiosity and creativity." It seems, looking at Debi's life, that that is exactly what she did do. She reveals, "I did not want to become a teacher. That unfolded because of a summer job. I didn't plan to go into business, no less the wine industry. It unfolded because of a curiosity of what two fellows were doing that I thought I'd like to learn more about. I'm fortunate that my parents weren't pushy about a career; they allowed me to pursue different things that captured my interests. I never felt pressured, so I was able to truly let things unfold based on my own comfort level and what I felt curious about and where I was able to make a difference. I felt that I could be a good teacher, and I was a good teacher. When I met Donald and Karl, I felt that I had something to offer and that I could help them build their business. And I did. I felt that I could make a difference in tourism. And I did. I learned to trust my instincts and follow my curiosity and to go where I thought I could make a difference."

She continues, "It was a very sad day in November 2017 when Karl Kaiser passed away. After all the years together—the hard work, the frustrations, the successes, and the laughter—there were now the tears of sorrow and feelings of disbelief. It was so difficult, and still is, to imagine that all of us were never going to see that big Kaiser smile, learn more from him or taste his 'homemade' wines. I still think that my phone will ring, and Karl and I will have a chat about wine or arranging to pick him up to go to a function or to share his immense pride he had for his children and grandchildren. The sight at the winery of the Canadian flag flying half-staff in Karl's honour is still imbedded in my mind."

They were an unlikely trio: a talented Austrian-born winemaker, an ambitious young businessman with an agriculture degree, and a curious, open-minded schoolteacher who was astute enough to see exactly how her transferable skills could help their dream become a reality. What they had in common was tenacity, grit, and unshakeable belief in one another. Together, they would change the future of the Ontario and Canadian wine industry. Along the course of their journey, they spearheaded an industry, broke down barriers, forged alliances, and built an appellation of origin system with other like-minded visionaries: they transformed lives, communities, and the world's perception of our country's ability to produce premium wine from premium grapes grown in the Niagara

Peninsula. Most certainly, none of it would have happened the way it did, and with such care of people, if it were not for Debi Pratt.

An industry is built by collective forces and individuals, each pooling their unique strengths towards a common goal. Debi's public relations skills were essential in building the winery and its loyal clientele on a daily, weekly, and yearly basis. Inniskillin, as a trailblazer and, consequently, the Ontario wine industry, would not have had the same draw or credibility without Debi Pratt. It's comparable to a tower of blocks in that, if one were to remove one block (in this case one person) of the foundation, the infrastructure would not have the same strength to stand or continue to build and would certainly look much different that it does today.

Of this remarkable legacy, Debi says reflectively, "Professionally, I would like to be remembered as someone who worked hard and truly cared about people and their understanding of the amazing wines we can produce in Ontario so that they, in turn, could become our wine ambassadors. Personally, I would like to be remembered as someone who was not restricted by one career but had the self-confidence to follow where I knew I could make a difference. An intelligent, professional woman with a great sense of humour, as that gets you through everything!" She adds judiciously, "Others will pick and choose what they want to remember about you because of their interaction with you at whatever part in your life and job you intersect." Thoughtfully, Debi ends, "I think people just want to be remembered."

JENNIFER WILHELM

Tributes to Debi Pratt

Debi Pratt by Nick Fry
Professor, University of Western Ontario, and spouse, Cheri Lind

"It would have been early September 1976. We were driving along the Niagara Parkway one day and saw this vineyard. It looked like someone was starting a winery or something. So, we pulled in and drove up the drive. There was a lot of activity, and it seemed chaotic as the grapes were coming in. They didn't have this, and they didn't have that. We went down the road a bit and walked into a little office. We didn't know her then, but it was Debi behind the desk. We started to chat with her about what was happening. We were really interested.

"Up the drive comes a white Mercedes-Benz convertible. This man got out wearing a white shirt, open down the front with this gold medallion. The ladies in our group went gaga [said with a laugh at the memory]. Don [Ziraldo] comes in, and we start to chat with him. He finds out that two of us are professors at a business school. He tells us he is trying to finance the business transition from a garage operation to a respectable winery. Debi is part of the conversation, and it's pretty informal. Finally, I say, 'Look, in the course I teach, we've got student groups who do start-up studies like this. They go out into the industry and look at the prospects, study the businesses, and prepare a report for the owner about the next steps and how it might be financed.' Don was a great opportunist and said, 'That sounds really good!'

"So, we decided to set it up. The timing was perfect as school was getting ready to start up again. Don came into class to speak to the students. Now, you have to imagine the attitude of people at the time. It was essentially, 'What the hell, why would anyone want to start a winery in this country?' The students thought he was crazy and, in fact, one of the students even asked Don straight out why a bright guy would throw money away starting up a winery in Canada. There is a tremendous risk, and the wines produced here have a reputation for being plonk! Don was prepared for the skepticism and responded, 'My dad told me that if you're going to drown, you might as well do it in an ocean and not a puddle.' So, the students did the study, and Don took it to the bank and to General Kitching, and he got the approval. It was a two-inch thick report on the industry and the possibilities. It was a significant plus for Don.

"Don knew there was a big risk involved, but he had supreme confidence. Being the type of guy he was—a very smart guy—he knew his strengths, and he also knew that he needed someone to look after the details and provide continuity to the operation. Well, that was Debi. Over the years, she was the person who was the glue for the business throughout its various stages of growth."

Cheri interjects here and adds, "Debi kept track of everything and everyone, and she did it in such a way that it all looked so effortless. And she did it with kindness. She was always so kind. But she was also so competent that Donald just believed everything she told him implicitly and took every one of her suggestions."

Nick continues, "This was crucial. The whole thing would have crumbled without Debi. I can give you a dozen other case histories of entrepreneurs who could not run a business long-term. The ideas and promotion were great, but the details and implementation were often terrible. Don was so smart. He understood and valued everything Debi did. Karl was great, too, but he was the technician, and Don was the promotor. Who is coordinating the two of them and keeping it all afloat? Every breath Don took was promoting Inniskillin, no matter where he went. But Debi was the one holding down the fort."

Nick says, "It was a fascinating success story, and Debi was a big part of it. People like Debi are crucial and often underappreciated, but start-ups and small companies will never survive if they don't exist. Don was smart, and he valued Debi and made that known. He ensured she was challenged and knew she was a significant part of everything. Debi was the face of Inniskillin if you were to visit the winery. She was always there."

Cheri says, "We returned to the winery to visit, and I had forgotten Debi's name. I told her, 'I'm so sorry, I've forgotten your name, but I could never forget your eyes.' She has the most beautiful eyes, and she was just wonderful. We were always big fans of Debi."

Debi Pratt by Maria Moessner
Arterra On-Premise Sales / Sommelier

"While working in the Holiday Inn's dining room in St. Catharines during the late 1980s, I had the privilege to meet an incredible lady, Debi Pratt. At the time, Debi was the sales and public relations director for Inniskillin Wines. She had left teaching to follow her passion for wine and support the growing industry in Niagara. I would have never imagined she would become a mentor, great friend, and play such a pivotal role in my life and career.

"At the Holiday Inn restaurant, Oregano's, we had private-label white and red wines created by Inniskillin. To further our wine knowledge, Debi Pratt tutored our team, and she was a regular at the restaurant, along with, Inniskillin's founders Karl Kaiser and Donald Ziraldo. We were all in awe of Debi and inspired by her wisdom, skill, and passion; we aspired to be like her someday. Come to think of it, I'm not sure I ever shared that with her!

"Debi stood out to me. Her down-to-earth nature, professional demeanour, knowledge, and teaching skills left a lasting impression. I was inspired to take my career path to the Niagara wine industry.

"In 1989, I was hired by Debi at Inniskillin, and from that moment, she took me under her wing. Throughout my fourteen-year tenure at Inniskillin, she taught me many skills, honed my strengths, and empowered me to be the best I could be. So many unforgettable memories, so many memorable moments embraced.

"If it weren't for Debi, I'm unsure where my career path would have taken me. I'm genuinely grateful for her and her positive impact on my life."

SHARING A GLASS

Debi Pratt by Donald Ziraldo
Co-Founder, Inniskillin

"It is difficult to truly express proper credit to Debi Pratt for everything she has done for Inniskillin, for Niagara and for the Canadian wine industry.

"Debi first joined Inniskillin at the original winery site on SR #58, where Karl Kaiser and I had started Inniskillin in an old fruit-packing shed. She had been teaching at the Brockview School, located on the Jeffries farm, where I had planted 30,000 grafted grape vines (Chardonnay, Riesling, and Gamay). She started working with us initially in the nursery/winery office. It was basically a converted chicken coop! This alone illustrates her belief in the future of the Niagara wine industry. There were not many believers at the time, but Debi was one. She 'walked the talk' and continues to do so.

"Debi took a sabbatical from teaching and started full-time with Inniskillin in the mid-1980s. She began by looking after retail customers on weekends at the original winery/fruit packing shed and then assisted in converting the Brae Burn Barn at the current Inniskillin location. While the winery was under construction, she helped transform the barn into a barrel cellar and wine boutique. The barn's design is thought to have been influenced by Frank Lloyd Wright [from when he was] working for the Larkin family from Buffalo, New York. They had 2000 acres and three sets of barns 'in the style of Frank Lloyd Wright' here in Niagara.

"I point this out because this is an example of how Debi was always fostering partnerships. In this case, not only did she invite Eric Lloyd Wright, Frank's grandson, to speak at Inniskillin, we additionally hired architect Bruno Freschi, dean of architecture at Buffalo State University. He had been in charge of restoring Buffalo's Darwin D. Martin House, designed by Frank Lloyd Wright. Bruno completed the Millennium Project, which was a twenty-year plan for Inniskillin.

"Debi's experience as a teacher served her very well. She used those transferable teaching skills to engage and educate visitors, whether they were professional sommeliers from around the world or local school kids visiting the winery. Often people would politely say to me, 'Donald, if you cannot make it for the tour or presentation, we would be delighted to have Debi present.' When people visited the winery, I always let Debi do the tours because she would do a much better job of 'telling the story' than I ever could.

"The other area where Debi was enormously influential was winery tourism. She quickly saw the potential of Niagara Falls and its thirteen million visitors as an opportunity to get them to come downriver and visit Inniskillin. We hosted dignitaries of all kinds, including presidents and kings. Not only did Debi brief me fully about each visitor, but she would also often fly the flag of the visiting dignitaries. At events we attended, sponsored, or poured at, she would always pick out famous individuals, quickly make a beeline, and introduce me. President of the Soviet Union Mikhail Gorbachev, US President Jimmy Carter, the Prince of Luxembourg, and F1 race car driver Michael Schumacher, were just some of those. Debi was also very aware that all these people coming to see the Niagara Falls could become great ambassadors for our region since few knew we grew grapes in Canada.

"Debi was always creating unique and innovative ways to share the cost of marketing and to reach new customers. 'Partners in Excellence' was a theme that she focused on in various sectors. We worked with Shaw Festival, Toronto International Film Festival, and American Express. Toronto Symphony Orchestra celebrity fundraising during Icewine harvest included Jim Cuddy, of Blue Rodeo; Ron MacLean, Hockey Night in Canada; and Geddy Lee of Rush.

"One of the things that became apparent to me when I left Inniskillin in 2006 and began making my own Icewine back at a vineyard I planted at the original winery site, was that I realized how invaluable Debi and all the staff at Inniskillin were. Under her leadership, they did so much work that I took for granted. I could arrive anywhere—in Japan, New York, Singapore, etc.—and everything was always ready. The wines were properly chilled and presented, all the information at my fingertips. Wherever I was—whether Vinexpo or Vinitaly—behind the scenes, Debi and the staff had invited wine media, sommeliers, distributors, and licensees to attend. I noticed when I had to do all those things myself at Ziraldo Estate Winery! Debi and her team worked hard, making Karl and I look good at all times while modestly taking little credit for all the hard work.

"Debi also represented the Niagara Region and Canadian wine industry at many events where she was asked to speak, especially on winery tourism. She worked very closely with tourism industry partners, media, and government officials. She would coordinate visits by travel writers who might not otherwise recognize Niagara as a wine region, often touring inbound travel writers, thus extending the demographic we reached and enhancing agritourism.

"Debi contributes numerous other activities to the community. Not only does she sit on the Niagara Community Foundation, but she is also the unofficial 'mayor' of Niagara-on-the-Lake. If you want to take the pulse of our incredibly unique town, speak to Debi.

"The other passion she spends a considerable amount of time on is looking after friends and family to whom she is a caregiver. She has touched so many, often assisting them through difficult times. At Christmas, she will pack and distribute gift boxes to needy families. Every time I speak with her, I discover yet another humanitarian act she has undertaken. She has been acknowledged, and rightly so, by numerous organizations, for her many contributions to Niagara."

Debi Pratt by Ann-Louise Branscombe
Niagara Community Foundation, Director
Branscombe Family Foundation
Branscombe Pathstone Mental Health

"I met Debi over twenty-five years ago, in the early 1990s. I wanted to organize a Friday afternoon wine tasting at our little Town and Country Plaza in Niagara Falls. It had been suggested to me that I speak to Debi in her capacity as a spokesperson for Inniskillin Winery.

"It would not be of any consequence to Inniskillin because it would be on such a small scale, but Debi was very welcoming and immediately said she would help me and donate a few bottles of wine. Later, Reif, and Château des Charmes joined in. But Debi supported me first, and I was so grateful.

"In the years since, I have known of her other involvements in philanthropic and cultural projects in Niagara-on-the-Lake. I currently sit with her on the fundraising committee for Niagara-on-the-Lake, a part of the overarching Niagara Community Foundation.

"Everything Debi tackles, she does with passion, care, and thoughtfulness. We are fortunate indeed to have her in our community."

Debi Pratt by Heidi Fielding
Director of Sales & Marketing,
Fielding Estate Winery

"In 2001 when I joined the then-Vincor team to open Jackson-Triggs Niagara Estate Winery, I had the pleasure of getting to know Debi. There is no other like her in our industry. When Debi enters a room, you are first greeted by her warm smile and then captivated by her magnetic personality. She has a true gift of sharing her passion for wine. The stories of her adventures while working at Inniskillin are entertaining and inspiring. Beautiful, classy, and smart, she was the perfect spokesperson for Niagara wines."

Dr. Helen Fisher

"It was a different era; politically correct wasn't even a concept yet. I never thought too much about what people thought about me being a woman in this role. When it did occasionally cross my mind, I told myself, To hell with it. I'm here and I've got work to do, *and on I went about my business. I wanted to do the best work I could and that had nothing to do with gender."*

It is a hot July day in Niagara when I meet up with Helen Fisher. Southern Ontario is under another summer heat advisory with severe storm warnings. The temperature is 32 degrees Celsius, 43 degrees with the humidity. As I pull up to the local pub where we have decided to meet, Helen sits, in the filtered sun under a canopy, unbothered by the heat, sipping a local craft beer and reading the newspaper. She smiles when I ask her if she is okay sitting outside. "You know what my first job was, Jenn? It was planting strawberries in the blazing sun in west St. Catharines. By the end of day one, I was burnt to a crisp and the colour of your shirt." [It's bright pink.] "I'd rather be outdoors in than inside any day" she states.

It's important to preface this telling by sharing a few critical details about this down-to-earth, extremely humble [to the point of self-deprecating), extraordinary human.

Her signature line following emails is telling, more because of what isn't included, rather than what is:

JENNIFER WILHELM

K. Helen Fisher (retired)
Department of Plant Agriculture/Vineland
University of Guelph

Let's start with the fact that most PhDs let us know right away that their prefix is Dr. They have a well deserved right to be proud of earning that title! With Helen, we must read between the lines to see her many remarkable accomplishments and contributions. She doesn't brag or self-promote. Nowhere in this message will you find credentials, or even roles. She doesn't disclose more than meets the eye. One would never know the obstacles she has overcome, the triumphs to be celebrated, the heartaches behind this fascinating woman.

Retired. Now don't associate images of southern flying, beach lounging, poolside lunching retirees with Helen. (Although that sounds pretty good to me!) Retired, for Helen, means working fewer than sixty-hour weeks, but still includes driving from Niagara to Simcoe or southwestern Ontario or Prince Edward County to check on vineyards and connect with farmers. It still includes teaching several college and university classes and mentoring numerous students. It still includes securing finances for grants and student programs. It also includes organizing and cataloguing 250 boxes of personally stored archives pertaining to the Ontario grape and tender fruit industry.

K. Helen Fisher. "What does the K stand?" for I inquire. She was named Kate Helen, after her mother Kate Lillian, but has gone by Helen her entire life to avoid confusion with her mother, though Helen claims that they would still get each other's mail as the bank and other businesses would confuse them on paper.

Helen was born in England and immigrated to Canada with her parents and two older siblings when she less than a year old. It was a difficult crossing, sailing the north Atlantic in December. The family spent their first Christmas off the coast of Halifax and then at Pier 21 like many of the other immigrant passengers. Their new home was meant to be Baie Comeau, Québec, where her father had been hired by what was known at that time as the Québec North Shore Paper Company (Quno). However, hazardous winter conditions made it impossible to access the town since there was no all-weather road and the coastal freighters stopped running in the winter. They settled in St. Catharines, on Chaplain Avenue before heading to Baie Comeau in the spring. The family moved back to Niagara in 1954 when Helen's father was transferred to Quno's office in Thorold.

Helen spent her early school years in the city before attending Havergal College, a girls boarding school in Toronto. Founded in 1894, Havergal's claims proudly to be "thriving today and leading tomorrow." Their website states that "Havergal's mission is to prepare young women to make a difference and to take on an ever-changing world with confidence, resilience and global-mindedness. Our supportive, stimulating environment gives them the future-ready skills they need to lead with purpose and thrive no matter what tomorrow brings."

Helen feels that she did come away from her school years there with confidence, self assurance, and independent thinking, which she put to use immediately.

Upon graduation, Helen headed off to university. She chuckles when asked how she decided on an agriculture degree at Guelph University. "It was kind of by mistake," she reveals. "I was actually registered for General Sciences but, on the first day, after spending five years at an all-girls school, I decided that the people, young men to be specific, looked a hell of a lot more interesting in the agriculture line! So, I switched lines," she laughs mischievously. "In those days, everyone just went into a big gymnasium and lined up in front of their program tables to register. When I got to the table, I just told them there had been a mistake and I was supposed to be in BSc Agr, not BSc. And that was that!" Eighteen-year-old Helen was already blazing her own non-conformist trail.

She enjoyed university and claims that the first year was, in her words, "a piece of cake." Helen says, "I had come from a school that concentrated a fair amount on science, especially for girls in those days." She tells of her Grade 13 French teacher who, in a broad Scottish accent, told young Helen firmly, "Dear, you have a far better ability in languages than you do in science." At Havergal, Helen had taken double-English, double-French, and double-Latin up until Grade 12. Although she admits to "sneaking in a little art and music, in amongst the geometry, physics, algebra, trigonometry, chemistry and physics," Helen knew even then, despite her French teacher's advice, that she was more interested in science.

She reveals that she didn't have a clear idea of what she wanted to do with her degree at the end of it but feels that it was serendipitous that she made her way into that agriculture program line all those years ago. Insight came from her summer jobs. After the first year of university, Helen's father encouraged her to write to a letter to local farmers. Having never spent time on a farm growing up, he felt she needed some experience.

"He wasn't displeased that I made the switch to agriculture, but he was surprised. So, I took his advice, and I wrote to one of the prominent fruit growers. My first real job, other than pulling weeds for Stokes one summer in high school, was planting strawberries. On the first day, after spending all year indoors in a classroom, I was in the open field, in the wind, full sun, on the back of a planter, trying to put the strawberry plants right side up in the planting wheel." She shakes her head and grimaces. "Every so often I'd hear this yell from behind me 'PALM TREE!' which meant that I hadn't separated the plants properly and they'd gone in root side up. Between my sunburn and my embarrassment, I was bright red. When we got back to the barn, the older Italian women took me under their wing. 'The skinny little white girl,' they called me. They insisted I join them in their big lunch of salami, bread, cheese. 'You must eat!' they demanded.

"Decades later, in 1992, my father was in Shaver Hospital. I recognized the name of the head nurse, as the same as the supervisor I worked under that first summer. 'Oh yes!' she said when I asked about a relation, 'that was my husband!' I asked her about the tiny little woman who came to visit the man, in the bed beside my father. Turns out she worked there, too. I remembered how kind those women had been to me. I went to her husband's funeral to pay my respects. It was all in Latin and Italian, but I was glad I went.

"In those days, Schenck was a leading propagator and supplier of rooted geranium cuttings. When we weren't in the fields, we were in the greenhouses. We were cleaning beds in between crops and in those days, plants weren't grown in individual cell packs. What we had was a bench, with sides, filled with peat, into which we would plant the geranium cuttings. In between crops, those beds had to be completely cleaned out, steamed, and new peat put in. So, this tiny little woman would get at the end of the bed with a bushel, and we would sweep all the peat into it. Wet peat. Now a bushel of wet peat probably weighs forty to fifty pounds, but this little woman moved them like they weighed nothing. I remember watching her and thinking, 'Damnit, I'm going to have to do that, too!' I learned how to work and to work hard with those ladies. I had to keep up and it wasn't easy!"

The following year, with further academics behind her, Helen took a job as a research student with the Horticulture Research Institute of Ontario in Vineland Station.

Helen reveals that while it wasn't expected, in the 1960s, that she graduate from university and build a career around her chosen studies, her parents were pleased and proud of her. Her BSc class from the University of Guelph was made up of 250 students, only twenty-five of whom were women. Approximately 150 students saw their degrees through to graduation, and the ten per cent ratio of women remained at the end. Despite her love of science, Helen confesses that she struggled through the second year of university. There were so many interesting things to do that didn't involve sitting at a desk studying or writing essays. By year three, she found her stride and had begun classes that truly held her interest, rather than the general science prerequisites of the first two years. Ultimately, she graduated near the top of her class and decided to continue in her academic studies. At that time, it wasn't common for women to pursue a master's degree.

She was hired by what was then The Wine Council of Ontario as a field person for the new grape trials in Southwestern Ontario, identifying varieties across Essex and Kent counties and ensuring that the plots were correctly labelled. Ron Moyer, a well-respected grape grower from Grimsby, had started a farm there, and Helen spent two summers working with him and the other co-operators. While working in the area, the fruit extension agent position, with the Ontario Department of Agriculture and Food, came up and Helen decided to apply. When it was determined that she was the most qualified applicant, her would be supervisors had to get approval from the minister of agriculture to hire a woman—the first in the provincial agricultural field advisory service! She became the fruit extension specialist for Kent and Essex counties.

"It was summer in the 1970s. I was all of five feet two inches tall, and I'd go out to meet the farmers in short shorts, short tops, and wooden sandals. I remember heads turning in amazement when people realized who I was. There was often a Mrs. peering through the farmhouse curtains or screen door to make sure I wasn't up to anything with her man!" Helen chuckles and shakes her head remembering.

"I loved those Doctor Scholl's wooden sandals. My colleagues would joke that they could hear me coming from miles away. *Clunk! Clunk! Clunk!* One year at the Christmas party in Harrow, they even had a spoof of me! My friend Joan dressed up in this plaid lumberjack jacket and, wearing wooden sandals, clomped across the stage. The whole room started laughing and clapping. 'It's Helen!'" Helen herself is laughing so hard here, retelling the story. She's the first to laugh at herself, says it keeps us humble to laugh.

The work was interesting, and Helen enjoyed being outdoors. She built friendships and recalls with a grin some of the ways they would have some fun after work. "My friend Ed was a good one. We were both single and had an absolute hoot going out together as friends. In those days, the growers held a big bash at Christmas time. We would have a great time! Oh, we would dance! Now, picture this. I'm five foot two and Ed was about six foot six." Helen is doubling over telling these stories, revelling in the memories of merriment.

Helen made many of her own clothes in those days, cloaks, dresses for dances, and the like. She recalls her friend Ed arriving to pick her up for a dance and she wasn't quite finished sewing her outfit. (It's already been established that Helen is a great procrastinator!) The trouble was the hem. The fabric was plaid and getting that hem to look straight on a circular cape was no small feat. "I was living on a farm then. Fortunately, my landlady was a wonderful seamstress and we just laughed and laughed at the dining room table trying to get this cloak done in time. My landlady was really my only female friend. She was also a well respected member of the local Anglican church, and I would go with her every Sunday. I went to her quilting club, too, and that was actually a lot of fun! The quilting ladies would poke fun at me good naturedly. My eyesight wasn't very good, so I had to hold the fabric right up to my face to see. 'Helen, you're going to stich your nose right into that quilt!' they would say.

"I honestly can think of only one other female friend at the time. I was surrounded by men in all areas of my life. Luckily, there were a few good guys who looked out for me and were happy to just leave it as friends. Smelt fishing was great fun back then. It was usually at night, and we would go to Point Pelee. I'm pretty sure it was illegal to catch fish there, but there we were!"

Helen recalls that during smelt season, the wait to get beer and smelts was sometimes well over an hour long. "The pubs were divided into the men's side and the women's side back then. The pool tables were on the men's side with nothing at all to do on the women's side! I wanted to learn to play pool, but oh no, that was a men's game." She rolls her eyes. "They were those little bumper pool tables, and it just would not do for a woman to be leaning over one of those tables in a pub!" Another eye roll, accompanied with a laugh and shake of her head. This was in the early 1970s. Eventually, it became the decision of the pub to decide if the genders should remain on separate sides of the establishment.

Helen tells of going with her friend Ed to an old French pub in Chatham. "You had to walk through the men's side to get to the ladies and escorts side. Ed would send me off first so that he would take the flack. The men would whisper loudly in outraged French, which I understood, but Eddie didn't. I just laughed. I didn't take any offense.

"I had to laugh. I was a real oddity at the time you see. I was over eighteen and single. The local community couldn't make sense of me. I had no desire to marry and raise a brood of kids. So, when, after three years in Harrow, I saw an ad in *The Globe and Mail* for a botany professor at Fairview Agricultural and Technical College in northern Alberta, I decided to apply, and off I went.

"I was on a vineyard tour that was run by the *Eastern Grape Grower and Winemaker* magazine [now defunct] at the time. We started off in Washington State and ended in California. The folks at Fairview College wanted to interview me for the professor position, so they suggested that I fly over to Vancouver, then to Edmonton for the interview. I would catch up with the rest of the tour afterwards. I booked a flight and a hotel room. I got to the airport in Edmonton and climbed into a taxi. The driver looked at me funny when I gave him the address. 'Do you know where you're going?' he asked me. I said no, I had never been to Edmonton before. 'Well,' he says, 'you're in a pretty sketchy neighbourhood. When we get there, don't get out of the car. Pay me in the taxi before we get out, and I will come around and escort you in. You will be okay. They built the hotel thinking this part of the town would improve but it hasn't.

"When we arrived, he let the front desk know I was there, but then informed me, 'You'll have to wait a little, the receptionist is dealing with a flimflam man. He gives you a whole lot of bills and asks for change, then gives you a whole lot of change and ask for bills. It's a shell game. If you don't keep your eye on all the moving parts, you lose.' While I wait, a fight breaks out in front of the hotel. At this point, I'm feeling pretty frazzled and I'm on my way to an interview!"

Helen recounts the events. Her interviewers decided she was the best person for the position but couldn't offer her the job on the spot because she was a woman. No woman had ever taught in the agricultural department. "The same damn thing again!" she exclaims incredulously with an irritated shake of her head. Without knowing this detail at the time, Helen headed to the airport and got ready to board the plane to catch up with her colleagues on the conference tour. She was so focused on navigating the airport that she didn't hear her name being paged over the intercom. It was the folks from Fairview College paging her to offer her the job. This is pre cellphone days, so they were trying to intercept her boarding the only way they could.

She accepted the position and held it for two and half years ("My years in the bush!" she says) before returning to Niagara in 1978 to join the Horticultural Research Institute of Ontario (**HRIO**). Once again, she was met with a hiring barrier because of her gender. Once again, it was determined that she was the best candidate for the post and permission was granted to hire her. Shortly thereafter, both of Helen's predecessors retired, leaving her to inherit not one but two positions: plant physiologist and grape breeder. She enjoyed this role as research scientist at **HRIO**, transitioning to associate professor with the University of Guelph in 1996 when the government divested itself of the research and education divisions of the Ministry of Agriculture and Food.

A condition of employment with HRIO was that their new scientists obtain a PhD. At the time, the closest university offering a doctorate program in viticulture was Cornell University in Ithaca, New York. Helen completed her PhD from Cornell in 1988, studying part-time while simultaneously holding her job as research scientist with HRIO. She laughs as she recalls that she only got one speeding ticket on the NY State Thruway during that time. She feels grateful that she worked closely with John Ghetti from Brights, Jack Monroe from Jordans, Earl Sullivan from London's, Bob Wilcox, and Jim Rainforth from ODAF. "These guys really took me under their wing." Helen recalls fondly. "They kind of squired me around and I learned so much from them."

When asked if there were any other women working in the grape growing industry at that time, Helen names just two: Madame Bosc from Château des Charmes, and Donna Lailey. She knew of Debi Pratt, but their paths hadn't crossed yet. At a conference for the North American Grape Breeder's Association, Helen was the only female attendee. Her fellow scientists at the research centre were all men. She remembers the environment being intimidating and the language and comments bordering on offensive. She summarizes with the observation: "Let's just say politically correct wasn't even a concept yet." She guffaws and rolls her eyes.

"It was a different era. I had to be tough. I just kept my head down and tried to do what was expected of my job. I actually never thought too much about what people thought about me being a woman in this role. When it did occasionally cross my mind, I told myself, *To hell with it. I'm here and I've got work to do,* and on I went about my business. I wanted to do the best work I could and that had nothing to do with gender. I also liked being out in the field. I got chastised for it sometimes. It was assumed that I would publish more academic papers but, honestly, I didn't like that work. Consequently, my publishing record was very poor. Abysmal, I was told, several times." She shrugs.

It wasn't that she didn't like research; she quite enjoyed gathering information about various plots, vineyards, and clones. What she didn't enjoy was deskwork. She remembers loving the openness of the conversations she had with growers and farmers. They were just six main wineries in Ontario at the time: Brights, Jordan, Chateau Gai, Barnes, Andres, and London, with Inniskillin, Château des Charmes, and Hillebrand newly established.

Much of the province was planted with hybrid varieties, mostly Marechal Foch, Chelois, Seyval Blanc, Aurore, and De Chaunac, soon followed by Baco Noir and Vidal Blanc. Helen begins listing clone numbers by memory. Most of the new variety research in the fifties and sixties was proprietary, however, and not shared among the wineries. The Canadian Society of Oenology and Viticulture was urging the industry to communicate information about clones, site, and soil selection, from an academic perspective to improve grape growing and winemaking for the whole industry. This began collectively in earnest in the 1980s, with a shared goal of increasing quality and consumer perspective of Ontario wines. Helen remembers this as an exciting time to be a part of such positive change, moving from labrusca to hybrid grapes with a further desire to fully embrace vinifera varieties. There were already experimental plantings of vinifera, albeit at much higher inputs than hybrids, but also resulting in much improved wine quality.

She tells of the division in the industry that arose then. Those with a goal of quality rather than quantity were willing to put in the resources of money, time, effort, hand labour, and research that growing vinifera would require. As a plant physiologist and grape breeder, Helen was all for advancement. There were powerful visionaries in Ontario, of which Helen was one. She was instrumental in these critical changes. She believed that change could happen. She recalls the work being done to identify locally adapted varieties. As a young research scientist, she was privy to heated conversations about LCBO policies banning labrusca/hybrid blends. Shifting consumer perception and buying patterns regarding Canadian wine was happening, but it would take time and dedication. Helen has been more than dedicated to the viability and success of vinifera grapes in Ontario.

Interestingly, Helen is a beer drinker, preferring a pint over a glass of wine. She attributes this to the fact that most of the scientists she worked with in the early days were teetotallers and there was a clear separation between the field and the winery. Additionally, she was required to participate in sensory panels, and declares that she simply didn't enjoy it. "I didn't have the patience or interest in sensory analysis past the fruit component stage. Besides," she laughs, "I just couldn't get on board with some of the observations." She puts her nose in the air and adopts a haughty tone: "Ahhhhh, it smells like the saddle leather from a Spanish racehorse."

We both burst out laughing. She is a scientist, after all, and although these aroma descriptions are critical to detailed wine quality analyses and the general marketing world; they are not part of Helen's lab reports. Still, she is strong supporter of local wineries, always gifting and proudly pouring Ontario wines at home when friends and family visit. She even had a shirt in the 1980s, which garnered much attention with its statement: "Conserve Water. Drink Wine."

The servers at the pub know Helen by name and greet her with smiles and friendly conversation as they deliver another pint of beer. She asks after their health and their grandchildren.

She says her partner Billy was her biggest supporter and sounding board. Billy had a stroke in 2009, an event that changed both his and Helen's lives drastically and played a big role in her decision to retire that year. Helen became his main caregiver.

About retiring, she confides, "I was just finished at that point. I was told that I had to move down to this little cubbyhole with no windows in the basement lab after thirty-five years in my upstairs office. So, I hired a moving company. I said, 'Pack up all the stuff in this office, my upstairs office, my corner of the library, and my stash in the barn.' So, 225 boxes and a dozen filing cabinets later, I put it all in storage. It's still there!' She laughs before continuing in a more serious tone. "It's been there for eleven years now. I keep thinking that I need to go sort it out. Maybe quickly. I've been making a list about who else could look after it just in case I pop off suddenly! Who would have any knowledge of it or appreciation for the material? The trouble is, a lot of it is just wonderful old books, and nobody collects books anymore since most things have been digitized. I can't even donate them to the library. But there are some important documents in there that should be preserved.

"For instance, the documentation of the original importation of the French hybrids that were brought here after the war, directly from the breeders in the south of France. And all the correspondence between the Ontario government [Vineland/Toronto], the federal government [Ottawa] and France [Paris and Aubenas]. They had to get special permission to import the materials in 1946 or '47 when they started this because they couldn't deal directly with France right after the war. Everything had to go through Ottawa at that time. It was initiated by Brights and the Department of Agriculture at HRIO. It's fascinating literature, especially when you read the dates on these documents. It took a letter two days to get to Ottawa and a day to get back. When you consider the context of when all of this was being done, it's really very interesting.

"When I think about those boxes, and I break down the time required to sort them.... If I take ten each week, that's still twenty-five weeks—half a year! And then there's the filing cabinets.... Ahhhhhh! I should probably just go weed the garden. The thistles are taller than the roses right now. In fact, I have a thistle that's grown up between the slats of the bench on my front porch! It's flowering, and it actually looks kind of cool. I keep meaning to send a picture to a horticultural friend of mine, and label it as an objet d'art. He will love it!" She chuckles with glee at the thought. "We met in a plant taxonomy class. I was taking extra taxonomy classes because I really liked it. I didn't even get credit for it because I already had too many classes. I just took it for fun."

Helen suddenly breaks into laughter. When she finally catches her breath and wipes her eyes, she confesses that she and her classmates used to steal the cannabis samples out of the herbarium. "It was horrible stuff! It had been dried for twenty years!" She also recounts that hemp used to grow prolifically in Essex County. It was used as a shelter crop to protect row crops. It would self seed abundantly throughout the area. "I'd be out along the fence lines scouting for chokecherry, which harboured peach X-disease. I would find the wild hemp, cut it, and hide it under some grass clippings in my trunk. I gave it to my friend, who said, 'Helen, this is like smoking old lettuce leaves! It's awful! Save your energies.' It wasn't easy or even legal to buy cannabis back then. So, we'd sit around and drink beer instead."

It's a surprise when Helen names staying focused as having been one the biggest challenges in her life. To clarify, she says she is easily distracted by so many other things she wants to do. "So, I do the interesting things and procrastinate on the less interesting tasks, like boring desk work or submitting expenses. They would tell me 'Helen, your expense account is too big. And PLEASE send your receipts in more than once a year.' She laughs. "That kind of accounting is just boring, so I procrastinate." She chuckles but admits that it often works to her detriment. Like when she was required to complete and submit her promotion and tenure documents. "I put it off, put it off, put it off. Then it was actually too late to apply, so I got a zero, which is next to being fired in the university world. I was ready to retire anyway, but it was a bit of a sour note to leave on."

The challenges in academia and agriculture differ, in Helen's opinion, in that "academia has to do with numbers and data, and agriculture has to do with perception. Most of the time, in agriculture, if you came across confident or able to demonstrate physically what the issues were, you were viewed as successful. In academia, the expectations were that you would publish as much as possible, and that just wasn't for me. I'm a boots on the ground gal. I was confident in the work I did in the field. I enjoyed it, and I think I was respected for it. One of the most rewarding parts of my career has been consulting. It is gratifying. And to get paid for it!"

Helen has also quietly taken some glee in what she calls "flying under the radar." She recalls some early times when she was underestimated because of her gender and petite stature. She wasn't the only one.

She starts to chuckle before recounting a story about her friend Margaret in Prince Edward County. She's smiling describes the scenario. "Marg is a bit younger than me, but we are considered 'the two old ladies of the County!' We had so much fun! There were two other ladies in our group, a teacher, and a grower. One day, we were touring some of the farms and vineyards there and Marg had some of her students with her. It was an official tour, so we had some government cars, ministry vehicles with government logos on them. We were looking at a tiny vineyard, a high-density plot, metre by metre, that had been planted on a slope right across from a small municipal park. We happened to notice a man sitting on his porch at a house across the street. Next thing we know, a County municipal car pulls up and the driver wants to know what we're doing. We told him we were looking at this vineyard and discussing whether it would work.

"Turns out that the chap across the street had called and reported some government people inspecting the area. Being that we were all women, the assumption was made that we must be there to scope out a location for a new playground. Oh, we laughed! 'The playground police' we called ourselves after that! It never occurred to anyone that this group of women could be grape scientists with the government!" Helen laughs uproariously remembering. That's Helen. She is able to find the humour in most situations, many of which would have others feeling offended. "Water off a duck," she says. "I just didn't waste my energy on other people's opinions about me." She becomes thoughtful here. "Maybe that's why I was always surprised when my work was recognized with awards. I could always think of someone else who was far more deserving of the recognition."

Hearing this humble confession, I am speechless, and more than a little sad. I clearly remember the overwhelming support and outpouring of love for Helen when I put forth her nomination for Lifetime Achievement Award with the VQA Promote the Promotor program in 2019. Of course, she was presented with the award. Helen and her work are critical factors in our industry's success, a reality well known across North America. In addition to being the recipient of numerous prestigious awards, a wine was made and named in her honour by renowned Vineland Estates winemaker Brian Schmidt as part of his Game Changer series, paying homage to those individuals whose dedication shaped the grape and wine industry. Helen's is called *D'Vine Doctor.*

Helen admits "I did get an American award that I was tickled about. I was sitting in the back of the room listening to the speaker describe the recipient and it dawned on me that they were talking about me! That was the American Society of Enology and Viticulture Eastern Section, outstanding achievement award, 2013.

"I don't know that I will ever stop working. As long as I can, I will. I love the work, especially now that it's on my terms! And I've always kept busy. I remember one day a friend of Billy's came over and I was darning socks. Does anyone do that anymore? Anyway, he said, 'Geez, Helen, don't you just ever sit and relax?' I guess I didn't back then." She's quiet for a moment before adding, "These days though I do find myself just sitting more often. Lost in thought I guess, or just staring off into space." She breaks the reflective mood with her characteristic laughter. "That's why I'm so brown! Sitting on the porch in the sun. I look around at the thistles and say, 'To hell with it... They can wait until tomorrow."

While conceding to slowing down a bit, Helen feels it's important to keep our brains busy. She loves crossword puzzles and looks forward to the big ones that come out on New Year's Day and other holidays. "They can be challenging," she admits. "There are often no parallel words. So, if you can't get this word or this word, there is nothing above or below it to give you a clue. But they're fun. I read weird books, too. I like second hand bookstores. I recently found a book called *Chronicles of Wasted Time* by Malcolm Muggeridge. Right up my alley!"

Like Helen, Malcolm Muggeridge is known for his interest in many subjects and world matters and has the tendency for tangents. Helen laughingly tells of an instance teaching in class during which she found herself looking out onto a sea of glazed student eyes. She instantly got their attention when she adopted a deep gruff voice and begin reciting Lewis Carroll:

> "Beware the Jabberwock, my son!
> The jaws that bite, the claws that catch!
> Beware the Jubjub bird, and shun
> The frumious Bandersnatch!"

The surprised students were sitting up straight, eyes wide, most of them had no idea what she was talking about or who the poet was. The next day, Helen brought in the book and read the class the whole poem, as well as "The Walrus and the Carpenter": "The time has come, the walrus said, to talk of many things." This was a science class, likely about soil composition or ampelography. She knew the subject material was tough for many of the students. She encouraged them to read poetry and other great works. Most of Helen's students will recount that while her subject matter was serious and often dry, Helen herself was neither of those things.

Despite the curriculum, they loved coming to class because they loved Dr. Helen, her quirky nature and humour, her tangents and industry stories, and the fact that she genuinely cared about them. She would frequently stay late to answer questions and she always encouraged curiosity.

When asked what advice she would give young people starting out, Helen doesn't hesitate: "Just put your nose to the grindstone. Keep your stick on the ice. Stay focused. Work hard and never let anyone put you down, but take criticism seriously. If you mess up, pack it in your memory, and do better next time. Don't be afraid to change course. If something else is better than your original plan, head off in that direction. Don't worry about conforming. And make sure you vote! Otherwise, you are throwing away your responsibility."

Helen is keenly up to date on politics and world events. She chooses not to have a TV but listens to a lot of radio news and reads two newspapers a day. Throughout the conversation, she changes the subject several times, claiming that other people and topics are much more interesting than she is. The 'master changer' I say, only half jokingly, and we both laugh.

When asked what advice she would give young Helen, she rolls her eyes, and with a grimace states, "'Don't get distracted,' I should tell myself. I would add, 'Keep dry,' but that would be so boring!" She raises her pint of beer and laughs her signature laugh, a combination of glee and mischief. Then thoughtfully, she adds, "There are many times I ask myself, 'Do I feel crappy because I had too much to drink yesterday, or just because I feel crappy? I don't sleep well. I have too much on my brain—like those boxes in storage! Either way, it is what it is. We must enjoy life while we can."

Amen to that Helen. Amen to that.

She finishes her beer. We chat for a few minutes in the parking lot before she pulls her petite five-foot two-inch frame up into her huge Canyon four-by-four extended cab truck, with the licence plate "GrapeDr" (a gift from Billy).

As I watch her drive away, I marvel at the life this extraordinary woman has led. She was ahead of her time, breaking barriers in industries traditionally dominated by men: agriculture and advanced science academia. She was unconventional, bucking systems and customs, including marriage at a time when that was the expected norm. She forged her own path and earned the respect of her colleagues through hard work, tenacity, and commitment to a cause and an industry. Short in stature but abundant in her zest for life, care of others, her indomitable strength, infectious laughter, and one-of-a-kind sense of humour. They broke the mold for this remarkable woman, and she broke down the walls for future generations of women to follow.

Thank you, Dr. K. Helen Fisher.

JENNIFER WILHELM

Tributes to Dr. Helen Fisher

Dr. Helen Fisher by Dr. Wendy McFadden-Smith
Tender Fruit and Grape IPM Specialist
Ontario Ministry of Agriculture, Food and Rural Affairs

Helen has been my colleague and dear friend for thirty-two years. I want to be Helen if we ever grow up. She has an encyclopedic knowledge of not just viticulture but science, arts, and the world. She is passionate about sharing her knowledge with students and growers. She's engaging and completely down to earth—Birkenstocks and all.

Her office at HRIO was legendary—stacks of papers and books three or four feet high all around her. It looked like complete chaos, but she knew exactly where everything was. Or so she claimed!

I remember the first time I helped Helen with harvesting Icewine plots. There we were at 2 a.m., working by the headlights of her ancient trusty Volvo, freezing our fingers and various other body parts off. She went to get into the car to move it down the row but... the keys were locked inside! She managed to pry an opening to reach the lock because the part between the front and back doors was broken. And we continued to harvest.

Helen holds a special place in the hearts of grape growers and students from her many years of history with them. Whenever I went to a meeting with Helen, everyone was so happy to see her with hugs from all her colleagues and growers.

She has been honoured for her contributions by the Lifetime Achievement Award from the American Society of Enology Viticulture and the Award of Merit from Niagara Peninsula Fruit and Vegetable Growers Association.

Helen has "retired" but continues to manage research projects, participate in the scientific review of proposals, and teach a large online course at University of Guelph, as well as courses at Niagara College, [where she has taught in the Winery and Viticulture Technician program since its inception]. Her students say she's tough, but they all say they learn a lot from her classes. She has inspired so many young minds.

Helen has been my role model for being a female researcher and extension person in a male-dominated environment. [Helen would say] "Don't make a big deal of your gender—just get the job done!" I'm proud to have worked with and continue to work with Helen until we both go to that great vineyard in the sky.

Dr. Helen Fisher by Brian Schmidt
Winemaker, Vineland Estates Winery

I can clearly remember the first time I met Helen Fisher. My father hosted a collection of industry people at Vineland Estates Winery. I had only been in Ontario for a brief period, and I was not familiar with any of the people gathered there that day.

I recall nervously standing there, plotting my escape. Sensing my unease, a woman in jeans that carried the dust from wandering in the vineyards, and boots that had clearly been worn as work boots, came up to me and introduced herself. "I'm Helen, you're Lloyd's son, your dad is amazing." She spoke about some of the projects they had collaborated on and then she added, "I know you're new to Ontario. Please feel free to call me anytime; I'm here to help."

That evening, my father commented, "I see you met Helen. If not for her, Ontario wine would not be what it is today." A truer statement could not have been made. The ripples of Helen's work extend far beyond the outer limits of our little corner of the wine world. The students she taught, the growers she advised and the ideas she explored have shaped and formed the foundation of grape growing over much of the eastern seaboard of North America.

In 2014, we introduced a series of wines called Game Changer. This wine honours and recognizes the people, places, and things that have defined the Canadian wine industry. In 2017, it was Dr. Helen Fisher's time to be recognized. I named the 2017 white wine blend *D'Vine Doctor* to honour this humble lady who was so kind to me the first day we met.

This wine celebrates a remarkable woman who helped shape our modern-day grape and wine industry, which has now evolved and grown in no small part due to the body of work, the passion and creativity of Dr. Helen Fisher.

Dr. Helen Fisher by Dr. Jim Willwerth
Assistant Professor, Grapevine Physiology
Department of Biological Sciences
Researcher, Cool Climate Oenology and Viticulture Institute (CCOVI)
Brock University

"Dr. Helen Fisher is a barrier breaker, an innovator, and a true inspiration and mentor to many, me included. Helen has been a huge part of my life and career from the moment I met her as a student in 2003 while studying grape and wine science at Brock University. Through the years, I have learned and witnessed the many contributions she has made to the grape and wine industry across Canada and internationally. In addition to her research contributions to viticulture, Helen has dedicated a significant amount of time as an educator at the University of Guelph, Niagara College, and Brock University. She has been a role model and mentor to many, including a growing number of women now teaching and working in the grape and wine industry themselves. Many of these women have made tremendous achievements in their own careers and would acknowledge her role in supporting them.

"Not only has Helen broken the glass ceiling, she has shattered it. Women in STEM have (and continue to face) many challenges but being one of the few women performing agriculture research focused on grape growing and working with farmers made her a pioneer during a time highly dominated by men. This includes her time as a graduate student at Cornell University, working at HRIO and the University of Guelph, and all her research and outreach working directly with growers. Helen is not one to talk about her accomplishments or success, usually brushing it off or explaining that while the results are promising, more years of data are needed. She has, however, made many significant contributions to the grape and wine industry.

"This includes her grape-breeding efforts, pioneering work on sub-surface drainage that is now a standard practice in viticulture in many parts of Canada and the East, soil management and remediation, mechanical thinning of grapevines, training systems and vine spacing, and rootstock evaluation and development (of which she continues in retirement!) just to name a few. She has also played a tremendous role working with industry stakeholders and serving on committees with the Grape Growers of Ontario, Ontario Grape and Wine Research Inc. and others helping with initiatives such as production guidelines, wind machine use and best practices, or reviewing proposals that will fund new research and innovation that will shape the future of the industry.

"Personally, Helen has been a tremendous mentor who I have so much respect for. She taught me aspects of viticulture and soil management as a student where I learned key practical concepts of vineyard management. Helen also helped guide my PhD studies as one of my graduate committee members. We still talk research and spend time in the field together but now as colleagues, and I feel very fortunate that this is the case. She has served as a mentor to many of the university's lab technicians and students over their careers. Helen's influence always shines through when we share stories about her, working at the grape station together, one of her lectures, or just Helen being Helen.

"Helen has contributed so much, but she has also done so with tremendous humility and with a great sense of humour. She has probably forgotten more than many have learned. I appreciate our conversations and time together with her as a mentor, colleague, and someone I can truly call a friend. Please raise your glass to Helen for all her contributions and, if you know her well, perhaps that will be a bottle of warm Labatt 50."

Helen Fisher by Stephanie Bilek
Field Operations Manager

"I first met Helen when I was enrolled in the Oenology and Viticulture program at Brock University in 2005. She was teaching a portion of the viticulture classes I was taking, and she made an impression on me right away. Helen is brilliant, eclectic, and unlike any teacher I had had before. Most of the students in the program were set on winemaking, and at the time I was as well. Helen changed all of that for me. Listening to her lecture, being in the vineyard with her, her enthusiasm and her love for all things vine and soil were apparent and contagious! She made the most mundane topics riveting.

"In 2006, I slightly exaggerated my experience with farm equipment (sorry Helen!) and got the coveted position of Helen's summer research student. I spent three summers working with Helen, and it truly was working with her, instead of for her. She allowed me to be involved in every aspect of her projects and we became fast friends. She affectionately referred to me as "Stephie" from that point forward. Thanks to Helen, I had found my niche in viticulture and am still working in that field today.

"Helen's contributions laid the base for many of the successes of the Ontario grape growers. It's not just about all her research contributions, which is impressive enough. It's also about who Helen is and the impact she has on people. She has taught and mentored so many students who have gone on to make large contributions to the industry. Her ripple effect is huge. Her brilliant mind, her work ethic, her dedication, tenacity, wit, and humour are just a few of the qualities that make her such an amazing researcher, teacher, and friend. Generations from now, people will still be talking about Helen Fisher and what she contributed to the Ontario grape and wine industry. Helen is now retired but still teaches and is still doing research. She's still out in the vineyard and collecting samples in the worst winter weather. I am still fortunate enough to cross paths with her professionally from time to time and have been able to work on some of her projects recently.

"I often drive by the old grape station on Cherry Avenue in Vineland and reminisce on the wisdom she imparted, the laughter she so readily shared, and the impact she had on me and many others. The grapes have been pulled out and replaced by apples, but I can still see the layout in my mind. The museum block, the blocks where Helen taught me about her grapevine breeding work, the training trial, and spacing trial blocks. Helen is a trailblazer for women in viticulture, an icon, and a memory bank of nostalgic history. At the end of a long workday, there's nothing better than having a beer with this legend, likely a warm Labatt 50."

Donna Lailey

"When I look back on my life, it will be the days I spent on the farm and in the vineyard, with no cellphone, often with my family and friends, which were the best."

Sitting in her Niagara-on-the-Lake kitchen on a bright spring morning, Donna Lailey is an impressive figure of well-being. The years of physical work and dedication to her health show in her lithe and muscled physique. She walks every day, plays golf, is active on many committees, and joins her daughters and grandchildren on family skiing vacations.

Growing up in Nova Scotia in the 1960s, Donna was involved in a wide variety of sports and always thought that she would make a career out of athletics. Her mother, however, had different ideas and wanted her daughter to be a nurse. The next wise career choice for women at that time was teaching. Donna conceded, but with her own plan. After completing teachers' college, Donna taught grade two for one year before returning to Dalhousie University to study her first love: physical education. At the time, she was living with five young women, all teachers, whom, after graduation, planned to go west to Alberta and British Columbia where the jobs were. Donna claims she just never got around to filling out the forms to join them but admits later that she actually didn't really want to leave the East Coast. She stayed and began teaching physical education at

West Hill School in Bedford, Nova Scotia, the only native Nova Scotian teacher at the time.

One evening, one of her roommates saw an ad for a teaching position in Belleville, Ontario, and suggested that Donna call. On a whim, she did. When asked for a reference, Donna gave the name of her principal. Her gymnastics team had won the area championships just that day and her principal was loathe to lose the talented coach and teacher. Donna was proud of her team and the work she was doing. She decided that she was content to stay in Nova Scotia. But the Belleville school called back and offered her almost twice the salary she was making on the East Coast. Donna decided to give it a try and packed up her car and drove alone to Ontario. First impressions were not good. Upon arrival, she received a frosty welcome from the woman assigned to meet her, who was out of sorts after apparently being required to leave her cottage to greet the newcomer.

Initial impressions aside, Donna liked teaching in the Belleville school and remained there for two years. It was during this time that she met her now husband David, also a teacher. Their plan was to get married and take a year off to travel. This plan was derailed when David accepted a job in Toronto. The couple relocated there for a short time before moving to Owen Sound for two years. That summer, shortly after their first daughter, Jennifer, was born, they came to Niagara-on-the-Lake to visit David's parents, William and Nora Lailey. The Laileys had been growing tender fruit since 1945 and had recently added some hybrid grapes to their farm on the Niagara Parkway.

On that visit, Donna remembers looking around the bucolic orchards, the nearby river rushing along its banks, the sunlight reflecting on the fruit trees. It was quiet and peaceful. After so many moves and now a new mother herself, Donna was ready to put down some roots. She recalls thinking, "This would be a nice place to live." David, however, wasn't thrilled. Having grown up on the farm, he knew what life as a farmer would entail. But Donna prevailed, and in 1970 they purchased the farm from David's parents.

Donna recounts clearly in her matter-of-fact way, "We moved in on July 1st and the cherries were ripe. David was going to summer school in

Toronto, and I had a six-month-old. I hired some pickers and a babysitter. We picked all day, and then I took the cherries to market. When I got back home, I had just enough money to pay the babysitter and the pickers. I picked up the phone and called David. I said, 'I'm not doing this.'"

At that time, in addition to cherries, the farm had peaches, pears, and a few grapes, but nothing that Donna really wanted to grow. The couple had spent two months in Europe before the birth of their daughter and Donna had an idea to grow vinifera grapes. She signed up for a wine course at Inniskillin taught by Andrew Sharpe. She believed that if Niagara was going to have a successful grape-growing industry, they needed to plant what the rest of the world was growing. She ordered and planted several vinifera varieties, most of which died that winter. But Donna was determined. The next year she ordered her vines from Europe. She planted them herself and remembers proudly walking the rows with the head of Vineland Research and Innovation Centre who promptly and with certainty told her that the vines wouldn't survive the Ontario winter. She says now, "I could have stopped right there and then, but I said no. I persisted." She now adds, "And this before we knew how climate change was going to affect us!"

She goes on to confide, "The farm was costing us a lot of money. I knew someone who was buying vine cuttings to ship to New York State, and I decided to do that. I remember sitting, with baby Jennifer beside me, as I cut and tied shoots into bundles of 500. The going rate then was about two or three cents per shoot. That was my start of making money, any money, in the grape and wine scene. It was peanuts really, but I persisted."

It's no secret that managing and working a farm is hard work year-round in the blazing summers and freezing winters of Ontario. David was teaching at a local high school all week and, in the summer, taking classes at Brock University, which were mandatory for teachers at the time. This meant that most of the day-to-day work and decision making fell to Donna. She recalls a day in 1980, "a really, really cold day when I was outside pruning, and I had this pruner with a motor that was a bit of a pain, but it was easier on the body. Still, it was so cold that I came inside. Terry Fox was running across Canada and when I turned on the radio, they were interviewing him. I said to myself, *If he can do that then surely I can go out and prune!* And I went back out."

Donna remembers her mother and sisters worrying about her and the life and livelihood she had chosen to build with the land. One year, when she was once again unable to leave the farm to vacation with her family on the East Coast, her family decided to visit her instead. Donna recalls them taking the train that autumn and arriving to find her alone in the vineyard in the pouring rain, attempting to get the grapes off by hand before the weather could damage them. She says, "They dropped their things inside and came out to help me. Together we got the grapes in." Her mother, her sister and her son, her mother's sister, "they all arrived and picked. That's when my mother realized how hard I worked."

As a grape grower, one is always at the mercy of the elements. Sleepless nights during hailstorms, frost advisories, and rainy harvests become ingrained in the life of a farmer. Donna recalls the sense of panic one year when, upon returning from a rarely taken vacation, their cab driver from the airport informed them of a terrible wind and hailstorm that had occurred during their absence. They returned to the farm to see row after row of damaged vines. They worked hard to salvage the vintage that year.

Admittedly, it wasn't a life that everyone would find fulfilling, but Donna says with a soft smile and far off eyes, "When I look back on my life, it will be the days I spent on the farm and in the vineyard, with no cellphone, often with my family and friends, working with our hands, talking with our friends, which were the best. When I first moved to Niagara in the 1970s, women my age [she was referring to her early thirties] at that time, wanted to get together but also to contribute, to do something helpful and productive. My friends would come in from the city and it was a great time because we could work with our hands, get things done, and talk about all the things that women needed to talk about. And I would pay them of course so it was good for all of us. David's parents had people who had worked for them for years who really knew the farm and the fruit trees, but they didn't particularly want to work in the vines, so we needed new people. David and I did the pruning and we hired people to help us with some of the other tasks."

In about 1983, Donna began selling her grapes to a few individuals. She insisted on a fair but premium price for premium quality. The wineries, however, were in the business of making money and didn't want to pay her what she was asking. "So, in 1985 I opened a business to sell my juice to the home wine market. That was probably the most successful thing, though we didn't have any cold storage when we started. David would come home Friday after school and we would work till midnight or later, crushing, pressing, getting the pails ready and everything organized for the customers who would come on Saturday. We did that for about ten years."

Donna estimates that she had about 300 customers, from Quebec to Thunder Bay. As the demand grew, equipment had to be purchased and upgraded to include new presses, destemmer and, quite expensively, a cold storage facility. This made life much easier and further improved the already superior quality. Donna says that this is when she mastered the fine art of negotiation. Buyers would come and tell her that her juice was too expensive and demand to speak with her husband, claiming that she was much too difficult to deal with. She says she learned to start prices off high and let them think they were talking her down and getting a deal. In the end, she got what she wanted, and buyers went away happily thinking that they had bested her. Donna admits that sometimes people would go elsewhere, but that they usually came back for the quality that she provided. She confides with a proud smile "My juice got known."

At that time, much of the juice that was being sold to home winemakers was often what the growers didn't actually want themselves. That's not the way Donna operated. She refused to compromise her standards, no matter the buyer. This resolve fuelled her to advocate for other likeminded growers, and in 1986 she became a grape negociant—buying, processing, and reselling grapes to winemakers wanting quality fruit from Ontario's most meticulous vineyards. Her reputation for distinction began to expand beyond her own vineyards.

In 1991, Donna was named Grape King, in recognition of her standards of excellence. The selection, crowning, and celebration of the Grape King is an annual tradition in Ontario that dates back to 1956. The title honours grape growers who exemplify excellence in vineyard management and knowledge of and commitment to the industry. Each year, the named Grape King represents Ontario's grape and wine industry throughout Canada, beginning with the Mayor's Grape Stomp in Montebello Park and including an appearance on the Grape Growers float in the Niagara Grape and Wine Festival's Grande Parade. Donna was the first female grower to be crowned Grape King and had hoped that the role would be a platform from which she could be a voice for women in agriculture.

Donna was also vice chair of the Grape Growers Marketing Board (and the only woman at the time). She remembers coming home from meetings "just livid" and David saying to her, "Donna, you don't have to do this." But her experiences as a grower selling to wineries were fresh in her mind and she says, "I felt so strongly about certain issues that I persisted." Her determination to affect change and fight for fairness fuelled her commitment to persevere and speak out against injustices in the industry.

She remembers timing at a swim meet at Brock University (both of her daughters were swimmers), when a woman rushed up to her and breathlessly exclaimed, "I've been sent to see YOU. I just came from a conference in Hamilton for women in agriculture and the stories the women were standing up and sharing about how they were being treated were horrendous. They told me to come and see Donna Lailey. So here I am."

Donna said this treatment was considered the norm at the time. She tells of a man and his wife who came to her farm wanting to pick and buy grapes. The man said he wanted two bushels, but he had piled up the grapes in them to the tune of one and half each bushel. When Donna insisted that he pay for the grapes he planned to take away, he became irate and demanded that his wife stay and work off the other bushel in the form of picking for payment.

As archaic as this seems today, at the time, exploitation of women extended past the home and into their careers. Donna wanted to be a part of changing this. She began where she could and has since been a trustee, director, and active member on approximately fifteen boards and committees, including the following: founding member of the VQA and on the VQA Technical Committee; founding member and Chair of Ontario Wine Producers; Director of the Niagara Credit Union; Niagara

Parks Commissioner and Director of the Agricultural Research Institute of Ontario; and vice-chair, Ontario Grape Growers Marketing Board. She has also served on the Niagara College Board of Governors, adding her voice and mentorship to future generations.

Of her time on these boards, Donna states the alliances and relationships forged with like-minded visionaries to be the most rewarding aspect. Sometimes, she says, it's not the always the work you are able to do, but the people you get to know who make that time well spent. In this regard, she lists Donald Ziraldo, Karl Kaiser, Ann Sperling, Peter Gamble, the Konzelmanns, and Niagara College president Dan Patterson as some of these early visionaries. She wants people to understand what these boards were up against at the time. She tells of Monsanto coming in with its deep pockets, offering million-dollar endowments to these "lil ole farmers of Niagara" and the universities and colleges if they were willing to get on board.

In the midst of this dedication, there remained the farm to be managed under Donna's meticulous stewardship. The twenty-three existing acres were made up of Chardonnay, Riesling, Vidal, Cabernet Franc, and the temperamental and high maintenance grape, Pinot Noir. Thin-skinned, tightly bunched, and prone to rot, Pinot Noir notoriously lives up to its moniker of The Heartbreak Grape. When grown and vinified well, however, it transcends into its magnificent alter ego: The Holy Grail. Elegantly structured, with a purity of fruit that evolves into remarkable complexity, some refer to the wine as an iron fist in a velvet glove.

Donna believed even then that Niagara had the ability to produce spectacular Pinot Noir but admits that the grape tested her resolve yearly. She recalls a conversation with Paul Bosc Sr. about some of her frustrations, during which she laments, "I am never going to plant another Pinot vine!" Paul had valuable connections and helped Donna secure approximately 300 Pinot Noir vines of various clones from Burgundy. Donna believes that these vines are part of the success of Lailey Pinot Noir.

She adamantly states, "I would not let anyone else look after my Pinots because I knew what I wanted in Pinots." Around this time, she went to a seminar led by Scott Henry from Oregon. After spending thirteen years as an aeronautical engineer, Scott Henry put his mind to designing a trellis system intended to increase fruiting through splitting the vine's canopy. Donna remembers coming home perplexed and saying to David, "He's telling us to separate the vine half up and half down—but nothing wants to grow down!" Nevertheless, Donna was committed to progress and open to innovation, so she decided to follow his advice. "At that time, I was on the Niagara Parks Commission. My youngest daughter Tonya was home from university, and I was telling her about this trellis system. We went out and I showed her how to do it. Well, when I got home from my meeting she was fed up. She said "Mom, this is going to take forever to do this!" Never one to be deterred, Donna replied, "Let's go out after lunch and do it together." Donna grew grapes for quality, not quantity. Over the next fifteen years, they transitioned all of their red grape vineyards to the Scott Henry trellis system.

In 1998, Donna hired farm workers from Jamaica to join the team, claiming that this was one of the best decisions she made, emphatically saying, "They were absolutely marvelous and became part of the family." The crew members were hard working, and a respect developed between them and Donna that evolved into friendship. Donna's appreciation was evidenced by the above average wage that she paid them, and the same crew returned each year.

As her reputation grew so, too, did the demand for her quality juice and the number of wineries willing to pay her premium prices. One of those wineries was Southbrook Farms in Toronto where Derek Barnett was the winemaker. Donna's daughter Tonya was completing her master's degree at Queen's University while working at a winery and said to her mother, "Mom, it would be a lot easier to sell our wine than somebody else's." Donna conceded, saying, "We are selling a lot of juice to Southbrook. Go talk to Derek." This conversation was the beginning of Lailey Vineyard transitioning from growing grapes for other wineries to becoming a winery in itself. In 2000, Derek and his wife Judith joined the Laileys as business partners.

Derek is a talented and personable winemaker with a fan following. Donna is an astute and realistic businesswoman, with a pragmatic manner of making decisions, which didn't always win her friends but did always hold the bottom line of the business as paramount. The two balanced each other out and, with Tonya's help, Lailey Vineyard became a sought-out destination winery. The winery itself was designed by Donna's brother Barrie. It's a stunning structure of wood, steel, and glass, sitting lightly on the land with a veranda overlooking the vineyards. In front of the winery, at the end of the long winding driveway, past the family home and under a canopy of trees, was a bicycle zone with racks to encourage cyclists along the Niagara Parkway to stop in, enjoy a glass of wine, and savour the unique beauty of this special place.

A certified sommelier and experienced winemaker herself, Tonya Lailey skillfully handled the winery's marketing and licensee sales, developing strong relationships with industry partners, restaurants, and wine lovers across Canada. Before long, the company's wine club was waiting list only. Smartly structured and well managed, members had access to highly anticipated pre-release tastings and buying opportunities, which often saw entire vintages sold out in an afternoon. On weekends, Derek could often be found leading tastings or manning the grill on site at intimate BBQ luncheons. Derek's talent and love of winemaking were palpable as he walked guests through the vineyards and barrel cellars. Handsome and charismatic, with a soft English accent, his fan base grew as wine lovers flocked to taste with and learn from him. Derek prided himself on crafting wines that reflected their terroir and showed a sense of place as well as a purity of fruit that has since become his signature style. Shortly after releasing the first vintage of Lailey wine, Derek was named Ontario Winemaker of the Year.

Lailey Vineyard was one of the first wineries to add Canadian oak barrels to its existing French, American, and Hungarian lineup. Those guests fortunate enough to secure a ticket were treated to a unique portfolio tasting showcasing the effects of the oak's nomenclature and usually left with several bottles from each barrel. It was a brilliant business plan and one that seemed, to consumers, to be a natural evolution from dedicated grape growers to thriving winery. Lovers of Lailey wines and the team followed the transition and the building of the winery, rejoiced in the success, and felt somehow a part of the magic that was happening on this special parcel of land. By all accounts, this is a story of hard work, passion, and perseverance, culminating admirably in great triumph.

Donna Lailey is a trailblazer and lived in tenacious pursuit of her dreams and goals, undeterred by the challenges and obstacles thrown in her path by finances, hard work, weather, or the naysayers who told her that it could not be done.

She remembers feeling frustrated when people would say to her that Ontario could make decent white wines but not red. While Donna admits that the province's weather can be challenging, she stands behind the Pinot Noir and Cabernet Franc being made here. She recollects with a smile the Cabernet Sauvignon from 2007 and 2010 and says, "When you have a good year, the wines can be marvelous. When you work in the vineyard with the Cabs in July and August, you try to judge what kind of year you are going to have and decide what to leave on the vine accordingly. When you're going after quality, it's a lot different than when you're going after yield." She continues, "It's been a really interesting journey learning all of this." Donna also planted Muscat, Malbec, and Petit Verdot with the belief that it is crucial to determine what we can grow here and on which sites and soils.

Donna takes a moment here to mention the Marynissens, another of Niagara's pioneering grape-growing and winemaking families dedicated to understanding local terroir and planting suitably. John and his wife Adrianna began planting *Vitis vinifera* grapes at their Niagara-on-the-Lake farm in 1976. Today it's home to Canada's oldest commercial plantings of Cabernet Sauvignon. Donna identifies the Marynissen Cabernet Sauvignon as early undeniable proof that the grape could be grown and vinified impressively well in Niagara. She emphasises research as crucial to understanding our unique cool climate terroir and how Niagara grapes and wine will be impacted by climate change. She speaks admirably and fondly about Dr. Debbie Inglis. Deb and her family worked with Donna in her years as a grape grower and négociant. Today, Debbie is the director of Brock University's Cool Climate Oenology and Viticulture Institute (CCOVI) and one of the core research scientists within the institute. With a PhD in biochemistry, her research focuses on priority areas of the Canadian grape and wine industry for premium wine production.

Having both come from the educational realm, Donna and David maintained strong connections to professors at other nearby universities in Niagara, Hamilton, Mississauga, and Toronto, many of whom were amateur winemakers and loyal purchasers of Lailey juice. Donna recalls one such client calling from Burgundy. His wife directed opera all over the world and they had a second home in Burgundy where they held concerts and events. He wanted to host an event showcasing Canadian wines in Burgundy. His plan was to bring in top wine people and organize seminars through the week if Donna could bring some Niagara people and their wines to pour for them.

Donna put the word out. She, Tonya, and Derek went to Burgundy with about fifteen other winemakers and ambassadors from Niagara. They spent a few days tasting Pinot Noir at the event and felt confident that their Niagara wines were on par, if not superior, to many of the Burgundian. Donna confided this to her friend who returned with a glass of Pinot Noir that Donna recalls as "absolutely to die for." The price of the bottle of wine was $200, far above what any Ontario wineries were charging. On the last day of the event, Donna was pouring Lailey Chardonnay and Pinot Noir. A group of men came and tasted, then went away whispering amongst themselves before coming back and asking incredulously, "You grew these grapes in Canada?" They were so impressed.

Tonya recalls that the people in attendance at this event were not looking just for delicious wines, they were looking for typicity of variety and region. At that time, she was living in London, Ontario, and selling Lailey wine to restaurants in London and the GTA, driving from London to Niagara two or three times a week. She made valuable contacts and did a fantastic job as a Lailey ambassador. When she moved to Alberta, it became challenging to continue heading up that sales channel. Donna had enjoyed working alongside her daughter and also missed Tonya's help in the vineyard and winery.

There was no replacement for Tonya at the winery but one of the many things the Laileys did well was hiring the right people to represent their winery and wines. Derek was invaluable, enthusiastically stepping into any role needed, from hand-pasting labels on bottles to selling and marketing, Derek was synonymous to Lailey. It wasn't uncommon for him to spend weekends personally delivering wine to Toronto, Stratford, Kitchener, or wherever else it was needed. His was often the face greeting visitors from the other side of the tasting bar. Tonya has so many fond memories of Derek. She recalls him generously pouring international wine from his own cellar to taste side by side with their own, looking for intricate parallels and differences. They also tasted their wines beside other local wines for comparison.

Donna feels that with any organization the people are key. The recruiting, hiring, and training are crucial but time consuming. Donna admits, "I like to see my people do what they are supposed to do." Never one to mince words, she voices her frustration about the often lack of understanding or willingness of many new to the wine industry with respect to doing the manual labour and preparation required in wineries and winemaking. She recalls being taken aback when a new hiree told her that he wasn't there to wash pails; he was going to be a winemaker. Having never turned her nose up at any of the tasks or energy required of her, Donna expresses concern about the possible industry misconceptions. As all trailblazers and pioneers, Donna's standards were far above the average person. Fortunately, her daughters shared the same work ethic, and her husband was supportive of her dreams, rather than crushing of her visions for his family farm.

Over the years of grape growing and winemaking, Donna and Derek have each mentored and impacted countless students, interns, and aspiring growers and winemakers. Their unified belief that great wine starts in the vineyard is unshakeable and they have passed this conviction on to many other talented individuals. On a recent visit to Big Head Wines in Niagara-on-the-Lake, Donna was greeted warmly by owner, grape grower, and winemaker Andrzej Lipinski. He reminded her that years ago when first arriving to Canada from Poland and struggling to speak English he, too, had worked side by side with her in her vineyards, absorbing her knowledge and love of the vines.

In the fall of 2014, in the height of harvest and winemaking season, a fire broke out in the garage that housed Lailey's fermentation bins, valuable equipment, and investments, along with cases of finished wine awaiting pickup. Donna remembers coming down East West Line and seeing the smoke. The fire department was able to extinguish the blaze before it spread to the family house but not before it destroyed the partially fermented wine in bins and the other contents of the garage. David suffered dangerous levels of smoke inhalation and was taken by ambulance to the hospital. News of the fire travelled as quickly to the industry as the flames had spread over the winery building. Nearby wineries rallied to create space for Derek to complete his wines that vintage. The outpouring of support was testament to how the industry felt about Derek and the Lailey family and team.

With this near devastation and added stress and expense, Donna began to feel the weight of the demands of the vineyards and business. With Tonya's departure, David's declining health, and her own advancing age, Donna sadly admitted to herself that she was tired. She was seventy-four years old. She had been faithfully and meticulously tending this land for forty-five years. But the needs of a farm and a winery make no concessions for fatigue, illness, or age. After heartbreaking discussions with Derek and their respective families, Donna began to reach out to other reputable growers and winemakers to gauge prospective interest in continuing stewardship of her beloved vineyards and winery. It was their deepest hope that someone with values and beliefs aligned with their own would be willing to carry Lailey Vineyard forward. She recalls sleepless nights, walking alone on the nearby path of the Niagara Parkway, praying for guidance during these tenuous times.

They held out for this illusive buyer as long as they could, to no avail, even willing to stay on as consultants and investors. On July 1, 2015, the sale of the property closed: forty-five years to the date that Donna and David had moved onto the family farm, so full of dreams and hope, during the height of cherry season that summer of 1970. On July 21, 2015, the second stage of the sale, which included the winery and business, was complete. The new owners, insisted on keeping the name Lailey Vineyard. Despite their urging, Derek Barnett decided not to stay on as winemaker and business partner. With heavy hearts, Donna and David handed over the keys, along with their life's work, their family memories, and a large piece of their hearts.

The sale of Lailey Vineyard signified the end of an era and a turning point in the Niagara grape and wine industry that left supporters and wine lovers stunned, mourning, and with a sense of unease about what was to come. Restaurateurs recall with sadness passing the message to their regulars that Lailey Vineyard was no more. With horror, locals watched as the new owners tore out some of the revered Old Vines and Brickyard Vineyard and interplanted among the rows to change the goal from quality to quantity. The Lailey family home came down and was paved over to make space for large tour buses, which were previously not a part of the small, personal experiences the Lailey team sought to create.

When asked who she turned to for support in the midst of her challenges with David teaching all day in the early years and later after his heart attack and illness, Donna recalls with gratitude the quiet support of her migrant farm crew turned family, and her neighbours, the Adams and the Ahluwalias. She also names Dr. Helen Fisher, renowned vine biologist at Vineland Research and Innovation Center as one of her main supports. Donna thinks that most of her mentors and supporters never knew that they filled that role for her.

Donna was intricately bound to not only her vineyards but also to her community and committees, which sometimes called her away from the farm and her family. When asked, "Was there truly a life balance? How did you fit your young family and home obligations in around harvest and the needs of the farm?" Donna says, "I was always there. I was there to get the girls off to school and most days I was still there in the vineyards when they got off the bus at the end of the day."

It is difficult for consumers to understand the price paid by grape growers and winery owners in pursuit of excellence. We are all conscious of our dollar and want value for said exchange. But in the unpredictable climate and precarious tax structure of the Ontario grape and wine industry we must pay a fair price to growers and winemakers alike if we want our local entrepreneurs to prevail. Families like the Laileys were pioneers and role models. They invested everything they had: finances, time, resources, the forfeiting of family vacation, life balance. They admittedly couldn't do the things that other people did because of the farm and the winery. It was a sacrifice. They traded traditional herbicides and irrigation for the long-term trade-off of sustainability, quality, and purity.

Of her journey, Donna feels it was worth every drop of tears and sweat. "When you give of yourself and get back what we did, it is simply marvelous." With a smile and a tilt of her head, she admits, "And I would still grow Pinot, despite the care it involved. When I had a little bit of success along the route, it lit my fire. If we could grow peaches, we could grow vinifera grapes, and if we don't maintain standards, we will have nothing to build on. I believe that whatever we are we are going to do, we need to do with quality. That's why VQA and labelling was and is so important. If you loosen this and loosen that, bit by bit, we will lose it all."

Donna has found the transition to retirement to be challenging. When asked if she is ever able to hear a weather report without thinking as a grape grower she says, "No. They may not be my vines, but they are somebody's vines." She also finds waking up without an endless to-do list difficult. Donna believes that everyone needs a purpose in life. In the absence of winter pruning, she and David prioritize their health, family, and community. It's a far cry from the nights when they slept under the stars, in a half-finished farmhouse, on a mattress on the floor with the phone beside them so they wouldn't miss any orders for juice. They were in the midst of construction, and for most of that summer, there wasn't a roof on the house. One night, feeling the first rain drops of an impending storm, Donna woke David and the two of them climbed onto the roof to put a tarp over the walls. These memories are bittersweet today.

These days, Donna continues to work tirelessly to promote Ontario wines. She formed a tasting group a few years back at which she showcases Ontario wines in blind tastings to members. She loves facilitating blind tastings in which she includes ringers from Niagara to keep international palates aware of the quality being produced here. With a proud smile, she says they are always impressed. Having people taste wines blind mitigates their preconceptions getting in the way and opens their minds to our wines.

Donna's most recent project is as a board member for Music Niagara. The goal of the festival is to bring musicians and music lovers (who often happen to be wine lovers as well) together while simultaneously showcasing the region's fine wines and wineries at each event. The festival's tagline is engaging and concise: *Music Niagara: Where the World Comes to Play*. Donna continues proudly, "We attract musicians from all over the world. You could hear them elsewhere, but you'd have to go to eleven countries to do it!"

Now in its second decade, the festival held an event at Lailey Vineyard almost ten years ago. Donna's five granddaughters sat, rapt, listening to a young violinist. The music, the performers, the venues, and the wines come together to create unforgettable experiences for attendees. In 2019, the festival drew more than 100 performers from eleven countries, showcased at thirty concerts around Niagara. It is Donna's fervent hope that Ontarians embrace, endorse, share, and celebrate the province's wines at every opportunity. While some of the larger wineries have venues to host concerts, Music Niagara is a way to involve the smaller wineries and give attendees a taste and appreciation of their wines. Donna says, "Music and wine are both culture and if we come together, we can spread the news of Niagara wine this way."

Among the supporting wineries for Music Niagara is the now well-established Big Head Wines. Happy to support one of his early Ontario mentors, owner Andrzej fondly remembers Donna and he as they communicated with their hands and smiles while they worked together in the Lailey Vineyard that long ago summer of 1990.

Donna is incredibly proud of the wines being produced here and believes strongly that they can hold their own next to those from any of the world's great regions.

On this topic, Donna takes a few moments to proudly speak about her daughter Tonya, without whom Donna claims there would have been no winery at Lailey Vineyard. Today Tonya remains a passionate ambassador of the Canadian wine industry, proudly pouring the wines against top wines from around the globe. A certified sommelier, she works with and represents premium, craft wineries such as Westcott, and Sperling Vineyards, through her own agency, Origo Wines. She also has a masters in political science and a second masters in fine arts. A writer and a poet with a love of music and culture, Tonya's first love was the vineyard. She was passionately committed to the success of Lailey Vineyard and the winery. Donna says that to this day, people ask her how Tonya is, often following the query with a personal memory of how Tonya made them feel or how she listened to exactly what they wanted and found the perfect wine for them.

Donna believes that the story of Lailey Vineyard would not be complete without her daughter Tonya. In fact, Donna insists that the winery itself would not have come into existence were it not for Tonya's urging and subsequent hard work and determination. Donna tells, "One year my mother was visiting, and my other daughter Jennifer was heading off to a summer camp she loved. I thought Tonya would love it, too, but out from the house came this dejected little girl, head hung low, and a ball of twine in her hands. When I asked her what she was doing, she looked up with tear filled eyes and said, "I don't want to go to camp. I want to stay here with you. I can help you tie."

Tonya, joining in the discussion, admits that she didn't always love the farm. "When my sister Jennifer and I were about seven and eight, we hated working the farm. It was hard work, and we were young, so we got the jobs like weed pulling and hand hoeing. I didn't like the farm when I was a kid, not in a conscious way. I loved the space and the mood of it and the smells and tastes, but working on the farm was another matter." She confesses "The real reason I went outside that day to be with my mother is because I was afraid of going to camp and was already feeling homesick. Otherwise, I would NEVER have chosen to work on the farm. But I did learn a lot from the work and certainly value it now." Tonya spent the first nineteen years of her life on their family farm before heading off to university. Even then she returned to work alongside her parents each summer. It's very clear that Tonya holds her mother in high regard. When asked to offer a few words to describe Donna, Tonya doesn't hesitate. "Dedication to the vineyard at all costs. Willingness to take on new and challenging methods of growing and all of the labour-intensive things that were required to produce quality. It would have been very easy to decide not to do them. They were hugely expensive and hugely labour intensive. She was an early adopter of hand harvesting and thinning at appropriate times, multiple times throughout the season. She was always trying to move towards sustainable practices like not using herbicides. Consequently, we were hand hoeing the entire farm. Today, there is automated leaf removal, but we did it then by hand. Yes, it was a lot of hard work, but that's the essence of farming for a living; the land owns you as much as you own it."

Tonya recalls the hailstorm that occurred the one year that her parents were away and says, "The hailstorm is a great illustration of how the best-laid plans of mice and men often go awry."

She and Donna both laugh at loud here, nod, and share knowing looks. They each add to the sentiment that as much as you give of yourself to the land, the land gives back to you. It's a dynamic. There is a deep humility. There are so many variables and no guarantees. You can plan and plan and plan but ultimately the weather factor, over which you have no control, determines the outcome to a degree, every year.

Tonya reflects thoughtfully. "Now that I am older, I am in awe. I mean, my mother was sixty years old when we started the winery. I now appreciate what that means. To be that open and interested and excited to take on something new and huge like that was amazing. And to me, honestly, it was a gift to have parents who were willing to do that, which then gave me the experience."

Donna injects good naturedly, pointing at Tonya, "She's responsible!" to which Tonya replies, frankly, "Yeah, maybe, in some way, except that I didn't have the capital, I didn't have the farm." Tonya feels that everything was there, in a perfect location. "It was poised to be a winery," she says. Tonya brought the idea, commitment, and legwork, and it was she who reached out to Derek, but it was Donna who gave the go ahead, without which the winery wouldn't have been born. Born it was, in the year 2000, bursting onto the scene with as much excitement and disruption to a family as the arrival and responsibility of a new child.

"My mother always had a willingness to experiment, whether in the vineyard or the winery, both of which are connected, of course. We played with all aspects of canopy management to assess the best techniques for our grapes and wines. We harvested small amounts of grapes, at various times, from various vineyards for small batch wines. Derek would ferment these batches separately and then we would taste meticulously to determine if they should be blended or bottled individually. There was a lot of this kind of thing. If a winery were just concerned about the bottom line, they probably wouldn't have bothered. I always felt that there was a lot of attention to the craft."

Tonya recounts the release of their first wines, sold out of the front of her parents' house. "We had these dinky little signs. Think lemonade stand. People trickled in. Due to some mix up, our Sauvignon Blanc was in hock bottles." She recalls trying to keep her cool the first time a person said that they would take a case. She said, "I was like, oh yeah, sure that happens all the time, very nonchalantly. I'll just grab that. Meanwhile in the back I'm like, 'Woohoo! Yes!!'" She and Donna burst out laughing with this retelling. Donna says, after catching her breath, "I can still see you in the front of the house." She looks affectionately over at Tonya with a smile.

Tonya recalls her mother devoting a tremendous amount of time volunteering her efforts to the furtherment of the wine industry and its politics. Along with other visionaries, there was a big push for truth in labelling, to speak with politicians, to reach the ear of LCBO officials. She notes Donna's work on the marketing board and how she was able to see that everyone wins if we all commit to quality and develop an identify that is clear. Tonya recalls her mother's commitment to mentoring students from both Niagara College and Brock University, her role on the Niagara College Board of Governors. She sums it up as a consistent theme to the industry at large and the ability to see that this unifying is more beneficial to all than a competitive approach.

Tonya wore many hats at Lailey, one of which as a sales rep. She recalls some of the challenges of selling Ontario wine in those early years. The industry was still young and just building its reputation and identity. Many consumers were confused by labels like "International Canadian Blends" and "Cellared in Canada," bottles that were located directly under the big "Canada" sign in the LCBO. When choosing these wines, most customers thought they were drinking Canadian wine made from Canadian-grown grapes. It was understandably confusing and awareness of the VQA at that time was uncommon. Tonya had her work cut out for her and spent much of her time educating consumers. She likens this practice to the clothing industry when some labels declare Canadian yet are actually made from internationally sourced and produced materials.

Tonya mentions with admiration her mother's curiosity and thirst for travel in her quest to ascertain if there was indeed a Niagara flavour of Pinot Noir. To discover if there was an expression of Cabernet Franc that's distinctive to Niagara across the region and, more specifically, to Lailey. Tonya says this mapping was fun to do together but also frustrating; when selling wine, she was always being asked to compare it to other countries. For example, consumers asking if she had a Cabernet Sauvignon that tastes like California Cabernet Sauvignon. She would patiently and repeatedly explain that that's not what the goal was. The goal was to create wine that tastes like the place where the grapes were grown, in this case, that meant at Lailey Vineyard in Niagara-on-the-Lake, Ontario, Canada.

Tonya identifies the small, emerging slow food and farm-to-table communities as more embracing of this taste of place. She feels that the local food movement was instrumental in helping to pave the way in embracing regional flavours and back to roots origins of agricultural products as whole. She surmises that they understood that the local tomato grower was driven by the same curiosity to learn more about their crops as the grape growers were to learn about theirs.

"We did a ton of outreach and relationship building to cement this. There were countless chef and winemaker dinners with Derek, events on and off site, and tastings with even small groups of people. There was a lot of foot work, but it was truly enjoyable, and I still think it's the best way to sell wine when you are a small producer. It's personal, it's intimate, it's the story, and it's tasting. Our philosophy, rather than buying ads, which we couldn't afford to do anyway, was just to give of ourselves and pour the wine. So that's what we did. Over and over. As people started to cellar and open our wines with their friends, there was the added value of word of mouth. It was also a lot of fun to introduce people to wines fermented and or aged in Canadian oak. It was completing the identity of Canadian wines."

She also identifies the location of Lailey as ideal for reaching visitors from both sides of the border, especially with Icewine. Donna interjects here with a fond memory of a couple from Buffalo, who told her excitedly that this was their fifth visit to the winery. They went on to say admiringly that they just love the building, the wine, and the experience every time. Donna says that these interactions made every day special and feels fortunate that, as a grower, she got to connect with visitors and hear these accolades firsthand. She said it further increased her motivation to grow for quality.

Tonya says with pride and a wide smile, "I have to say, it was just an awesome time, being able to sell wine from your family vineyard and winery." Being frontline in the tasting room, surrounded by her family and side by side with a connected and personable winemaker, Tonya says was just an amazing experience. To hear this feedback daily, as an invested partner, truly allowed the team to complete the circle. The joy and pride that each of them brought to the visitors was palpable and infectious, adding to the unique and wonderful experience that was the essence of Lailey Vineyard. There was a precious sense of belonging there, familial yet extended to everyone who made their way up that gravel path to the tree-lined property, through the glass doors and into the bright tasting room.

Tonya reminisces, "It was the perfect winery in my vision. The size itself, and I loved the building that my uncle designed. I loved our philosophy, and the creative freedom that we allowed ourselves. It's the coolest thing to be able to taste wine that often too because you start to see how wine evolves. When you're tasting the same wine all season long you really get a sense of it, how it ages, and its subtleties. You know each vintage, and the vintage of each variety. I gained a much better appreciation of all of that and then it becomes so much more than just a product. This makes the sales aspect a leap, because there's our appreciation for what is grown and crafted and then the market is demanding something else. Even though people are aware of vintages, they still want consistency. We would often hear, 'We loved the Chardonnay from that year; when will it taste like that again?' For us, it was work but there was such beauty and appreciation in that work, and in the process of moving the through the seasons and growing and putting that year in bottle." She pauses and takes a breath from a far-off place. "It's a rich life in its own way," she sighs, her voice full of emotion and nostalgia.

The land is demanding, year-round, and makes no concessions when life doesn't go as planned. You still must get up every day and do all the tasks involved, not just in maintaining the farm but also the business, the winery, and the frontline selling and marketing of wine. It's expensive and you do accrue debt to operate at the standards you demand.

Tonya recalls the family struggling to maintain the farm and winery as her parents battled age and illness, and she herself struggled through divorce. She notes that when all of this is happening on the land on which you also live, it becomes much more intense with the infrastructure and the constant traffic on the property. You are aware of everything, always, and your energy is pulled in so many directions. There is no place to go to recover from illness, grief, or to just find some stillness in your mind.

Tonya is asked to think about Lailey Vineyard and winery as it was at its highest point, about her role and connection, her parents, Derek, and everyone else who was so intricately woven into its success and identity. How does she want them to be remembered by others when people look back on that time?

This is a hard question, fraught with so many emotions: love, pride, heartbreak, and a myriad of everything in between. She takes a deep breath. Her voice cracks as she replies, "I find this hard, because I feel like the way the sale went undermines what I would want the legacy to be. It was incredibly sad that the winery and farm had to be sold, but I understand why it did. My parents worked so hard their whole lives. There were so many challenges. And then the fire. It was time, but it was still sad. It would have been beautiful to find a way to keep it going, and to keep it in the family somehow. We so hoped someone local would have it, but there just wasn't the capital here." She swallows hard and looks out the window. Thoughtfully, she says, "I want people to remember commitment. Commitment to vintage, and to willingness to experiment. And the intimate evenings and dinners we had with people at the winery or at restaurants that carried our wine. I felt that when we had people to the winery, we really welcomed them. I hope they felt that. We tried to create a sense of community and a celebration of flavour. There was a simplicity and openness to that."

She lights up with a memory and smiles, "Behind the scenes was kind of crazy sometimes. We made so much of our own food, we got pretty good at catering. We did have relationships with amazing chefs. Bryan

Lavery from Murano in London, Ontario. He was the person who introduced me to the Slow Food movement and with whom I founded a slow food convivium. When we had our Italian picnic, the chefs from Murano restaurant made a massive eight-foot sandwich. We set the event up in the orchard under the cherry trees to celebrate the last harvest before we converted it to a vineyard. These were the trees I grew up climbing, laying under when they were in bloom, eating the cherries when they were ripe. We set up barrels and put big bowls of cherries on top of them, there were tables with white linen and flowers, and a canopy under which the chefs were preparing delicious antipasto and the massive sandwich, which we all shared. It was lovely, but the sun got so strong and hot. My mom and I ran over to the house and got umbrellas and all of these random straw hats that we had in the laundry room. We passed out the hats and people wore them! We served gelato and played bocce ball. It was beautiful."

Donna injects, "Remember the year we had Music Niagara there? The granddaughters walked over from the house in their pyjamas to watch the little girl playing the violin."

"What about the corn chowder event?!" laughs Tonya. "One year for a passport event we made homemade corn chowder to serve with our Chardonnay. The toppings were really good cheddar cheese and bacon bits. We had no idea that literally hundreds of people would be coming. It was very important to us that we didn't use disposable cups and utensils, so we used these little chowder mugs. What that meant was that we kept falling behind throughout the day because we had to wash all of these cups in between." They both start laughing and shaking their heads. "We made a second and then third batch of chowder on the fly and people just kept coming. It was insane. There were dishes piled up everywhere." More laughter. Tonya says, "We were exhausted; it took us days to recover. We knew we couldn't do that again. We just didn't have the infrastructure. But that chowder... It was so good. The next year ninety per cent of the people came back for the chowder!"

They exchange smiles. Their faces are beaming with shared pride and happiness as they recount these stories. Tonya confides that they spent so much time planning and setting up these experiences. She declares to this day that the Chardonnay and corn chowder pairing were a fabulous match, leading to terrific sales of Chardonnay, and visitors who couldn't wait to return for another magnificent experience at Lailey.

Donna recalls she and David returning home from a visit with their daughter Jennifer's family in Thunder Bay. Donna tells, "It was about midnight, and we walked into the kitchen, and there was Tonya, peeling tiny onions to make boeuf bourguignon for an event at the winery the next day. She was so committed. She always has, and still does, give so much of herself to presenting and marketing the wines. She's a people person and people love her." Donna looks over at her daughter with radiant pride.

With a smile, Tonya jumps in, "That was the Julia Child recipe! And you changed your clothes and came down and helped me. It's a great dish when you're making it for eight people, but that's a lot of pearl onions to peel for one hundred! I was coming in from London and I would often underestimate the time these things would take. We challenged ourselves," she admits.

"Oh, didn't we?! Donna chimes in. "We laughed a lot though. You have to, don't you?" "It was a great adventure" Tonya finishes. "I have no regrets."

It's so clear that they enjoyed the events as much as their guests. It was demanding work, yes, but it was fulfilling to see visitors turning with wonder and delight as they took in the surroundings so carefully and lovingly prepared for them. What they were able to visualize and create was magical. People carried, and still carry, this magic in their hearts when they remember their time at Lailey.

It is difficult to convey the powerful emotions present this afternoon when Donna and Tonya Lailey invited me into their home. They welcomed me so warmly, and graciously poured me a glass of 2013 Lailey Vineyard Chardonnay—the last vintage the family made and one of a few precious bottles remaining. I was stilled by their generosity. I held it reverently, breathing in the distinctive Lailey bouquet before slowly sipping the trademark elegance with which Derek Barnett lovingly transformed the precious fruit into a snapshot in time, a vintage of bottled memories.

We may not have been sitting at Lailey Vineyard today, but Tonya and Donna still made me feel, without a shadow of a doubt, that I was somewhere special and with truly, truly, extraordinary people. Together, in turns, they shared with me so much of what their life and their journey was like. They locked arms together, celebrated together, commiserated, laughed, and cried. They've grown and reflected and shared their stories and their journey with the rest of us. Tonya calls it a great adventure. When we think about an adventure, and the characters therein whom we faithfully follow, they are strong, innovative, and resourceful. They persevere through and triumph over challenges, ultimately stronger for them. These two women are all of that and more. They are strong and innovative and resourceful and committed to their cause and their craft, to raising the bar. Alongside the Barnetts, they've given the Niagara wine industry and, by ripple effect, the Canadian wine industry, a gift—a powerful, memorable gift for which we are humbly indebted.

Lailey Vineyard, and the winery, as they created it, may not be today what they had hoped it would continue to be, but that wasn't for lack of trying, it wasn't for lack of commitment. Life happens, aging happens, health and illness happen. This unravelling is heartbreaking and happens within every family. For this family, it happened very publicly. At some point, if we are wise, we say it's time to call an end to this chapter, while we are still strong, while what we are leaving behind is still our best and is still special. These women, this family, were wise enough and strong enough and cared enough to do that. Instead of us as a community, an industry, a province, and country seeing a winery and a brand that began to decline because of their inability any longer, despite trying, to maintain that standard, this incredible family, in partnership with the Barnetts, said, "We must do what's right here." The unavoidable sale of the winery did not take away from the magic they created. As a result of their great strength, the rest of us are left with a memory of one of the most exceptional places, wineries, and families in the Ontario wine industry. For that, we should be eternally grateful.

Note: Faik Turkmen bought Lailey Vineyard in 2021 from the couple who purchased it from Donna and David Lailey. Turkmen's intention is to return Lailey to a quality-focused operation. He hired Ann Sperling and Peter Gamble to oversee the winemaking and vineyards. On June 1, 2023, Donna and David Lailey were invited to pick up shovels and plant the very first vines for the replanting of Lailey Vineyard. The new vineyard blocks were generously and respectively named Donna's Block and David's Block in their honour, paying homage to the work they did and impact they had on that farm, and on the local and Canadian wine industry.

SHARING A GLASS

Tributes to Donna Lailey

Donna Lailey by Natalie Gorejko
Early employee and family friend

"It was early 2002 when I first met Donna and Tonya Lailey. I was in my third year of Brock University's Oenology and Viticulture degree, and an eight-month placement was required that incorporated a combination of hospitality, viticulture, and winemaking. Although this was not my first interview in the wine industry, this time something instantly felt different. I didn't know at that time how big of an impact the Laileys would have on me, both personally and professionally. It would also shape my formative years in the Ontario wine industry. I did, however, realize within the span of the interview with both Donna and Tonya that I could learn a lot from both women and that Lailey Vineyard was the place I wanted to be. It was small, family run, and I would have an opportunity to learn many facets of the vineyard, winery, and hospitality.

"The interview ended with a firm handshake, and I anxiously awaited their decision. I wouldn't be writing this if they didn't decide to offer me that intern position. I later found out that my firm handshake was one of the reasons Donna decided to hire me and because of that my grip has never wavered.

"To say that Donna was a hard worker would be a gross understatement. Attempting to keep up with her through the growing season and harvest was a challenge in itself. Although I appreciated the time in the vineyard, literally learning from the rootstock up, I also quickly learned that farming and grape growing is difficult. It takes a very specific type of person to be able to do it and, at that time, Donna had been doing it for thirty years. Up to that point, I had considered myself a hard worker, but it was Donna who directed me to be detail oriented, to go that extra little bit further to focus and make sure I really nailed the task. This attention to detail became part of my work ethic which I carry to this day.

"Donna practiced a no-nonsense attitude in her approach to work and people. The bar was set high for those of us working under her tutelage. She had zero tolerance for excuses, but if you showed up, did the job to the best of your ability, and were open to learning, there was a world of experience to be gained.

"I also gained a second family that became a support system in my early wine industry years and for this I am very beholden to the Lailey and Barnett families. In such a male-dominated field to be able to work closely with a woman who is a pioneer in Niagara is an opportunity that not many of us get to experience. To be able to do that in an environment that both pushes and nurtures you is special. From my heart to you, Donna Lailey, thank you!"

Donna Lailey by Albrecht Seeger
Grape Growers of Ontario Board member (25 years)
2019 Niagara Agriculture Lifetime Achievement Award recipient for more than forty decades of growing

"Donna was a very hard-working entrepreneur. She didn't wait for others; she saw opportunities and took matters into her own hands. She had the foresight to develop an incredibly successful juice business. That had never been done before. Her juice was in demand all over Ontario and always sold out. She was well known and well respected among Ontario winemakers, professional, and amateurs; back then there were many home winemakers.

"She came onto the board of the Grape Growers of Ontario and went up the ranks very quickly. Back in the 1990s, Niagara was a conservative generation, Donna was very instrumental in changing perspectives and making progress.

"We belonged to the same wine club and were personal friends as well as colleagues. Over the years we discussed a lot about the industry. There wasn't an idea she had that she didn't try to push through, and she wasn't easily defeated!

"If I had to sum her up in a few words I would say she was a determined, hard working, well respected, visionary. The grape and wine industry were lucky to have her, she made so many significant contributions and changes."

Donna Lailey by Dr. Daniel J. Patterson
President of Niagara College, 1995–2020

"Niagara College were thrilled to have Donna join its Board of Governors. Donna was an active member of the board from 1993 to 1996. I spent a great deal of time seeking Donna's advice on a range of topics in addition to her tremendous insights to the grape growing industry. As we were in our early stage of development of our campus, she provided valuable input on how we linked to the Niagara Escarpment Commission and how we could grow in the agri-food sector.

"She was passionate about education and gave voice on how important it was for Niagara College to have a strong economic mission that opened the doors to the college developing our learning enterprises and help grow the next generation of grape growers, winemakers, etc. Donna recognized that having a strong labour force to support the growing grape and wine industry would be critical to that industry's future. Having her advocacy at this early stage of the college's desire to grow in this area, was a real blessing. At board meetings, she was always active and provided sage advice on many topics. On a personal note, I saw her as a mentor to me as I worked with governors to create a strong board, that provided us with long-term strategic advice and assistance.

"While I do not see Donna regularly now, when we do connect, it's very magical for me. We are kindred spirits and share so many of the same value-based leadership qualities that I think are important for a robust community."

Donna Lailey by her daughter Jennifer Lailey

"A significant thing I have taken from growing up with a woman as determined and passionate as my mom was about wine is that caring about something and fighting for it truly does make an impact. It comes at a cost, but one shouldn't be afraid to speak to something that matters to one, let alone apologize for doing so. So many young women grow up with the belief that nice girls don't speak their mind or make other people uncomfortable. My mom wasn't having that, which was a pain in the ass sometimes but also empowering. I think about the poem 'Our Deepest Fear' by Marianne Williamson.

"My mother had a way of speaking truth to power that I admired. I talk about this in the past tense not because she no longer does, but because I am not around it as much and she HAS softened as she has aged.

"She also has an incredible palate and a sense for growing things. It's like an intuitive connection with the vines and the wine that comes from them. It took a long time for me to see this. As a child [to me], she was such a force and all business. I have come to appreciate her vision by the discernment and respect she is able to give to the product, even if she was completely biased toward her own. I have struggled with her aggressive style but have gotten better at recognizing why it was necessary and appreciating the fruit it has borne."

Dr. Linda Bramble

"I wasn't a critic of wine. I like to think that I was a chronicler of the stories that we were living and also an educator. I love to help students of wine discover."

I met with Linda Bramble over lunch, which began with her proposing a toast: "To friendship and everything that is to come, because there will be so many good things." She nods emphatically, makes eye contact and smiles. "There will," she says with certainty. We clink glasses and she says, "Shall we begin?"

Linda was born in Erie, Pennsylvania, moved to Indiana when she was four, and then to Buffalo, New York. She originally wanted to go to law school. Knowing that her family didn't have the money for law school tuition, she applied for a scholarship her last year in high school. "They called me to tell me that I came in first, but that since I was only going to end up as a housewife and mother, they had decided to give it to the fellow who had come in second." She went instead to the state college in Cortland, NY. "The only career choices in the 1950s for a young woman was you were either a teacher, or a nurse. I chose teaching and I loved it," she said with a genuine smile.

Linda came to Canada in 1974 when she got a teaching job at Brock University. At the same time, she was completing a PhD in philosophy and education at the University at Buffalo. As a single parent of two, Linda admits that those were challenging years juggling each of her roles but felt that her passion for teaching and dedication to education kept her motivated.

Four years later, she began teaching at Concordia University in Montreal, which she loved. She had just met her future husband Ben, but he couldn't join her in Montreal, so she relocated to the Niagara Peninsula.

For thirteen years, Linda worked at the Niagara Institute, a centre for the study of leadership and eventually became director of the Values Program. The mission of the Niagara Institute was to build stronger leaders and organizations for a better future. This has truly been Linda's life work for over forty years. Of her time with the institute, Linda reminisces fondly, "That was a wonderful interlude and some of the best years of my life. Oh! They were fabulous! That's how I got into leadership development. It was also how I got into the wine industry."

At the Niagara Institute, Linda held week-long seminars where leaders from government, industry, business, academia, and labour came to take a deeper look at the nature of leadership. Because their discussions were held in the beautiful nineteenth-century home of the Rand Estate, right in the heart of the burgeoning modern wine industry, showcasing Niagara's new wineries was a natural fit. But in the early days, the participants regarded Canadian wine as an oxymoron and felt confident in assuming that even the new wines were not going to be very good.

Linda explained that the wines of the old industry, were, indeed, wretched, but many of the new wines, based on premium grape varieties and not the old native grape varieties, were stellar. One night, she got so frustrated trying to persuade the participants be more open minded, she created what she called "The Great Canadian Wine Challenge." She asked each participant to give her the name of their favourite wine in the $15 to $20 range and she would match it, style for style, grape for grape, vintage for vintage.

She assembled the wines, and wrapped them in brown paper bags, with only numbers to identify the wine inside. The blind challenge was to first identify their favourite wine among the wines, and then identify the wines they thought were from Niagara. The word got around so new participants would request the same tasting. She never lost a challenge!

Linda, along with William J. Thomas (humor writer), Evie McTaggert (journalist), and Caroline Wilson (copyeditor) started a magazine in the early eighties called *What's Up Niagara*. Niagara didn't have a monthly magazine at that time. Linda's beat was crime and wine; she said she always loved a glass of wine while reading a good mystery! At that time, there were about twenty-two wineries in Niagara and Linda knew them all well. She began sharing their stories and writing about their wines in *What's Up Niagara* as well as other magazines. She said to herself, *If I'm writing about wine, then I better have some credentials!*

Linda began taking courses through WSET (Wine & Spirit Education Trust) and in 1999 she became a certified sommelier. She started writing in national magazines and doing a lot of travelling. At this point, she rejoined the faculty at Brock University, first in the Cool Climate Oenology and Viticulture Institute (CCOVI) and then as an adjunct professor in the business department, applying her business leadership development skills and experience. Says Linda about this time: "It was lovely, but the people who knew me in wine knew nothing about my business leadership development and vice versa."

By this time, she had written several books on wine touring in Niagara's (and Ontario as well) wine country. Her editor asked her whether she was interested in telling the history of modern industry. To make it more approachable, Linda chose to tell the history through the people who most lead the industry. That book, published in 2009, became *Niagara's Wine Visionaries: Profiles of the Pioneering Winemakers*, which she was delighted about because it connected her two interests: wine and leadership.

Linda has always had a love of history and of telling the stories of the people who shaped eras.

To select the individuals she would profile in the book, she consulted key members of the industry, and the people they all agreed on became the basis for the profiles she created.

Linda spoke highly of Linda Franklin, but she wasn't a winemaker. Franklin worked behind the scenes and, according to Linda Bramble, "she was vital." Linda Franklin was the executive director of the Wine Council of Ontario (WCO), now known as Ontario Craft Wineries, from 1994 until 2007. Those years were a time of great challenges and also great advancements in the Ontario grape and wine industry. At that time, the WCO was responsible not only for system-wide marketing of Ontario wineries but also government relations on behalf of the wineries. In *Niagara Wine Visionaries*, Linda Bramble includes a quote about Linda Franklin from Len Pennachetti, co-founder and CEO of Cave Spring Cellars in Jordan, Ontario, and the then president and chair of the newly formed Vintners Quality Alliance: "We were cowboys until she arrived. She taught us how to deal with the big guys in government."

Linda Bramble goes on to say, "Linda Franklin played a very significant role in helping to advance the industry. We probably wouldn't have had VQA as soon as we did without her." Although Linda Bramble is an accomplished writer, educator, and speaker, she reveals that she is an introvert. She tells of the days of *Cheers Niagara*!, a local radio show she hosted for a couple of years. In each episode, Linda spoke about wine and food and the evolving stories of the Ontario wine industry. She divulges, "The first time I did the show, I threw up when the ads came on. I would run to the bathroom, throw up, and come back. I was insanely nervous. It went away the more I got prepared, the more I had some certainty. I used to draw this big clock and divide into the time slots, and I knew exactly what I was going to do in each of the time slots," she laughs out loud, remembering.

When asked who her mentors and role models have been, Linda was quick to name two: Peter Gamble and Jancis Robinson. Linda had viewed Jancis, the renown British wine writer, as an example from the beginning of her wine studies, noting that she purchased and studied every one of Jancis' books. She had decided early on that if she was going to professionally review wine then she was aspiring to be the very best taster she could possibly be. When the opportunity arose later in her career to work with Jancis, Linda was thrilled and exuberantly recalls the experience as "just fantastic."

Linda notes that in this digital age it's much easier to get to know your role models and strongly suggests learning all you can from them and about them through books, other writings, courses, and online material. She advises fervently, "There might not be a mentor nearby, but if you find one, stalk her. Just stalk her. Or him. Just say I want to learn from this person and then you just go and find out how and where and when might work. That's my advice. Stalk that person!"

Linda counts herself fortunate that she did in fact have a mentor nearby in Peter Gamble, who was the then winemaker at Hillebrand, as well as an educator and internationally recognized wine taster. Peter later became the founding executive director of the Vintners Quality Alliance, and one of the people insistent on the formation of an independent tasting panel for all wines seeking VQA approval.

To be able to make a successful career out of doing something you love so much is what we all strive for. To this end, Linda brings up author Joseph Campbell and the archetypes he claims we all live by. She quotes Campbell: "Above all follow your bliss." She follows that by saying, "I know it's overused now, but in those days it wasn't. So, I thought long and hard 'What is my bliss? What is my bliss? My father died at fifty-nine. My mother and he never had an opportunity to do what they had planned to do in life. You know, life is too short. So, I said I would never do that. The other thing was I would never have toxic people in my life. If I felt sad in their company, I would take myself out. I think those were early lessons for me."

"When I was starting my studying, my goal was to become one of Canada's top tasters. Peter Gamble was my mentor. It was through his encouragement and the strategy he suggested that I follow, I grew into a fairly good one. He said, "At the beginning of every week, read about a grape variety. Buy five different examples. Taste them. Take notes. Invest in a nitrogen pump. By the end of the week, do it blind and see how well you do." That constant discrimination and differentiation of place, of style and of type, I did on my own. Then when I was ready to take courses, I was okay. And I learned a heck of a lot. I would research every wine, the winery, and the grape variety, of course. That's how I taught myself and that's how I taught students. So. Peter was the guy." This last part said with conviction and a satisfied smile.

Linda goes on to recall a time when she wanted to interview Peter for *What's Up Niagara*. She lights up and animatedly recounts the tale: "I told him, 'Okay, let's go on a picnic. I'll bring the lunch; you bring the wine.' We went to the Niagara River Parkway and, of course, it's against the law to drink wine on the parkway!" Linda giggles. "So, there we were, violating the law, and having SUCH a good time!" She laughs delightedly at the memory.

This story leads merrily into another in which Linda was writing an article about women in wine for *Winetidings*, a Canadian wine magazine. Linda describes the perfect summer afternoon with a group of talented female winemakers. "We sat on my back porch. The sun was at just the right level in the sky that no one got too hot. I had assembled a big platter of antipasti and we had lots of wine. It was Sandra Marynissen (Marynissen Wines), Sue-Ann Staff (then at Pillitteri Estates), Ann Sperling (Malivoire at the time), and Deborah Paskus (then at Tawse), Mira Ananicz (Jackson Triggs). I asked them questions for the article of course, but really, we just had a lovely afternoon talking. They truly captured the spirit of what it meant to be a woman winemaker. They laid it all on the line to show a real image of what it was like in those days."

Linda recalls Ann Sperling recounting a time when she was the winemaker at Cedar Creek in British Columbia and had just won an award for the best Merlot in Canada. Ann told of the salesmen coming to the winery to sell her equipment. They would talk really loudly and slowly, Linda says, adopting a deep voice and drawing out each word as she tells the tale, "...to hhhhhhelp Ann understaaaaand this guy stuff about a maaaaaachhhinnnne." Linda says Ann rolled her eyes in recounting this and said, "I knew more about this than he did!" but to placate and not to offend them, Ann would say instead, "Ohhh really; is that right?"

Linda says that was just the way it was. "I don't know the extent to which it is today, and I'm hoping it's not like that anymore, but at that time, in the eighties and nineties, there was a lot of condescension towards women in the industry, almost that some people didn't believe that they could really make wine."

She shakes her head and with an eye roll of her own says, "I'll tell you another story while we're on this topic. In the mid-nineties I was asked by the Australian consulate to go to Australia and write an article on Australian wine for a Canadian publication. They paid my way; they paid Ben's way, too [her husband]. We were there for a month. They had an itinerary, and it was absolutely magnificent." Linda says, "At one point, I was doing a radio interview and when I arrived at the studio the announcer looked at me and said, "You're a Sheila! You're a woman wine writer? Does anybody really listen to you?" She recounts this in a macho Australian accent. Linda shakes her head ruefully and says she replied, "'Your Australian Consulate in Canada seems to.' So those were the days. Just appalling condescension. We had to have persistence and fortitude."

Linda goes on to say in a strong voice, "When you could get your foot in the door and demonstrate—demonstrate that you can write, demonstrate that people follow you, demonstrate that you're a good taster and a good judge, and then to get accepting people. Like Tony Aspler, Canada's pioneer in wine writing, editor of *Winetidings* magazine and organizer of the Ontario Wine Awards. Tony was wonderful. He paid no attention to that. He was open. He just wanted to get the best people to be judges. When I first started with Tony, about three-quarters of the tasters were men and then it became about half."

When asked about the accomplishments or impacts she is most proud of, Linda grows quiet and thoughtful. "Hmmm," she muses. Then, in true Linda fashion, she turns the tables and says adamantly, "Top. Top. Is to see students like you do so well. I adore it. It's so gratifying." She smiles. I smile. And I melt. To know Linda is to love her. Truly.

Of teaching wine, Linda almost gleefully proclaims, "I had so much fun. I spent every penny available to be able to present the students with the best possible array of wines. I loved every minute of it. I also taught courses in the business school, and I loved that, too." Her happy laughter rings out with this account.

Linda has an extraordinary gift as a teacher. To be a student of Linda's is an incredible opportunity. She is invested in each and every student, getting to know them, engaging and motivating them through numerous teaching methods, developing meaningful relationships that build student efficacy and add meaning and value to the learning experience. She imparts her bottomless knowledge with great enthusiasm, peppering each lesson with personal anecdotes and stories about the wines and the people behind them. One comes away from time spent with Linda excited, motivated, and with renewed passion and dedication to their field.

As an educator myself and lifelong student of Linda's, I have always found myself striving to channel my inner Linda Bramble during interactions with students and colleagues, often asking myself, *What would Linda do in this situation? How can I too, be impactful, encouraging, compassionate, and inspiring like Linda?* A tall order! Linda leaves us transformed and determined to be a better person, student, teacher, friend, and colleague—to come away from each experience having contributed something positive.

Linda understands that some of the most effective ways of learning and retaining information is through shared experiences and collaborative learning. Retention is much easier when knowledge is linked to positive emotions and memories; the connections evoke recollections of details, dates, facts, and conversations. The great Maya Angelou said that "People will forget what you said, people will forget what you did, but people will never forget how you made them feel." With Linda, you never forget how she made you feel but, miraculously, you also never forget what she said because the way in which she says things is so impactful.

Linda's love of wine and of teaching spilled over into her family as well. Gatherings and celebrations almost always included thoughtful conversations around the appreciation of wine and the people involved in making it. Her family members have themselves absorbed so much of Linda's knowledge and enthusiasm. On a recent trip to Italy, Linda's grandson found himself being schooled by a restaurant sommelier regarding which wine he should order. He realized that he knew with confidence and certainty which wine he wanted and said to the sommelier with pride and pleasure, "Do you know who my grandmother is?"

When pressed, she admits that she's gotten some awards that have also been gratifying. "It's nice to be recognized, I guess, and validated. When I got the RBC Business Award, I was so proud. They called me up to the podium and then wanted me to sit down after receiving the award and I said, 'No, I'm not finished talking,'" she chuckles. "I was so proud of the award. I was proud of the Promote the Promoters Award for Lifetime Achievement. I was proud when I got the Dean's Award for Excellence in Coaching in the MBA program at Athabasca University, which was very rewarding."

SHARING A GLASS

The following announcement can be found on the Athabasca University website:

> This distinguished award for excellence in coaching is given annually in recognition of the notable achievements in the following areas: excellence in presentation of subject matter, innovation of delivery, sustained achievements in coaching, and high standards of service to students.
>
> This year's recipient is Dr. Linda Bramble, Academic Coach, Leadership. Linda's students and colleagues had many kind words to share with her. "I am a better leader for her guidance and I found what she taught me immensely valuable. I'm using this every day at work now, it was my good fortune to have been in her class," said one of her students. Faculty of Business Dean, Dr. Deborah Hurst, shared kind words about Linda as well, "your exquisite brain is something to humble all of us."

Upon receiving the award, Linda said that she was, "very grateful to be among such wonderful, thoughtful, caring leaders and educators. Just to be among all of you—such dedicated people, it's just a thrill for me."

On the topic of recognition, Linda continues, "It's always nice to be validated but I never went into what I did for that reason. Ever. Ever. I do think one of the top things in my life was getting my PhD, under stressful circumstances. I was a single parent, and I knew I had to make more money so, you know, you do what your strengths may be."

To the question, "If you could give advice today to your twenty-year-old self, what would you say?' Linda replies, "Be prepared. Know your stuff impeccably. Never lie. Be kind. Be generous. Relax. If you are prepared and you know what you are going to do, whether it's teaching or talking to groups, if you're prepared, you can leave your notes and then be free and enjoy the encounter with other people."

As an industry, Linda feels we have so many things to be proud of but notes taking the challenge to move to vinifera grape varieties from the domestic labrusca as the foremost. "I don't think everybody realizes what courage that took. Nobody knew for sure what was going to happen, and they lost a lot of crop. They brought in terrible material at the beginning. Thank goodness for Lloyd Schmidt, who sourced some good material. Nobody really knew what to plant where, so it was a lot of touch and go. So just the courage of that. It's such a low margins industry to start with. It was just a total transformation. Total. A disruption in the industry and then transformation. From the ground up! Literally."

Linda also names CCOVI and Niagara College as achievements to be proud of. "We're just a small speck in the world of wine, but yet we have all of the necessary ingredients for real greatness." She notes that going forward, with regards to grape varieties, "We don't have to please everybody. Here's what we do best. Focus."

Linda carried the idea of focus into all aspects of the business through her teaching and training, in and outside of the classroom. She believes that each of us play a part in the industry's success and should always strive for excellence, whether grape growers or front-line hospitality. In 2003, she developed and taught Brock University's Excellence in Wine Sales and Service. In 2007, Linda contributed to a chapter entitled "The Development and Economic Impact of the Wine Industry in Ontario, Canada," in the book *Wine, Society, and Globalization: Multidisciplinary Perspectives on the Wine Industry.* Most recently, she collaborated with Carman Cullen on the Canadian chapter 'Creating Winter Wine Festivals in Niagara' in *Best Practices in Global Wine Tourism,* which was awarded Best Wine Tourism Book in the United States, and Best Wine Tourism Book in the World 2017, at the International Gourmand World Cookbook Awards. While passionately speaking about the Ontario wine industry at Brock University's 2014 Experts Tasting, Linda referenced Phil Alden Robinson from the movie *Field of Dreams,* "If you build it, they will come." As an industry, we have Linda's dedication to thank for much of our building success.

In this vein, when asked the question, "What can each of us do, going forward, to advance the industry" Linda states, "Be educated, especially women. Get all the education you can. Be persistent. Without losing the qualities and virtues of one's gender do what you do well. Be prepared.

Be ethical. Never take shortcuts. If you can't do it well, don't do it. Figure it out. Put the time in, plan and do it well so you can be proud of your excellence. And continue to study; never stop studying. That's beautiful thing about the wine industry—it's brand new every year!"

Lastly, when asked how she would like to be remembered, Linda answers with a sigh and a thoughtful nod, "For being kind. For being generous company."

Back home, surrounded by my notes, several of Linda's books, and the recording of our meeting, I am overcome by emotion. To capture the essence and impact of such a woman within a few pages is daunting; it's barely skimming the surface of a fascinating life and mind. I mentioned to Linda that sharing her story is comparable to trying to photograph an iceberg: she is the iceberg, in that only a very small yet striking portion is visible to the world while so much magnificent depth lies beneath the surface. With only a few pages, I can convey but a small glimpse into the life of such a remarkable individual. Linda has given us a true gift with her time, her insights, her wisdom, advice, and stories. One of the most marvelous things about recollecting these times and events is that the teller, and the audience, are both rapt in the sensations of the story—reliving the joy, the laughter, the insecurities, the determination, the triumphs, the friendships, the feelings of being united by a common goal, and the exhilaration derived from the pursuit of those goals. This is what life is about. Living to the fullest. Finding and following our bliss.

Linda told me many years ago, and repeated it ardently yesterday, "Life is meant to be lived. I don't want to get to the end well preserved. I want to be all used up and live to the fullest every minute." I believe she has always done just that and with such style and aplomb. She is a true inspiration and a powerful role model. She has transformed us, and we are better, individually, and as a whole, for knowing her.

JENNIFER WILHELM

Tributes to Linda Bramble

Linda Bramble by David Hulley
Director of Customer Experience
Vineland Estates Winery

"As I opened the near worn-out door to the legendary downtown St. Catharines diner, I saw, for the first time, in the restaurant's dim light, Linda's shining smile. That encounter was more than thirty years ago, and that famous, caring smile has not lost one ounce of its lustre to this day. Linda's bright, steady, and inquisitive eyes cut right to my core. Here was a person of infinite substance and gravity and I knew in a moment that I needed to bring my scholarly A game just to sit at her table. The meeting was at Diana Sweets Restaurant and Soda Bar, a much-loved institution and now lost to history. Linda had invited me to coffee so we could become familiar with each other's stories and passions. Little did I know that the beginning of an important, lifelong friendship was just steps ahead. In truth, it was the beginning of a love affair. I love Linda's energy, her compassion, her wit, her humanity, her charm and, easily underpinning all that profound weight, is her prodigious intellect. Linda was and continues to be impressive.

"Mostly, what caught me by surprise was her grace and warmth. Linda was the model of hospitality. Even though I knew that I was in the presence of wine "royalty," I felt immediately at ease. As she stared over her steaming cup, the quiet and informal interview began. I was simply unaware. Linda possesses the unbridled wonder and curiosity of a child and is always keenly interested in those around her. She is a seeker. Linda calmly looks for the pure essence in others and gently digs out their truth in a safe and comfortable environment. You cannot help but give it up. She's naturally caring and a master at her craft; the result of sharing with Linda is a far deeper understanding of oneself plus the issues at hand. Regardless, Linda had a plan the day we met over coffee as she wanted to gently ease me towards teaching in the wine industry as part of my career. She could see into my instinctive mentor's soul and nourished it. I will be forever grateful.

"Besides enjoying many conversations, collaborations, and glasses of wine over the years, I also had the privilege of interviewing Linda during a fine meal at Vineland Estates Winery. It was for one of the many honours she has received over the years. Now, we certainly had work to do, but just breaking bread and catching up with Linda was reason enough to make time. With my pen and pad ready, I started with some basics that quickly swirled into an in-depth conversation. The next thing I knew, Linda was interviewing me! She just cannot help herself. Her quizzical and curious nature just spontaneously guides her down interesting roads of discovery. I had to hold up my hand and say, "Wait a minute. It's my job to interview you!" Linda replied with that soft and engaging smile, "Oh David, just take my hand. We'll get there eventually." Okay, Linda."

Linda Bramble by Barb Tatarnic
Manager, Continuing Education and Outreach Brock University | Cool Climate Oenology and Viticulture Institute

"A love letter to Linda,

What a true privilege it is to write about wine industry icon, Linda Bramble. Having the honour to have known and worked with her since 1997 when I joined the Cool Climate Oenology & Viticulture Institute (CCOVI) at Brock University, quite simply has been a joy. When I think of Linda, the following words come to mind: integrity, brilliance, selflessness, curiosity, love, and a generous pinch of humbleness. Humbleness? Yes, she never makes anyone feel less than she or anyone else. In the wine world, she is keenly aware that there are no silly questions and wrong answers are always met with gentle words. With the early beginnings of the wine institute, Linda was front and centre advocating for its academic program, building CCOVI's outreach to the community, and advocating for what was to become the Canadian Wine Library (a permanent, revolving collection of Ontario's finest VQA wines judged ageable by its directors and housed within Inniskillin Hall at the Cool Climate Oenology & Viticulture Institute, Brock University).

As for myself, along the way, Linda quickly became a mentor, as she did for so many. Without hesitation, she brought me into her world, this beautiful woman taught me how and why we all need to work every day to be your best self. She also taught me so much about the wine industry, the people who work so hard in it, and why. Hers was the first work colleague home telephone number I committed to memory in all my years at Brock University and the wine industry! She was always there for me. I was new to this industry, I was a nobody, but she brought me in and how lucky am I that she became a coveted friend as we travelled the path together.

There were so many workshops we did; she took on each challenge without hesitation and always with infinite creativity. We would laugh so much but knew each other so well that when it came to an end result, it was always executed to perfection. Another result was that everyone in the room was left inspired by this wonderful woman, not just from the perspective of what she was teaching them about wine but simply because this beautiful human being became everyone's Linda Bramble.

The grape and wine industry has benefitted from Linda in so many ways, the books she has written, the courses she has taught, the community events she has hosted and the people (and purposes) she has advocated for. But when I think about it, it's all the people who have read her books, the lives she's touched through the courses she's taught, or the community that's been in front of Linda who are the true benefactors of Linda because with each of these things she gives a part of herself and we, in turn, are all the better for her generosity.

By the way Linda, if you find a mason jar of gin at your door, it's from me ☺

Barb"

Linda Bramble by Tammy Kruck
Senior Manager of Customer Relations & Sales
Malivoire Wine Company

"Few people in my adult life have positively affected my professional life more than Linda Bramble. When I was searching for a career path, Linda came into my life through the Institute for Enterprise Education with a program designed to educate a new class of individuals who wanted to be a valued part of the growing wine industry in a sales and marketing role. The program was designed so the participants could fully understand the industry by learning about the product and its environment. Linda was responsible for teaching the wine portion of the program, but she was so much more than a teacher following a curriculum. Linda's energy and commitment were an essential part of her authentic desire to see everyone succeed. She had a way to bring everything to life. Linda provided a space where this adult class could make mistakes and still feel worthy. She lives through example, as when she says, "Be bold!"

"One of many examples happened when Linda explained stemware's effect on wine tasting. She was very excited to educate us all about Riedel stemware, both how functionally elegant and surprisingly strong they are. She demonstrated these attributes by striking the bowls of the stemware together! We are all shocked and amazed. Linda then showed us how you could even strike them harder, as we all winced with disbelief that they could handle this punishment! But with the third deliberate and forceful strike of the elegant bowls, they shattered! While we were all shocked and disappointed for Linda, she laughed with disbelief and grace in front of the class. Linda has always taught through example.

"Only a short time after our course finished, I was taking another wine class to further my education. When faced with an opportunity to share my thoughts with the class, I was hesitant, unsure, and scared to be ridiculed for saying something completely wrong. Then I remembered Linda's advice and heard her voice, "Be bold!" I want to tell you that it ended well, but like the Riedel stemware demonstration, my sharing started strong but turned into my worst fear. I had gotten it wrong but, like Linda, I was able to laugh off the "failure." I learned instead.

"Linda's presence in my wine career has continued over the last twenty-plus years. She has always been there to assist and mentor me with challenges along the way. She is so smart, kind, modest and authentic in everything she does and with everyone she meets. I know that she has been a positive force for more people in our industry than she could imagine, and we are not just better industry colleagues for it but better people. I am proud to know Linda Bramble."

Linda Bramble by Britnie Bazylewski
Tourism Development Officer
Town of Lincoln

"Dr. Linda Bramble is undoubtedly one of the most influential women in the Canadian wine industry. As a revered mentor, educator, author, and industry trailblazer, Linda's constancy to purpose in this industry has never wavered. However, it is not because of these attributes that my affection for Linda began but rather because of Linda's humanity and how she shares herself so selflessly with the world.

"I will always remember my first interaction with Linda. As a young, burgeoning wine lover, I courageously took a leap of faith to explore the world of wine in my last year of university. I left behind a traditional career path far more ideal for my parents and societal norms than for me. Terrified of the unknown, intimidated by wine's elitist narrative, and faced with a lack of female representation in the industry, I felt alone and anxious, despite also feeling anticipatory.

"As I entered the classroom, a petite, unassuming figure echoed from the front of the class, "Welcome! Great to meet you! No need to sit all the way back there. Get close—we're going to get to know one another really well over the coming weeks." Linda was immediately disarming. The gut-wrenching nerves that plagued my car ride to class had suddenly melted away, and I felt myself begin to let go, leaning in enthusiastically to everything Linda had to say. Each week in class led to more of the same. Warm greetings, genuine care, and concern—in fact, this industry legend gave out her personal cellphone number to our entire class should we face a challenge in the future that could use a little Bramble sparkle!

"Not once did Linda pontificate about her impressive portfolio to me or my fellow classmates. With great humility, Linda shared examples of her impactful body of work to inspire our class to know what was attainable in the industry if you were to follow your passion, commit to the hard work, and conduct yourself with kindness along the way.

"As a collector of mentors and moments, I attribute my early successes in the Ontario wine and tourism industries to incredible women like Linda Bramble, who have blazed the trail before me. I am forever grateful for the decades of learning and lessons that Linda navigated knowingly or unknowingly for myself and my fellow female wine professionals, as we could not stand here today without her contribution. She set a standard for excellence and integrity that I strive to emulate and carry on every day. It is my hope that these stories of women in wine will be shouted from every rooftop, continuing to give hope and blaze trails for the next generation of icons, just like Linda Bramble did for me."

Linda Bramble by Tony Aspler
Author, Wine Writer

"Linda Bramble is the consummate wine professional. She brings an academic rigour to her writings, to her tasting abilities in competitions and to her lecturing—and she does all of this with great flair and humour. Countless young wine students owe their success in the industry to her mentorship. Linda's books on the Niagara region are required reading for anyone who wants to learn what makes this region such a magical place to grow wine."

Linda Bramble by Elena-Galey Pride
Submission for Woman of Distinction Nomination Letter

Seldom has the YWCA had the opportunity to consider a nominee for "Woman of Distinction" whose credentials more closely reflect the credo "above and beyond the call." Linda Bramble is an integral part of the Ontario wine scene and the industry, and her community is healthier because of her.

Understandably, with a PhD in education, Linda sees herself foremost as an educator. She is also a writer, a broadcaster, a researcher, a trainer, a facilitator, and a consultant. She is behind the scenes, behind the keyboard, behind the microphone, in front of the audience, and in front of the camera. And, luckily for the Ontario wine industry, she has a pride in and a passion for our industry and has made it the focus of her incredible energy. She is our cheerleader, our teacher, our mentor, our conscience, our philosopher, our historian, and our friend.

Linda shares her passion—she can't seem to help it. It bubbles up and spills over and so impresses those around her because it is genuine and intense. As an educator, Linda demonstrates her pride in the industry, coupled with her sense of responsibility to it. Both wine consumers and wine professionals benefit from the opportunity to sit in any of Linda Bramble's classrooms, as hundreds of students can attest. But perhaps the most interesting aspect of Linda-as-educator is her personal commitment to her students. Having sat in several of Linda's classrooms, I can vouch that she makes a promise to each group of students to "be there for them" as a resource, a coach, and a mentor, not just while they are taking the course but at any time in the future. And from personal experience, I can also assure you that this is no idle promise. Students take her up on it over and over, and she not only welcomes it, she thrives on it.

I've left out more than I've included about Linda's qualifications to be the YWCA's Woman of Distinction. In the truest spirit of selfless devotion to the betterment of her community, Linda Bramble deserves to receive this honour this year.

<blockquote>
If Linda were a fine wine—
Jewel-toned, crisp and clear, with good concentration.
Youthfully exuberant, and very approachable.
Complex structure, with layers of fresh yet
intense peachiness,
that open up to an earthy mid-palate and a spicy or even
nutty top-note.
Sweet with just the right touch of acidity.
</blockquote>

Elegant and beautifully balanced, with lingering richness on
the finish.
Very well made. Rare.

Respectfully submitted,

Elena Galey-Pride

Elena Galey-Pride
(then) Director of Customer Experience
Southbrook Vineyards

Debbie Zimmerman

"Many of the things and experiences which have shaped me most were the ones which pushed me out of my comfort zone. I had to keep doing them. Sometimes it took a lot more faith than I had in myself. What I did know is that I did not want to look back and realize that I had repeated the patterns of the past. If something wasn't working, I had to find another way."

Debbie was born in British Columbia, the fourth child of seven, to parents Murray and Pearle Roy. With hindsight, she halfway jokes that her birth order, right in the middle of seven children, or as she says, "the youngest of the oldest and the oldest of the youngest" may have contributed to her trait as an impartial observer. It meant that she had to learn how to quickly assess situations, consider all options, and shrewdly balance outcomes. Invaluable qualities which would play a critical role in her future.

The Roy family moved from Burnaby, British Columbia, and settled in Grimsby, Ontario. Both Murray and Pearle became active members of the then still small town, instilling the importance of community in their children from a young age. Debbie recalls that her mother was always volunteering and contributing to their community and society in numerous ways. Her father volunteered with the Rotary and Kinsmen service organizations.

It was a busy household. "Since there were seven of us, it was fend for yourself in some ways. We were a typical family in that because there so many of us, there was never enough money, but weren't troubled because we always knew that we had a place to belong."

With a deep sigh Debbie reveals, "We had other challenges. My older brother was killed in a car accident shortly after we moved to Grimsby. He was eight years old. That changed the dynamics of our family a lot. It was hard on us as a family. It was so traumatic. As a child, I didn't quite understand but, as I watched the family dynamics unfold, I was changed. We all were. It shaped our emotions and interactions with one another and within the family and community. We soldiered through it, but you can imagine that that was difficult for all of us as kids. We were changed. But the strength of the unity of the family was always there."

Debbie feels she came from a traditional 1950s family but also notes that her father was determined to ensure that she and her sisters developed their own voices as women. She includes reflectively, "Not so much with my mom, mind you; he treated my mom like a 1950s homemaker. He paid the bills, did the things, and gave my mother an allowance to run the household. And that bugged me. That always bugged me that he gave my mom a set amount that HE determined for her to run the household. There were always debates about that in my house. Interestingly, my father never wanted any of his three daughters to take a back seat to anyone; that was made very clear to us as we grew up.

"Politics were frequently on the table at our house. Dad and Mom were very good parents, but they were very vocal about politics in our household. There would be big fights around election time. My dad died a Liberal and my mother, who is alive still, is a staunch NDP [supporter]. My mother would tell him, "I don't care you what you say, Murray; my vote cancels yours out anyway!" Debbie laughs and says, "She took great pride in saying that."

She continues. "My mom went back to work after years of staying home with us kids and she went on to be very successful in her career. While Dad still thought she should stay home, he did not want that for his daughters. It was a bit a bizarre, but he still had traditional expectations in some ways, like asking me when I decided to run for election who was going to cook my husband's dinner!" She laughs in bewilderment at this juxtaposition.

After high school, Debbie enrolled in and graduated from Niagara College's journalism program. She remembers being drawn by the idea of having a voice and her love of the written word. Following graduation, she took a position as a reporter with the community newspaper, the *Grimsby Independent*. Her early exposure to politics at home and her natural observer's ability to intuitively perceive all sides made her a perfect fit to cover local issues.

"My decision to run for city council grew out of a problem we encountered in the community. It was a simple problem, so simple it was silly, really. The town had decided that the tennis club would determine the hours of the public tennis court. We were frustrated about the fact that we paid taxes, and why should we have to pay additional money to join a club?! My friends and I were sitting down one night, talking about it and I said, 'This is just awful; we should do something about this. We should go to city council.' And my friends said, "YES, and YOU should do it!"" (She laughs, here remembering).

"One of the people I worked with said, 'I bet you can't get one hundred signatures.' [At the time you needed one hundred signatures to run for city council.] "I felt challenged and so I took the bet! I knew people, and I had a strong community presence because of my family and my husband's family. So, I went out and I got those one hundred signatures!"

Debbie recalls, "I was twenty-two years old. I was so naïve about the concept that women were unable to run for things and about the pushback that I would encounter. It didn't even occur to me. I would knock on doors and the husband would open the door and say, 'What are you doing out here? Why aren't you home cooking dinner for your husband and family?' Meanwhile, his wife would be standing behind him giving me two thumbs up."

Debbie entered the then male-dominated realm of politics in the 1970s. As a young woman, she encountered mixed reactions to her decision. While some people cheered her on with admiration, others were taken aback by her nerve and perceived social impropriety. At the time, she was working as a journalist for a local newspaper, a job she loved, and which fed her curious mind. When she decided to run for candidacy, it precluded her from continuing to investigate and report on local political news. Debbie says she was fortunate that the publisher of the *Grimsby Independent* allowed her to move from this department to another so that she could maintain a position there while running.

Debbie confesses, "I was terrified at my first candidate debate. I overstudied, and I walked into the room looking ridiculous, carrying about five feet of binders, thinking I could possibly find the answer in a twenty-minute debate. The interesting thing about my first election in 1978 is that I ran against an NDP candidate and my public school principal. Two very well-known older men and another young man from Grimsby.

"Being young helped, I think. I think people liked the idea that I was young and what was wrong with change? I will admit that there was a lot of indulgent patting on my head saying, 'Ohhh, it's good for you to try, but don't be disappointed when you lose.' However, I believe my oddness in being young and female appealed to more of the voters than I realized.

"Still, we had so much fun and that was also key in those early days. My husband and family were incredibly supportive. As were my community and all my neighbours. They came out and helped me fold my brochures. I was so naïve about what it meant for me to be doing this as a female. I just figured I would have to work twice as hard. So what if this guy didn't like me? I would just get two more votes from this another household! And I knocked on every door.

"I was starting something new, and I didn't have any clue about what I was signing up for." She laughs and adds that that was probably a good thing, because if she had known she may not have even gotten started!

"My family always accepted the fact I enjoyed politics. My parents, siblings, husband, and children were so supportive. My dad was proud of me but old fashioned enough to worry about my marriage and family life. Unfortunately, he died before I became the head of regional government. That would have made him very proud."

It is very clear that Debbie's upbringing and family, nuclear and marital, were and are so integral to her character and strength. She speaks of both of her parents with such appreciation for exposing her in in her young life to politics and the concept of varying views and opinions in any given situation.

"My dad had a penchant for bringing strangers home for dinner or lunch. My mom never knew who he was bringing home. They were always interesting people of varied and diverse backgrounds and led to interesting discussions and viewpoints." Debbie fondly recalls the gentleman who owned the shoe store on the main street of Grimsby and later became a family friend. She says with gratitude. "He was one of those wonderful, very balanced people. If there was something going on in my life, I knew I could go there, sit down with him, and talk it out. We would sit in his shoe store and have long these conversations. He was always so encouraging. I appreciated his perspectives."

When she speaks about her mother, her voice is full of admiration and pride in her mother as a woman and a parent, even if Debbie herself wished for greater equality for her mother. "My mom is and was vigilant about our up bringing. She was strong and wise and a very good teacher. She raised very strong daughters, all of whom are extremely accomplished, but she also expected her daughters to follow the idea that the head of the household was your husband and breadwinner. While I respected her beliefs this [marital hierarchy] was an odd concept for me. Still, I tried to fit both that idea, and the independence I craved, into my own life."

With passionate conviction Debbie adds, "I don't want to be disparaging, but I watched my talented mother fight so hard to have a life outside of the family home, even after we kids were grown. My dad was just so against it for some reason, and I remember thinking that I would NEVER take direction from anyone or anywhere but within myself about what my life would look like. I just could not comprehend that anyone, male or female, should be telling you what you should be doing with your own life. It was beyond me to accept that your life would become someone else's picture of it, rather than what you wanted for yourself.

"There were always moments of reflection when I was carrying out homemaking obligations when I shook my head and told myself, *I am not repeating this! This will NOT be what defines me.*" She feels it critical to add,

"I am not disparaging these important tasks and roles; within them there are challenges and opportunities to affect change."

Debbie had earned respect for the ways in which she challenged boundaries and inequities early in her life. She had remained close with her school friends and their children were in kindergarten together. As these friends had pushed her forward to advocate for their rights to use the tennis courts long ago, they now appointed her spokesperson for their own children. She recalls them often calling to say, "We need you to come in and take charge of this or that issue. We will be right behind you.'" She tells of one situation when they had to intervene of behalf of their children.

"The head of the school board wouldn't change the boundaries for a school district, which meant that our children would have to walk an extra kilometre to school, even though there was a school in our backyard! We would not accept this decision! So, a mighty group of moms decided to invite him over for tea at my house and then we said to him, 'We are going for a walk.' So, we lined up our buggies and we walked him to one school and then we walked him to the other school. Then we asked him, 'Now which school would like your child to go to?' and they changed the boundaries!"

She says succinctly, "It was simply the only thing to do. If we were to make a phone call, it would have been too easy for us to be dismissed. I think this goes back to me being an observer. Observers sometimes have an ability to stand back and see opportunities or alternative ways forward. I began to see that we as women needed to demonstrate that we should be valued for what we knew. I was driven by thinking that my young son would have to take that extra long walk through town, because they didn't provide a bus, when there was actually a school right in our backyard. That was lunacy! I was driven by the love of and safety of my children, as we all were that day. We would just not accept that those changes couldn't be made."

Debbie reveals, "My biggest challenge early in my career was figuring out how to be heard at a table largely directed by those that felt you should be seen and not heard. I knew to be successful you needed to be clear, concise, and firm when putting your ideas forward but also considerate of others' views. It took years of watching many successful people before I got this right."

She recounts an incident early on in this learning curve that left her feeling embarrassed by an individual who publicly humiliated her. "He called me out and said I basically didn't know what I was talking about. I felt about an inch tall. I didn't go home and cry, but I definitely made sure that I was even better prepared the next time. So, I learned from him, too."

Throughout her life, and at each of the various stages of her career, Debbie feels grateful for her mentors who were generous with their time, support, and counsel as she forged her own path. She also recalls with warmth and appreciation the folks whom she says stepped up and supported her, with no personal agenda for doing so. She tells of a time during which she had launched a consulting business, thinking that it was a good way to be at home with her children while also building a career. In this particular instance, she was working on a project to expand the transportation in Hamilton, when a stakeholder boldly told her, "You aren't cut out for this home-based consulting business. You should be doing something different." At the time, she was considering running for regional chair and she told him so. He replied fervently "You should go for it!" She recalls with appreciation and a bit of awe, "He was just so positive, so supportive in his encouragement of me."

She admits that there were some naysayers, individuals who told her that she wouldn't amount to anything, that she was reaching too high or too far. She clearly recalls numerous people warning her of the glass ceiling she would eventually encounter. In a reflective, solemn tone she reveals, "That was tough because I really didn't see it. Then something would happen, and I wouldn't perceive it as the glass ceiling yet so I would just work harder and tell myself that I needed to change peoples' attitude about me, and about the given situation. To make them see that I could do as much and be as much as the male counterpart beside me." Her voice holds such a telling and emotional mix of sadness for what the circumstances were, and fierce determination for who she is and was in the face of it.

As a young child, Debbie developed strong character traits that would stand her in good stead as she moved through life and her career. She determined early on that she would not be sculpted or broken by the opinions of others. Debbie felt driven to affect change, break moulds, and improve lives. She perceptively assessed her environment and wisely chose her course of action. Debbie rose above challenges and learned from mistakes, both her own and those of others.

She names trailblazing female politician Nellie McClung as an inspiring example. A leading women's rights advocate, McClung was also famous for her influential and powerful public speaking. She was instrumental in earning women the right to vote and tenacious in her successful fight to help overturn the wording of the *British North America Act*, which, by referring to "persons" as males, excluded women from holding official positions of power. The Privy Council stated that "the exclusion of women from all public offices is a relic of days more barbarous than ours. And to those who would ask why the word 'persons' should include females, the obvious answer is, why should it not?"

Debbie herself also made it a point to question and challenge the norm and demand, "Why not?" She names Debi Pratt, Donna Lailey, Linda Bramble, Debbie Inglis, and Andrée Bosc as powerful women she admired in her own community. "Debi Pratt is such an incredible, elegant, and dignified individual. I am just in awe of her. I would step back and watch her and think to myself; she is amazing! Debi Pratt and Madame Bosc—they did things in a way that moved the marker for us in the roles that they played, in an era when that was very difficult." With a laugh, she says, "I was perhaps less elegant in my approach. I just kept questioning WHY NOT? Why can't I do that? Why do we have to allow things to stay the same? Why not move forward? We DID question the social norms of the time and we DID push boundaries."

She continues, confoundedly, "I work with mostly men, who hired me for goodness' sake, to work with them in a very male-dominated industry! I felt prepared because of my role and experiences as regional chair. But still, there were and are times when I thought I had proven myself, and yet I find myself having to do so again and again."

Reflectively she says, "Many of the things and experiences that have shaped me most were the ones which pushed me out of my comfort zone. I had to keep doing them. Sometimes it took a lot more faith than I had in myself. What I did know is that I did not want to look back and realize that I had repeated the patterns of the past. If something wasn't working, I had to find another way."

Debbie gives another example of this indomitable ability here. "At the region, we had a situation where the region's credit rating was so poor, SO poor that we were not able to borrow money affordably. So, we decided to showcase the region. We invited people from around the region, but also folks from the bond writing agency and other financial institutions. We rented and landed a glass-bottomed helicopter on the grounds of Vineland Estates winery, which was owned by John Howard at that time." Debbie says they flew leisurely over the Niagara Region, pointing out many of the features that made the area unique and worth investing in. By the time the helicopter landed, she and John had convinced the decision makers to lend Niagara the monies.

"John Howard was an important mentor to me. He stepped up when I needed him, and he has always been in my corner. Howard Staff was also amazing to me. And he was raising a strong daughter in Sue-Ann," she says with admiration.

She goes on to name some of her mentors as Gladys Huffman former mayor of Lincoln, Eleanor Lancaster former city of St. Catharines Regional Councillor, Ivy Riddell, Welland, and Dr. Robin Williams, former medical officer of Health for the Region of Niagara.

When asked what the environment was like for women at that time, Debbie replies with gratitude. "I had wonderful support from many women on regional council—in fact, back in the 1990s there were more women as mayors of municipalities than there is today. These women were and are my heroes." While women did hold council positions across Niagara in the 1990s, Debbie was the first female in the position of regional councillor for Grimsby. In 1997, she became regional chair, a role she held for six years, until she chose to step down in 2003.

Of her time with the Region, Debbie notes some of her most satisfying contributions as early learning programs for children, Niagara getting its own ambulance dispatch, which reduced the actual time ambulances would arrive, municipal transit, and the (still in process) idea of rerouting heavy traffic to an alternative highway.

On moving into her position with the Grape Growers of Ontario (GGO), she shares that, "I had watched the grape and wine industry from afar, but when I had a chance to get more involved by being at different events, it really intrigued me. From my role as a regional chair, I had seen the struggle the growers had putting their concerns on the table alongside the wineries. It bothered me how ill-equipped they were to get their voices heard. I'm so glad the opportunity came up to join the Grape Growers of Ontario."

"I was recruited by Bill George and Ray Duc, who were both chairs on the Grape Growers board. It was really interesting that they set out to recruit me because I had no intention at that time of leaving my senior role at the Region, but I was so intrigued by the industry and its possibilities, that I thought why not give it a whirl. The GGO's relationship to the grape and wine industry is unique but also intertwined. Our association is an independent marketing board.

"I was only on the job about a week when Donna Lailey reached out to me. I ended up going to Burgundy, France, with her, her daughter Tonya, and winemaker Derek Barnett. I was there just to learn about the industry, but I learned a lot a lot about Donna on this trip. She didn't do anything halfway. Her goal was to showcase the wines from Niagara against the best and she did that. She is just an amazing individual. Donna was the first at so many things: first woman Grape King, first woman grower in Niagara, and she guided me early in my career with the growers. She is an amazing woman who knew the challenges of growing grapes in a male-dominated industry. I saw people like Donna Lailey, and the formidable Austin Kirkby from Niagara-on-the-Lake as a driving force for growers and agriculture."

Austin herself was a councillor and longstanding member and chair of local irrigation and agriculture committees. She was an invaluable and extremely well-respected advocate of the farming community. In 2017 she was named Niagara-on-the-Lake Citizen of the Year.

On co-founding the Agricultural Task Force, Debbie recalls that this also evolved out of a problem, in that the agricultural land in Niagara needed to be protected but also economically viable and useable by the farmers for them to sustain their farms. To learn more about this critical issue, she recalls inviting a group of people from the industry, including Donald Ziraldo, Howard Staff, and Len Troup of the Grape Growers, to a meeting about this land. Remembering, she exclaims with a laugh, "This was three very strong personalities and voices in one room! I learned from that! There was such a difference of opinion, and each was valid. I listened to each of them. It was clear that the issues needed to be better defined for us to consider solutions and the economic impact of each on the industry. Out of that grew the Task Force. It changed how we viewed agriculture as part of our economic fabric. It gave agriculture a value."

When asked what keeps her motivated and driven today, she replies with certainty, "This may sound cliché, but I view my role as building on what the growers did who came before me—Howard Staff, Bill George Sr., Brian Nash, and so many others. I owed it to them to take the organization further. I am proud of moving the Grape Growers of Ontario to an organization that is respected and recognized for its role in producing great grapes for great wine and having a seat at the table both provincially and federally."

In many ways, Debbie's early role as a journalist helped equip her with some of the investigative tools needed to delve into, actively listen to, and present all sides of an issue. Listening is a rare and invaluable skill, one that is further honed when an individual truly cares about the people and issues at hand. Being able to filter through the many varied opinions and conversations to find feasible solutions for all at stake is rarer still. Debbie describes the relationships between the growers and wineries as intertwined, each needing the other, and the land.

Debbie names accomplishing change for the better as her constant goal, no matter the position she held, and across both her personal and professional life. Without question, her life was incredibly full and yet Debbie still gave her time and efforts to many voluntary boards and committees over the years, including the **YMCA** board of directors, McNally House Hospice, and as co-chair of the Pathstone Mending Minds fundraising campaign. She says, "My favourite fundraising role was for Pathstone Mental Health, a new facility to help more children that required support for mental health."

Debbie has been the recipient of countless awards including Niagara College's Board of Governors Award in 2001, and in 2003, the YWCA's Woman of Distinction award. In 2013, she was honoured with the Community Leadership Award by the Greater Niagara Chamber of Commerce. She was also named Local Food Champion by Friends of the Greenbelt Foundation for her dedication to local food and service to Niagara. She received an Ontario Lieutenant Governor General's Award in 2017 and was deemed a Friend of the Greenbelt for her work on the Provincial Review Panel.

In 2020, she received an honorary doctorate of laws from Brock University for her lifelong work and commitment to the Region of Niagara, an honour she finds incredibly personal as she confesses to secretly wanting to be a lawyer. Most recently she received the prestigious Lifetime Achievement Award from the Greater Niagara Chamber of Commerce at the 2022 Women in Business Awards in recognition of her forty-plus years of leadership and success. The purpose of the WIBAs is to "Encourage more women to seek out and reach for leadership roles in business, politics, and our community."

When asked if she held personal commandments and or values that helped guide her decisions, Debbie shares that early on it was to "Never give up, never give in" but admits that over time that has changed wisely to "Sometimes you need to compromise."

Debbie is often sought out for her advice and perspective, and generously offers her experiences and insights saying, "Mentorship is a gift we get to give to others. Sharing our experiences can only help to guide others. I was blessed with many, many mentors who took the time to offer advice, guide and support my ambitions—we all need to give back to those who will replace us."

Her advice to those just starting out is to "Be yourself and be open minded about what you don't know yet. Be flexible and be honest with yourself about what you can be. Anything is possible." She adds, "Do not be afraid to challenge yourself—that's the most fun—even though you might fail sometimes. Failure can help us to come back stronger and to dig deeper to achieve our goals. Take a moment to think of what you want to achieve and then live your dream."

To her twenty-year old self, she would like to advise, with the wisdom that can only come from experience and hindsight: "Be patient with yourself and take the time to learn more before rushing ahead."

Debbie feels that it is important for people to realize that lives and careers rarely evolve in a straight line. "I believe that we each come into this world with certain gifts that we have been given. It takes incidents or circumstances and experiences before we can understand our gifts. These twists and turns may not always be easy, but they shape us. Along the way, these unique gifts within each of us become layered with the things that happen to us. I think that when you start to discover these gifts, they begin to emerge."

When asked about her support circle, Debbie names her family and close friends as critical to keeping her grounded. Friendships, and relationships in general, are often based on commonalities of circumstances. As we grow and change, and our circumstances change, not all these relationships will grow along with us and our ambitions. Sometimes, it is not actually about us, but about the fact that our growth simply makes other people feel uncomfortable. Debbie has remained authentic and committed to her path and purpose, succeeding without climbing on the backs of others or resorting to unethical tactics. Instead, she has kept relationships and the greater good as her guide, turning to the sounding boards of her internal compass and those who knew and loved her to keep her going.

Debbie's journey is a valuable reminder that it is imperative for each of us to censor the voices we allow into our minds, the voices that whisper to us about who we are, where our place is, and what we are capable of. If we internalize the negative, discouraging comments, we may be become disheartened and lose faith in ourselves, gradually abandoning our personal dreams and goals. Debbie was able to rise above these voices and now lends her own powerful voice as a source of strength to others forging their path.

As a province, and as a community, we have benefited immensely from Debbie's drive to improve lives, from early childhood programming to politics, transportation, agriculture, public services, and mentorship. She is a tenacious and passionate trailblazer, a game changer, a leader, and an inspiration for all. She has risen through the ranks of male colleagues, while at the same time gaining their respect and friendship. She built and maintained a solid network of supporters and friends, intuitive early on that relationships were key. Always in the public eye, it is vital to remember that her personal relationships remained her priority. Her family is integral to who she is: a daughter, a sister, a wife, mother, and now grandmother. Debbie says, "I would like to be remembered as a 'good Mom' first. My kids mean everything to me. After that, I hope I am remembered as someone who was kind but determined to make changes for the good of the people I represented and worked for."

Debbie's children hold her in the highest regard. Her daughter Amy says, "My mom has always been the biggest supporter to my siblings and me. Her strength and determination in life are unmatched. From a young age, my mom taught us to love our community, help others, and the true meaning of family. She is also the most loving grandmother, daughter and spouse. She goes above and beyond for everyone. We would all be lost without her. She is an inspiration to me and to all women showing there is no limit to what we can accomplish. She is a true, fearless, authentic leader, and I'm so grateful she is my mom."

Her son Benjamin adds, "To describe how incredible my mother is in only a few sentences will be a challenge in itself! My mother, Debbie Zimmerman, is truly an inspiration to so many. She is my hero, my mentor, and my life coach. I have always been so proud to speak about my mom and always will be. Her achievements over the span of her extensive career show how much passion, drive, and devotion she has to making any place, business, event, or fundraiser her main priority and insuring it thrives with success and positivity."

Early in our interview Debbie had confided, "I always wanted to be a cowboy when I was growing up. I'm not sure why," she says with a laugh, "but that's what I wanted to be."

I think you did grow up to be a cowboy, Debbie. In a matter of speaking, you have been herding cattle, developing, and establishing frontiers throughout the greenbelt, and fighting for and protecting your community. If your idea of a cowboy meant being able to ride with and keep up with the men, being courageous, heroic, and trailblazing, then you are, indeed, a cowboy, Debbie.

SHARING A GLASS

Tributes to Debbie Zimmerman

Debbie Zimmerman by Cathy Dixon
Lifelong sister-friend of Debbie Zimmerman

Cathy describes her friendship with Debbie as more of a sisterhood. During a conversation punctuated with laughter, tears, and so much evident love and admiration, Cathy paints a picture of a cherished and enduring friendship spanning more than fifty years. Friends since the age of six, the girls met at school when Debbie first moved to Ontario, and they have been fast friends ever since. As Cathy tells it, both girls worked hard in school and at their part-time jobs. Cathy worked at her father's Grimsby restaurant, the Peach Bar, and Debbie at the local Dairy Queen before joining the town newspaper. With a laugh, Cathy adds that they were both too busy to get into too much trouble! Besides, Grimsby was a small town then and both of their families were well known through their involvement in the community.

Cathy recalls that Debbie was well liked, with a reputation as a hard worker who was friendly, dependable, and always willing to help out—traits that would come to mean a great deal in the campaign and political world she didn't yet know she would be entering.

After high school, the girls headed off to post-secondary school, Debbie to study journalism, and Cathy to nursing school. They connected during school breaks and in the summer, where they spent time at a family cottage in Manitoulin, hiking and swimming during the day and staying up late into the night discussing the details of their lives, debating world issues, and weighing in on solutions for both.

Their friendship endured and solidified, and they stood beside one another as they each married, had children, and moved through the many celebrations and challenges that life held for them. Cathy tells of a treasured friendship with long and honest talks, laughter, tears, and of the steadfast support the two have given one another through it all. Cathy remembers the day when, as young mothers with strollers, Debbie led the charge as they marched the local school board director to and from the local schools to demonstrate (and win!) the need for boundary changes.

The women were more like honorary aunts to each other's children, and their families are close to this day. Cathy's daughter worked with and was mentored by Debbie. Cathy feels that working closely with such a strong and independent woman has added to her daughter's own strength and success.

Adamantly, Cathy declares, "I have never heard anything, but good words said about Debbie, because, truthfully, there is nothing but good to say. If anyone says anything but, then they don't know Debbie! They don't know who she is and what she has lived through and withstood. She is the strongest woman I know. If you call Debbie and you have a problem, she will first tell you if it's worth pursuing and then she will give you strong, sound advice.

She is my lifelong friend and a friend I will have for the rest of my life. We were always there for each other. We have been through so much together since we were children, weddings—our own and our children's!—births, deaths, the loss of our parents. We talk about everything, and while we don't agree on everything, we still talk about it and respect each other's opinions."

They can, and do, still talk for hours, sharing memories and continuing to make more. In addition to their full-time careers, busy families, and extensive community involvement, they served together, until shortly after Cathy's retirement, for several years on the board of McNally House Hospice, a respected and valued place for the families and communities of Grimsby, Lincoln, and West Lincoln. Debbie is still a McNally House board member today.

Cathy sums up by saying, "Debbie is the strongest person I know. She makes an impression on people and lives. She has done so much good and will be missed by the Grape Growers of Ontario when she decides to retire. Though, she will be humble and say that the next person will be just as effective! I have always felt that Debbie should be mayor of Grimsby, but that wasn't what she wanted to do. I think she should have run for prime minister! But who knows what she will go on to do? She can do anything."

Debbie Zimmerman by Matthias Oppenlaender
Chair, Grape Growers of Ontario Board of Directors

"When Debbie first joined the Grape Growers of Ontario, she brought valuable political experience. She may not have known much about grape growing at the beginning but that didn't deter Debbie. She dug right in and committed to learning and committed to the farmers, their families, and the community. It's been seventeen years now and I have to say that she has been one of the best people I have ever worked with. When we sit down in the boardroom to reach an agreement, we consider all sides; most of the time we can come to a consensus with all parties, and that is largely due to Debbie's excellent leadership. I admire her and respect her. She is so fair; she is able to see all sides and she truly wants to serve everyone. She has such integrity. She understands that grassroots build a better community and society for all. She is willing to listen, and she genuinely cares. She also isn't a pushover. She will fight for what she believes is right and best for all involved. She is so passionate.

"Debbie is also very interested in building people. She sees them as a whole, with their personal life as well. She understands that if people are troubled, they can't bring their best selves to the rest of their life. She makes an effort to connect and make sure that everyone on her team is okay. She brings her best and she wants her team to bring their best, too. She genuinely cares for people and if they are willing to grow, she will pour her life into them. They become better leaders under her mentorship.

"She builds such strong relationships; you can trust her. She is always there for people, and they know it, and in return, they care about her and will be there for her. It's really remarkable to watch. She is the first one to reach out in a crisis and find ways to help. Whether picking up the phone to check in on someone, to send flowers or a note or, [during] COVID-19, to support the community through donations. The GGO donated a ventilator. Now, she is exploring ways to support Ukrainian families (since the war announcement). She always puts people first and as a result, people, and societies, grow along with her.

"We have been very fortunate to have Debbie as the CEO of the Grape Growers of Ontario; she has made many important contributions and the industry and community are better because of her."

Debbie Zimmerman by Doug Whitty
President, 13th Street Winery

"I remember discussion among farmers in 2003 when Debbie was selected by our board of directors to be CEO for the Grape Growers of Ontario (GGO) organization. Although Debbie was unlike our previous CEOs, the general consensus was that this was a progressive and necessary change for our industry. I do not remember many comments concerning her qualifications for the job based upon her gender, her ability to grow grapes, or indeed her knowledge or experience with the Ontario grape and wine industry. What I definitely do remember is that most grape growers recognized that our industry had become increasing complex and politicized, so what we really needed was an experienced and capable person with the political skills to lead us successfully into the future. Debbie was and is that person. From a very young age, Debbie learned the fundamentals of effective political discourse when she was encouraged by her family to discuss and debate the issues of the day at the kitchen table. She also witnessed and was taught that the ultimate goal of leadership in all its forms is to advance the common good. She has honoured that important childhood teaching in every leadership role she has assumed in her life, including two terms as chair of Niagara Region, her role as CEO of the GGO, and as she helped guide many charitable organizations.

"I admire Debbie. Leading any diverse group, including Ontario grape growers as they interact with their partners in industry and government can often feel like "herding cats." I am very thankful that for twenty years now, the GGO has been blessed with her strength, conviction, hard work, resilience, diplomacy, empathy, vast reserves of energy, patience, mentorship, and attention to detail.

"I feel very fortunate to have had the opportunity to know Debbie on a personal level. I often think of a story she once told me when I put on my good shoes to do something important. Debbie told me that when she was a young woman, local boys would come over to her house and want to take her out. Her father would always meet the hopeful suitors at the door. He would then inspect their shoes to see if they had taken the time to clean and polish them. It was his way of determining the young man's character, discipline, and intentions.

"That story reminds me to take care of the details, to do the work and to do it for the right reasons which is what Debbie Zimmermann has done and continues to do."

Debbie Zimmerman by Carrie Zeffiro
Senior Associate, Philanthropy Armstrong Strategy Group

"What I admire most about Debbie is her genuine passion and compassion for our community. She is a very busy person with what she does in her work life, yet she always finds the time to commit to organizations and causes she believes in.

"I had the pleasure of working with her as she co-chaired the Mending Children's Minds Campaign for Pathstone Foundation. This highly successful capital campaign built the Branscombe Mental Health building, which is home to Pathstone Mental Health. When we first started, Pathstone did not have the profile it now has and having Debbie in a leadership role brought credibility which opened doors for us. I am now working with her on the McNally House campaign, which will mean expanded hospice care in the Grimsby area and, once again, her commitment to this project is opening doors. We are so lucky to have Debbie care so much about her community."

Debbie Zimmerman by MP Vance Badawey

"Debbie has always been a straight shooter—genuine and caring—she always stood her ground. She was a trailblazer with vision that will benefit Niagara for future generations—issues related to transportation (transit, inter-modal hubs, highway infrastructure), disciplined asset management, early years learning, updating and building long term care homes, investing and giving attention to south Niagara to ensure the overall brand of Niagara includes all destinations throughout the region for business, tourism, and lifestyle. She worked hard to bring people together within the team at regional headquarters as well as throughout the region (residents and businesses) and abroad.

"Debbie knows how to bring people together, establishing strategies—attaching deliverables and action plans and working with people within their areas of expertise to execute. We got things done! She continues to do that to this day in many capacities."

Debbie Zimmerman by Cecely Roy
Communications Professional
Former press secretary to Prime Minister Justin Trudeau

"Debbie is my aunt and my role model. I grew up on the West Coast in British Columbia, and she was based in Niagara. Despite the geographic distance, ours was an important relationship to me, as a child, as an adolescent, into adulthood, and to this day.

"My father was always proud of his sister. We followed her career, and he would often share stories about her and the ways in which she forged a path and carved a unique yet critical role for herself in her career. As a young council member in Grimsby, in the newsroom, and various board rooms at a time where that wasn't common—especially in a small town. Big decisions were being made; she was influencing where and how power was being exerted, and she was exerting power herself. She was an example as a strong and successful woman in various positions of leadership, and particularly in politics, both regionally and well beyond.

"Women in public office were rare at that time. I was fortunate to have her as a role model, and a close family member. She cared about me personally and my choices as I was trying to determine what it was that I wanted to do in life and who I wanted to become. She was a huge source of inspiration and direction for me. As a young woman from a small town myself, I hadn't been exposed to many career options for women in public life. I was always politically engaged, but I wasn't yet sure where I fit in or what I wanted to do with my interests and passion.

I moved to Ottawa to study Carleton University. Being in the same province as my aunt, I could spend more time with her. I would spend holidays with her and our family in Niagara. If she was working in Ottawa, she would always make time for me. It was an opportunity to be exposed to a different life. She brought me along to sit in while she met with regional MPs. As a young woman of eighteen or nineteen years old, I had never been in these rooms, and this was very impactful. Being on "The Hill" and going with her to stakeholder meetings with elected officials was fascinating.

"Watching her interact with others, being firm but personable, left an impression on me. She was and is liked and well respected while also not backing down. She showed me how women can lead in roles and spaces traditionally dominated by men.

"I remember when she brought me to a fundraiser in Ottawa, during the Harper government years. It was an incredible evening with entertainment by Gord Downey, Randy Bachman, and Rick Mercer as the host. Justin Trudeau was there. It was an invaluable opportunity for me. I was just determining where my own partisan allegiances lay. She introduced me to anyone and everyone and told them 'This is my niece; she wants to work in politics.' She had this way of lifting me up and inspiring me to grow towards things and aspire to things that I couldn't quite put a definition on yet, but I had ambition and knew that I wanted to enact change. She gave me a window into a world that I might be a part of. She continued to do things like that.

"On another occasion, she and I were at the Château Laurier in Ottawa. Chantal Hébert, the incredibly accomplished media writer, happened to be there. Having been raised in a CBC household, I knew of her through my television screen. My Aunt Debbie walked up right up to Chantal, introduced me to her, and told her what a big fan I was of hers. Both Chantal and my aunt are very direct. It's a trait I admire. These are people that I had always looked up to. Debbie took the time to mentor and support me and helped shape my concept of the world and what I wanted to do.

"After I finished university, I moved to Toronto. I still wasn't quite sure what I wanted to do for work, so I reached out to her for advice. This led to me volunteering on my first campaign. This was during the 2015 federal election. I volunteered for my local Liberal candidate. That year, the election was won with a Liberal majority.

"Through her introduction and my volunteer work, I subsequently landed an internship at government relations agency, which led to a full-time job. This was my first foray into politics.

"Years later, I began working for Prime Minister Trudeau, as a press secretary. Debbie's belief in and support of me, were critical to my career start. She once told me, "I can connect you with people, but I won't always be around. You have to do the work and build your own relationships to make sure that you have these connections and opportunities down the road." That always stuck with me. I never took her support for granted, I never had expectations based on shared a bloodline. I remember also thinking that if I ever had the opportunity to make connections for someone, like she was making for me, that I would do my best to pay it forward.

"These are some examples of the fundamental steps and moments that led me to believe that I could do something, achieve something, that I had no direct reference point or role model for, with the exception of my aunt. She was an advocate and a positive, constructive influence on me. She encouraged me to think big and made me believe that I could set and achieve big goals.

I watched her, always knowing that she worked so hard, and persevered, at a time when women didn't have these types of roles or lives. On top of her demanding profession, she raised a family and became a pillar of many communities, where she consistently strove for progress. She is known and respected in every circle, locally to federally. When you mention her name in Ottawa, if the person knows of her, there is a big smile on their face. To be clear, I have never leveraged that relationship, but if I knew that someone was from the Niagara Region, we usually had a shared bond knowing that we mutually admired her and her work.

"Debbie and I stay in touch and connect regularly. I genuinely want to know how she is and what she is doing, and she is genuinely interested in how I am and what I am doing. She, and our relationship, have been so important as I have been growing into my profession and the person I am becoming. It's invaluable to know that she is there for me to touch base with for that gut check and guidance when I need it. But she is also there for me as my aunt and as someone who knows what life is like sometimes, because not a lot of people really comprehend the levels of pressure at times when working in the political sphere. It's a shared bond that we have and, frankly, it's good to have a reality check once in a while, to keep yourself grounded, because it's very easy to let this work consume you when you care so much. Having another woman who is successfully navigating this life and who knows me personally has been a gift.

"Over the last years, I have been fortunate to have had a series of supportive women in roles of leadership in my life, who have guided me. But it started with Debbie, and it always circles back. She, and the other mentors I have, are the reason I will always put my hand up if someone needs help or guidance. Sometimes the things we learn from them don't fully sink in until we are in that moment that we need their advice and then we remember what they told us, or taught us, and we are able to grow because of what they shared with us.

"Mentorship can be considered a burden to some, but I have always felt, and as Debbie has modelled, that mentorship fills our cups. These connections are so important, in politics, in life, and as a human being, to have people around you who you can trust and who know that they can trust you. That trusted support network is crucial, regardless of age, place, profession.

"There are barriers that are very much still present at the decision-making table. There is sometimes a perception that people at those tables often look and act a certain way. These perceptions can be limiting; it is integral to progress that these perceptions are disrupted. Debbie accomplished this and recognized the importance of being visible. She has and continues to pave a path for others, everywhere she goes. She is present, influential, impactful, and visible."

Ann Sperling

"Paradigm shifts don't happen when you keep doing the same thing. While I think that my first five or six years of winemaking were about learning the rules and staying in that safe zone, after that, my goal was to stretch myself–and the rules–to reach towards greatness."

Ann was born and grew up in Kelowna, British Columbia. Her great-grandparents, the Casorsos, first arrived in the Okanagan Valley from Italy in the 1880s. As survival was paramount, they began ranching, a relatively new livelihood in British Columbia. They then started clearing lowlands for vegetables and field crops and the hillsides for fruit trees and vines, just as they would have done in Piedmont. Ann's grandfather was one of eight sons who began experimenting with grape vines in the Kelowna area. By 1931, they had a productive commercial vineyard, primarily of labruscas and other multi-purpose grapes.

Ann recounts, "About this time, some young men from the prairies showed up looking for work, and my grandfather hired them. They showed an interest in the grapes, and since my grandfather was also interested in vinifera, they decided to work together. They became the 'grape specialists' on the farm. One of these men was Frank Schmidt. His son, Lloyd was actually born on our farm. [For context, Lloyd Schmidt started Sumac Ridge Estate Winery in Summerland, BC, before moving to Ontario in 1988 with his wife Noreen and their two sons Allan and

Brian, to work with Paul Bosc Sr. at Château des Charmes. Allan and Brian joined the newly established Vineland Estates Winery. Allan, one of the early Vineland Estates winemakers, currently serves as president. Brian took on the winemaker role in 1992.] Lloyd used to hang out with my uncle. Learning about grape vines was something the Schmidts and our family did in parallel together. Eventually, Frank Schmidt went to work for a landowner named J. W. Hughes. Because J. W. didn't have any heirs, he developed a program for the families he worked with; if they worked together for twenty-five years, he would turn the land over to their ownership. That's how the Schmidts started as grape growers and winery owners in BC."

Ann continues, "Besides grapes, we had a cow-calf operation. The cattle would come home in the winter to have their calves, and then in the summer, we would turn them out on the mountain range to graze. We focused on the fruit trees, vegetables, and grapes in the summer. In my lifetime, my parents converted nearly all the fruit trees to vines. Eventually, we had about thirty to forty acres of grapes.

"My father Engelbert, known as Bert, was very active on the Grape Growers Association in BC, so the development of the industry was always being talked about around the house. A lot was happening in the industry then. From the 1930s to the 1960s, the grapes were primarily labrusca, it was hybrids throughout the 1960s and 1970s, and starting in the 1980s, it moved to vinifera. In 1978, the family planted the Riesling Weiss 21 clone. All the technical aspects of planting, growing, and changing varieties in a developing industry had an impression on me."

When asked if she enjoyed working in the vineyard as a youngster, Ann replied that she was motivated by seeing her siblings (who were ten years older) gaining some independence by working. "I had a sister a year and a half younger and another a year and a half older. The three of us would always beg our older siblings to bring us along and let us help." Ann adopts a child's voice with a smile of remembrance, recounting how they asked, "If you're tying, can we wrap the vines ahead of you? That will make the tying go faster. You don't even have to pay us. We just want to be out there with you." She says, "That was a big attraction, just to be out there with our older siblings and to feel included.

"Tying was the beginning of the season for us. We would return from March break with money in our pockets and suntans," she laughs, "even if it was a farmer's tan and our classmates may have acquired their tans in Hawaii. We were outdoors, gaining independence and maturity and making decisions for ourselves. That was a big draw." Ann also remembers working with vegetables and picking cherries and other fruit, but as more tasks were required in the vineyards, working with the vines provided her with the most experience.

Ann's father and grandfather made wine, so from a young age, she and her siblings were tasting and experiencing that part of the culture. Ann says, "Winemaking was part of life on a farm. We preserved everything that we grew so that we could consume it year-round. As a family, we evaluated how things tasted and compared from one growing season to the next or one meal to the next. We were always assessing and evaluating. For example, coming in after school to find pasta sauce simmering on the stove. We would all taste it and say, 'This needs a bit more salt,' or 'This needs more oregano.' We were all major critics! We examined these things every day. Because we raised beef, there was always meat on the table. Sometimes it wasn't the greatest animal or cut, but we still had to make something delicious. We utilized various cooking techniques or ways of handling it so that it would be delicious."

Ann always understood they were responsible for taking what they had grown or raised and doing something wonderful. She feels that doing that with wines was the next extension. "Most of the time, we did have great ingredients because we tended everything ourselves, and it was fresh and ripe." Perhaps knowing from a young age that she could have a hand in delivering quality, and from the ground up, is one of the reasons that Ann chooses to refer to herself as a "winegrower" rather than a "winemaker."

"Growing up in a vineyard was an important impetus for wanting to join the wine industry. But it was also driven by what I saw around me all the time. In 1978, when I was a teenager, we planted Riesling. It was the first significant vinifera planting that we had, and that meant that winemakers—mostly German and other Europeans—came and visited. They saw our plantings; they gave their advice. They sat around our kitchen table, where all meetings took place in our home, and talked about growing Riesling. And I was overhearing these conversations.

Something about it stuck, and I thought, 'Hey, this is interesting. It's not just about pulling weeds in the vineyard. There's more to it.' Our family's friends were also planting vineyards and starting wineries, George and Trudy Heiss at Gray Monk, for example. It was in the news and getting lots of exposure. It was exciting.

"At the University of British Columbia, I studied food science, which was in the faculty of agriculture. Since there was no formal winemaking program in Canada then, I decided that what I could do at home in BC was to learn as much as possible about fermentation, processing, and those things. When Ron Taylor, the wine master at Andres [Wines] at the time, addressed our class, I was the only one with any questions relevant to the winemaking topic. When I graduated, there were twelve of us, and virtually everyone planned to be a lab technician in the food industry. I was the odd person in my class.

"Growing up in the family I did, in the place I did, and having guest speakers in my university program, these were all the pieces that united and reinforced my interest in the wine industry. As it happened, when I graduated, there were two production jobs, one at Brights and one at Andres." She laughingly notes that there was no Wine Jobs Canada website then! "The Brights' job was a temporary research assistant, and the Andres position was for someone to start in the lab and work over two to three years to become a winemaker with the company. It was meant to be a developmental position. That was the one for me. It was 1984. At that time, there were a few start-up estate wineries in British Columbia, but they all had family members who were the winemakers. These small wineries weren't hiring non-family. I could look to only the big wineries for a job.

"Even though I began my career with a big winery, within two years, I was also the 'fieldman' at Andres. When I started, an older gentleman had been doing that job for years. I spent two harvests with him; he showed me all the vineyards and told me all the stories, so I got the complete background. Shortly after that, I was the one regularly visiting over twenty growers. So even in that big winery setting, I wasn't just waiting for the grapes to come to the doorstep. I already had a role in what quality level we would bring in. And that just seemed like a natural thing to do."

Ann says she's always enjoyed meeting and talking with the growers. She concedes with a laugh, "Maybe at first, when they saw that they had a twenty-something-year-old inexperienced winemaker who was going to be interacting with them, they might have been surprised, but as soon as we had our first conversation and our first walk through the vineyard, they knew that I had experience in that area. I found that it was usually a positive experience."

She admits, "There were a few grumpy growers I had to deal with." With a chuckle, Ann confides, "One guy, in particular, had a huge reputation for being difficult as a grower back then. Yet today we are good friends and enjoy each other's company. I think we enjoyed the sparring we developed back then. I understood that he, and others like him, had their product to sell and to get the most money they could for it. They saw wineries come and go, and winemakers come and go, but they knew in the end that their vineyard was going to endure. Since I generally didn't back down, we developed a good respect for each other. For me, coming from the grower side, I knew that you must work with people, get the best outcome possible, and improve for the future. You don't want to destroy somebody along the way. It doesn't serve your purposes as a winemaker because if you don't have grapes, you don't make wine. It doesn't serve them long-term, either, to make it impossible for them to make a living. Keeping that in mind is the approach I have taken over the years. I have tried to work with people as much as possible. I hopefully recognize early when there isn't a good outcome possible, but even still, I always do as much as I can, for as long as I can, that is positive."

This is also fundamental to how Ann feels about organic and biodynamic growing. She says, "My earliest memories of the vineyard were of a much more 'organic' time. I remember tall grasses between the rows, for example. Back then, we were irrigating with furrow irrigation and not sprinklers. We didn't install sprinklers until the 1970s and 1980s. The water was delivered around the Okanagan by surface channels. There was this network of aqueducts that we called flumes. So the biodiversity in the vineyards was greater, with more flowers, insects, and birds inhabiting the vineyards. In the 1970s, when chemical herbicides became prevalent and 'clean cultivation' was everywhere, that all changed. Suddenly, everything else was gone, and all that was left were vines. A monoculture. That had a significant impact on me."

It was the 1980s when Ann first learned about organic viticulture. "I was at a presentation at the Summerland Research Station, and the speakers talked about their farming methods. Now, I know that it was biodynamics that they were talking about, but they weren't using those terms then, probably because they knew they wouldn't have had much of an audience. But these people were making no-sulphite wines and doing other things that would have been leading edge then." Ann recalls that she was one of the few people asking questions. "The rest were in the back of the room, arms folded across their chests, probably thinking, 'What is this crap?'" She concedes that it's difficult when you have a room full of growers because they have different concerns than winemakers who are trying not just to get a product into bottle, but to make something that represents the vineyard, represents the region and will be something lasting.

Ann affirms that her time with Andres was valuable in her career trajectory. "Andres was an evolving company then and still is today. At that time, it was an incubator for people to develop within. It may not have been easy for the business to constantly train people who left and went on to other things, but that's what it was. Many of us were there for three, four or five years, then moved on to smaller wineries or other projects. But there was a good attitude about developing people, and that was important.

"I think I had been with Andres for a few years at the point that I went to a national standards meeting. They had been taking place for years; however, the topic was the Vintners Quality Alliance (VQA) at this meeting. It had already been discussed in Ontario and was then suggested to BC to gauge their interest. My boss said I should be there at that meeting, so we went together. It was pretty cool to be there talking about the formation of the VQA and getting involved as it became more tangible."

Ann feels that being a part of the VQA was a significant part of her career, and her ten years on the BC tasting panel had a strong impact.

At that time, the panel was made up primarily of winemakers, but there were also people from other facets of the industry. Ann says, "Having the opportunity to share, taste, and judge many of these early wines put me in front of many good and great winemakers. The collective was very inspiring.

"There were significant women already working in the wine industry, like Lynn Stark. She was an early influence on me as a winemaker. She used to buy our family's grapes and had worked for Andres before moving to Brights. She led some significant research projects. That's what people were doing then—experimental plantings, experimental winemaking. The Becker project, conducted in the 1970s, planted German vinifera grapes and crosses such as Riesling, Gewürztraminer and Ehrenfelser to see what would survive and ripen in Canada. This project made way for other similar studies across Canada. We would all get together and taste these research samples, and it was an excellent opportunity to network and learn what was happening in the industry.

"The Vancouver Wine Festival was an important event on my calendar because many great winemakers poured their wines at tutored tastings. As a young winemaker, I got to attend those tastings. For example, one year, I tasted Amarone—from a barrel sample through to a 1940s sample. All from the same producer, all from the same vineyard. It wasn't every vintage, but we probably tasted fourteen wines that spanned that time frame. I recall how almost undrinkable the young barrel sample was. And then, by the time it had twenty, thirty years on it, you could taste how it had integrated and evolved into the style. I don't know of another tasting that has taken place like that. I was fortunate to be able to attend, and so I made a point of being there. Also very informative was the Society of Wine Educators, based in the US."

Soon, the organizers of such conferences were asking Ann to lead these valuable tutored tastings. Preparing these presentations forced her to examine her beliefs, theories, and practices. She also learned to organize her thoughts to create a compelling presentation. Additionally, it helped her present not only the "cellar" perspective but also that of the "seller." She looks back at this as key to her development.

Ann feels very fortunate to be a part of a group of people in the industry who had that pioneering spirit and the fortitude to keep quality at the forefront. Ann says, "It seems like every ten years, the industry cycles. There is change—the people most in the public eye change, trends change. I'm glad this book is being written so that people and their accomplishments will be remembered. It is so important that those coming after us know who the trailblazers were and why."

Ann names Deborah Paskus as a prime example, and she feels that Deborah should be remembered for being foundational in studying individual vineyards and sub-appellations in Niagara. She worked with many single vineyards in what is today known as the Niagara Escarpment and began using the term "Beamsville Bench" by the late 1990s. Ann exclaims "That appellation-like term was on her label more prominently than the name of the wine or the variety! She expanded the awareness that sub-appellations could and should be identified. Her work drove her. Working with Steven Tempkin, she made Tempkin-Paskus wines that garnered critical acclaim, scores and recognition that benefited Deborah and the entire region. With a masters in viticulture from UC Davis, her first work in Niagara was at Cave Spring, doing vineyard and winemaking trials assessing wine quality relative to vine yields. In 1997, Deborah worked with Martin Malivoire on his first vintage, and that's when I got to know her better."

When Ann joined the team at Malivoire in 1998, there was already an existing vineyard, which would later be named "Moira." The land where the winery stands today was a cornfield with a few old fruit trees and lots of poison ivy. Ann says, "The great wines Martin and Moira enjoyed were organic or biodynamic, so it was a natural fit for them to want to introduce those methods in their own vineyard. The fact that they lived in the vineyard was also an important consideration, as they questioned the health impacts of conventional pesticides." Ann admits that the move to organic farming was a huge learning curve, but she credits Martin for being on the leading edge. "In everything he did, he was always inventing or reinventing." Ann explains, "We didn't have the tools that are available today. The lack of depth of resources was a big challenge for organic viticulture in Canada in the 1990s. Certified inputs might have been available in the US or Europe but not to Canadian producers because manufacturers had not registered them.

"Thankfully, we now have a bigger organic community and more responsiveness to our needs. For instance, a mineral oil called Stylet was approved for use in US organic vineyards in the 1980s but wasn't registered in Canada. In the 1990s, when Canadian organic vineyards wanted to get it approved, the process took four to five years. However, more recently (2018), a group of organic viticulturists, headed by Joel Williams of Hidden Bench Estate Winery, applied to get a more efficient copper product called Cueva ® approved in Canada. With fifty producers signing the letter, it took less than two years. It's encouraging to see developments like this taking place. Like many things, early adopters can run into unexpected challenges that wear you down.

"But I am convinced that organic viticulture is the best way to grow quality, terroir-expressive grapes while also respecting future generations. To achieve the highest quality winemaking, every detail must be executed in both the vineyard and cellar which, in reality, is costly. To continue to be meticulous stewards of the land, top wine producers must command higher bottle prices. Ontario lags behind British Columbia and Nova Scotia's top producers that continue to have more success with local consumers for their top bottles. Ontarians are getting an amazing deal for the best wines made here.

"Looking at my career to date," Ann says, from the mid-1980s to now, "these times have seen consistent experimentation and learning—varieties, approaches, treatments, techniques—a steady stream of new developments. For me, appreciating and learning from each step has been satisfying.

"Something that I hadn't predicted, though, was the impact of the industry's growth. In the 1980s, the winery owners, who came from vineyards or winemaking backgrounds, were actively operating their businesses. They often took on other roles, such as developing standards for the nascent VQA appellation system or lobbying the government to improve the vine-growing or wine business environment. It was a small industry. Growth, including the contribution of our educational institutes and more diversity in the backgrounds of the people the industry has attracted, is impressive and satisfying. All these people, with varying skill sets, have come together to make the industry more dynamic today." Ann cites Linda Bramble (see Chapter 6) as an example of a positive force in the wine industry. She came with skills and aptitudes she honed in other areas and then applied herself in many different ways to the wine industry—none of which were winemaking.

"To see the evolution of Brock's CCOVI and Niagara College's programs makes it exciting and also brings hope that there is a critical mass in the industry that will keep us going and always improving, Ann says. "Our strength as an industry is the people. They are the drivers behind our success. We have a climate that can support wine grapes, but it's not the climate or the place itself that is making the wine. It's all the communicators, the winery owners, and the winemakers who are making the industry. It distills down to the people. The ones who have stayed with it and developed. What they have built has attracted more people at every level. In the end, it's all of us."

Ann believes it's essential for all of us to work collaboratively and share knowledge. When Brock University's CCOVI was being developed, she helped to raise funds. Her parents made a significant contribution to the cellar and donated $20,000. She has mentored dozens of aspiring grape growers, winemakers, and interns and is a consistent contributor and speaker at nationwide conferences. As a winemaker, one of her strategies is to work alongside her assistants and interns, always pitching in and exposing them to as many aspects of the process as possible. Ann's teams are small at each of the wineries she works at, and she expects as much from each member as she gives. She always has a vision of what she wants to accomplish and works towards it. Throughout, she's always observing what is happening in the vineyards, how the vines are functioning and performing through the season, and how these facets will impact the wine. These observations seasonally guide her decisions.

Ann continues, "When the time comes for harvest, you have to make decisions working with the best information you have and with that vision of what you want to create." Knowing what she wants to create makes all those extra hours and the attention to detail throughout the year worth it. If you take shortcuts, you will inevitably see the adverse effects in the vineyard and in the subsequent wines. She teaches a solution-oriented approach. "Nothing stops because something's gone wrong. It's just a step to solving the problem, so understanding what's happened is useful and important in order to improve or fix the issue." Within these small teams, Ann says it's essential to be accountable but also to realize that you can't do it all yourself. Furthermore, she assures that people have the skills and the empowerment to carry through and get things done when situations arise that she may not be there for.

Ann recalls a time in her twenties when she met an individual from a globally renowned winemaking family. They were the same age and were comparing notes. This person had many advantages, had tasted iconic wines, and was well travelled. Ann says, "I hadn't travelled anywhere, and my exposure to great wines was limited. Here I was, thinking I would make these great wines but not knowing what that meant!" She remembers feeling at a disadvantage then, so she and her husband Peter have made a point of opening those great bottles for people. Sharing and drinking them together, but critiquing them and sharing their knowledge, time, and insights, is all part of the drill. "We want to increase the knowledge and understanding of wine with keen young people. One of the themes in our household is, 'If you don't know what great wine tastes like, then how can you make it?' That's our excuse for drinking amazing wines on a Wednesday!"

She interjects here, with a sheepish grin, "It might seem kind of cheesy, but Peter has been an important mentor for me." She is referring to her husband, Peter Gamble. "He's nine years older and has been part of the industry for more or less the same amount of time, but he comes at it from a different perspective. It's been good, not only to have a spouse who understands why you come home tired every day at harvest and why you can't leave after ten hours or twelve hours or fourteen hours; but also to understand when you come home and say, 'I've got this problem or this worry.' Peter is always good to strategize with or to get help from to make a quality decision when you have to explain it to your boss when it might have financial implications. To have someone consistently coming down on the quality side with you is invaluable."

From a sensory perspective, Peter has mentored countless palates and has been instrumental in the standards committee for VQA. He and Ann have judged together over the years. While Ann says they don't always have the same opinions or preferences, they consistently recognize quality, reinforcing their standards. Individually and as a team, the pair also work as international winemakers and consultants, ensuring they are less likely to have a cellar palate, [a commonly used term for what can happen when a winemaker or wine professional becomes acclimatised to their own wines or those of their region] which many winemakers can develop if not regularly exposed to global wine styles and terroir.

Can you just imagine the dinner table discussions over wine? To this, Ann laughs and admits, with just a little bit of pride, that while their children may have found some of those discussions boring, if you ask them questions about the wine industry, they can give you a lot of information, even though it's not their primary interest. As Ann and her siblings did in their youth, her children have absorbed much knowledge about grape growing, winemaking, and the industry in general.

Ann explains that when asked about challenges, she looks at everything as a stage in the growing season. This allows her to address each issue as it arises, one thing at a time, rather than feeling overwhelmed. She says her strategy has always been to learn more, research more, and develop creative solutions. She laughs. "We're just making wine here; after all, we're not curing cancer!" She jokes, but I remind her of her conscientiousness in reducing chemical use in the vineyard and the great product called Bioflavia she helped to create at Southbrook. It's a powerful antioxidant derived from grape pomace. Maybe Ann's not curing cancer, but her actions are possibly contributing to preventing it!

"I hope that my wines are remembered. I hope something about them elevates that vineyard or place to a higher level of greatness. I know that the wines aren't going to last hundreds of years but, hopefully, we can get a couple of decades that leave an impression. Working through the medium of the soil is how I have always felt I would leave my mark. When you look around the world at where great wine comes from, often they are from biodynamic producers. I see the role of biodynamic production as channelling what is coming through the soil and the climate, without interference, to create the individuality and specificity of place."

What has kept Ann engaged and motivated over her career? She names continuous improvement as a driver. "I get to work with vineyards, see them from early plantings to the first wines, and then see how that changes as the vines mature. It never feels like the work is done; there is always something that can be built on or improved. I think the feeling that there is still more that can be done is ever-present. A new project is always fun because you are starting with a clean slate. You learn about the site before planting and then apply theories using the knowledge you and others have acquired. Then you test your theories by planting and developing that vineyard and making those wines. That's always fun. So now there are old vineyards, new vineyards, converted vineyards. Some differences happen when you convert from conventional to organic production. There are regional differences. So, it's infinite. Ultimately, satisfaction is gained when people taste and comment on the wines. There is also how those wines age. That's all a part of it. It's multifaceted."

There is absolute pleasure and gratification in her voice as Ann shares this insight. She finds reward and fulfillment in her work. To Ann, this isn't a job to be completed and punched out from at the end of each day or a yearly harvest to make it through; rather, the seasons, the vines, the fruit, and their subsequent wines are a gift, given her each year, and meant to be celebrated as such.

One of those moments of celebration came when Ann's 1992 Merlot from CedarCreek Estate Winery was recognized as having such promise that the Okanagan Wine Festival created an unprecedented platinum award for it. For Ann, the thrill was also in the ripple effect of what followed. She explains, "This particular Merlot vineyard was naturally low yielding due to its age and how it was planted. It was rooted, not grafted, and wasn't in a good location, so no one was excited about it. But tasting the fruit and working with it, it was obvious to me that it was different—it was better. I followed my instincts and was able to carry through and make a wine that people recognized for its quality.

"What was significant at that time was that in the Okanagan, almost no red wines were made other than hybrids and small amounts of Pinot

Noir. No big reds were being made from vinifera grapes. So the timing of that wine, and having it recognized that way, also coincided with the availability of vine planting material to grow some other varieties, like Merlot. What followed was a boom in planting Merlot. That changed the nature of the BC. industry. It also coincided with increased consumer demand for red wine and a realization that we could do something like that. I think that is where that wine became more legendary. Today Merlot is the largest acreage of red grapes planted in the Okanagan Valley."

Another exciting venture that Ann recalls being a part of in her four-decade winemaking career was being involved with a sparkling wine research project in the early 1990s. "While the sought-after outcome didn't happen, all of us who were a part of the research went off and eventually made sparkling wine, which leading up to the consumer demand for the millennium, was very timely. I was rewarded working with a group and seeing people go off and do great things, like Steller's Jay [a renowned sparkling wine from Sumac Ridge] and Blue Mountain sparkling wines. And now, finally, I get to make Sperling sparkling wines." Ann is smiling here with a far-off look. She says, "Good things come, but not necessarily right away."

This is true of the not-so-instant gratification of growing grapes and making wine. The delayed satisfaction requires copious amounts of patience. Numerous studies have been published about the specific character traits displayed by those who have climbed to the pinnacles of their industries: athletes, musicians, and even spelling bee champions. Many these people believe that the countless hours spent learning, researching, practising, and perfecting their talents were part of the journey and that perseverance and tenacity are mindsets curated to help them achieve their goals. They claim that their "Why" is so big that it is worth all the sacrifices required to achieve their goals. It seems Ann operates on the same premise, believing in the outcome and never comprising her standards along the way. Another commonality is the celebration of small daily wins, rejoicing in a job well done, a solution found, an innovation conceived. To me, this sounds like thriving. Thriving isn't living without challenges. It's found in the triumph of overcoming, despite the barriers.

Ann has been asked by countless interviewers what it is she likes to do in her free time, and her answer is always the same. "I like to make wine." This desire and passion for working with varying climates and regions have driven Ann to make wine in Ontario, return to her roots in Kelowna, and work on Canada's East Coast in Nova Scotia. In 2008 Ann and Peter purchased an almost century-old vineyard in Mendoza, Argentina, where they are crafting some of the country's most elegant and complex Malbecs.

When asked about life balance, Ann says, "Well, I don't really know about balance. Being healthy and recharging is important, but I don't use other things to recharge. 'A change is as good as a rest' is part of my philosophy. The beauty of being a winemaker/winegrower is that this time of year [spring], the focus is on the vineyards and in the fall, there is harvest and primary processing, and in the winter, you're looking at the wines and the blends. So every season brings those cycles and those changes, and that is refreshing.

"If balance somehow relates to hours spent, then spending the time to get good results is a better way of spending my time than to cut it off at 5 p.m. and consider my day done." She admits that the realities of having children and picking them up from daycare and school require being there on time, but that's only for a certain period of our lives. She is grateful that when daycare and school pick-ups were needed during harvest, Peter could be there when the kids got off the school bus. Ann says she is grateful that they each had a both a healthy family and career.

For some, balance means the ability to spend time aimlessly, unstructured and unfettered by an agenda. Not so for Ann. She finds balance in the natural ebb and flow of the seasons.

Did Ann ever want to do anything else? Ann laughs and shakes her head, recalling that she was a teenager in high school when she decided to pursue winemaking as a career. "My brother, who is twelve years older, was already growing grapes and had studied agriculture to be a grape grower. Since he was already doing that, I thought that winemaking was the next best thing for me. Connecting to the sensory part of winemaking was easy and natural; making wine, tasting wine and talking about wine became the thing that I was absorbed by.

"With winemaking, there are many aspects. There are intellectual parts of it, and there is craft, and then there is something tangible in your hands at the end of it. Those filled bottles of wine are the physical result of it. And, of course, it carries on for years because you get to taste those bottles, and you can evaluate how good your decisions were in the previous ten, twelve, or eighteen months before the wine went into bottle. You can recall the growing season and all that's within each bottle. I think having those tangible things has always been important to me. As a child, crafts were important, and making things was necessary, so preserving the vegetables and fruits for later enjoyment was something that just seemed like a normal and natural thing for me to do."

Of life lessons, Ann says, "We mustn't hesitate to research, apply, and try new things, to come up with creative solutions to solve problems. Don't stay in the same ruts that have been plowed ahead before you. Paradigm shifts don't happen when you keep doing the same thing. While I think that my first five or six years of winemaking were about learning the rules and staying in that safe zone, after that, my goal was to stretch myself—and the rules—to reach towards greatness. It's important to have that solid foundation to grow from, but continuous learning and innovation have always been a part of my philosophy. I think I've inherited it through the generations of my family. I want to share here that not all the work is done. Anyone who chooses can come in and make a difference if they want to. There is still ongoing evolution and development."

As if on cue, Ann's daughter Juliet arrives. Juliet and her husband Martin founded and operate Linc Farm, the biodynamic farm beside Southbrook Vineyards. As Ann did before them, they call themselves "stewards of the land." Like Ann, Juliet is a trailblazer. Appalled by the conditions in which animals are routinely raised and slaughtered, she came up with an innovative way to be a part of the solution rather than remain a part of the problem. At Linc Farm, they humanely raise grass-fed pigs, chickens, sheep, and cattle and ensure that the animals live happy lives.

One of the principles of biodynamics is to have a "closed loop," and Linc Farm supports this principle for Southbrook by providing the winery and vineyards with much of its manure for their biodynamic applications.

The farm and winery share the same values of sustainability along with holistic, regenerative farming and viticulture. The meat and wool are sold to local chefs and consumers. Juliet announces, "Tonight, we will be taste-testing bacon!" The conscious sustainability and sensory analysis gene has been passed down to yet another Sperling generation!

Post-chapter updates (2023)

In 2021, the Cambridge Food & Wine Society named Ann the Riedel Winemaker of the Year. The society recognizes individuals who have accomplished significant achievements in the global wine industry. Past recipients of this prestigious award have been Robert Mondavi, Miguel Torres, and Lamberto Frescobaldi, among others. Ann was recognized for her commitment to and passion for elevating and promoting Canada's wine industry and contributing to its international recognition. Ann's impressive global wine portfolio includes Southbrook Vineyards in Ontario, Sperling Vineyards in British Columbia, and Versado Malbec in Mendoza, Argentina. Upon receiving the accolade, Ann stated, "It's an honour to receive this important award. In our relentless pursuit of great winemaking, we have learned the high value and relevance of organic and biodynamic viticulture, and this has instilled in us a deep respect for the soil, water, and ecosystems upon which great wine—and our planet—relies. I am delighted to be recognized for these efforts."

In another noteworthy development in the Ontario industry, Ann and her husband, Peter Gamble, were recently hired by Faik Turkmen, who bought Lailey Vineyard in 2021 from the couple who purchased it from Donna and David Lailey (see Donna's chapter). Ann and Peter will oversee the winemaking and vineyards to return Lailey to a quality-focused operation. Faik also owns the Stonebridge Vineyard in Niagara-on-the-Lake. Ann and Peter will be making wines under both labels. This is exciting news for Niagara!

Juliet and Martin have relocated to River John, Nova Scotia, where they continue to practice sustainable farming and the humane raising of animals.

JENNIFER WILHELM

Tributes to Ann Sperling

Ann Sperling by Shauna White
Winemaker

"There is so much for me to say about Ann that it is a challenge to know where to start! From the moment I showed interest in the wine industry, my aunt Ann was there to support me and help me. We spoke a lot about schooling and what would be the right fit for me. I chose Niagara College and was accepted into the Winery and Viticulture Technician program. I needed to move halfway across the country to attend college, and Ann opened her home to me. The wonderful part about living with Ann, other than being able to pick her brain, was that the learning continued at home after class. The many experiences and wine tastings around the dinner table were memorable and impactful. Ann taught me so much about food and wine pairing and how to select the best wine for each dinner course. Blind tasting wine was a nightly tradition—and challenge! I learned about many wines and world wine regions. This nightly exercise helped me gain confidence in my senses and palate. I attribute my success in tasting classes at school to Ann's home blind tastings. On my final test for new world wines, I received a 96 per cent and nailed one of the wines perfectly—an uncommon 2005 Syrah from Chile.

"Ann continued to support and mentor me after I finished school and moved out. Ann helped me to get my practicum experience at Domaine Laroche in Chablis, France. This experience left me in love with Chardonnay. It encouraged me to travel to learn more from other winemakers and regions worldwide. Ann also introduced me to another great female winemaker, Louisa Ponzi, who accepted my request for a harvest internship in Oregon. This led me to meet more female winemakers as I continued to travel and learn overseas. When I returned home to Canada to pursue becoming a winemaker, Ann again reached out to me. She was assisting a new winery and providing them with a custom crush facility. They needed an assistant winemaker. I interviewed and was hired by Ravine Vineyard, eventually becoming their head winemaker. Ann's mentorship and guidance allowed Ravine and me to receive two Lieutenant Governor' Awards for Excellence in Ontario Wines.

"One of Ann's best qualities is her thirst for more knowledge. Ann is always learning, experimenting, questioning, collaborating, and sharing with others! Ann's experience and passion for organic and biodynamic practices make her a specialist and one of the longest-practising Canadian winemakers in this field. Ann shares her passion and knowledge about organics and biodynamics and leads by example in the vineyard, winery, at industry events, conferences and in her daily life. Ann will always answer the phone and provide advice and ideas when asked. I know many people, especially other women, whom Ann had inspired, mentored, and helped on their winemaking and viticultural journey. Ann is a true steward of the land, and she strives for the expression of place in every wine she makes. Ann is truly inspiring; the Canadian wine industry is so fortunate to have Ann as a leader, and so are all of us whom she has assisted on her epic journey."

Ann Sperling by Shiraz Mottiar
Winemaker

"I first met Ann when my Cool Climate Oenology and Viticulture Institute (CCOVI) class visited the then-brand new Malivoire Wine Company in 1999. Her focus on "eco-friendly" viticulture and gentle winemaking to maximize the expression of terroir resonated with me. That vision was hers and forever changed the Niagara wine-scape.

"A year later, I asked Ann for a position in the cellar, and we soon forged a great partnership of learning. Ann is always ready to explore new ideas, taking others along on a journey of discovery to better her wines AND the whole industry, enriching those like me to succeed in her wake. I'm eternally grateful for learning from such a giving mentor."

Ann Sperling by Elena Galey-Pride
Winestains

"One of the luckiest days of my life was the day that Linda Bramble introduced me to Ann Sperling. It was early 1999, and I was taking an intensive wine marketing program with Linda as our key instructor. In true Linda Bramble style (as evidenced by her own chapter in this book!), she was graciously connecting her students with key wine industry personages. And Ann Sperling was certainly one of those! Although she'd only been in the Ontario industry a brief time at that point, she was quickly gaining attention and building on the glorious career she had started in BC.

"Ann subsequently contacted me to discuss a winery project she was working on that she felt needed a dedicated marketing person on board, even though the doors were not yet open. That was my first evidence of Ann's strategic and far-sighted thinking. There were many more examples to come!

"That project turned out to be the Malivoire Wine Company, and after meeting and passing muster with Martin Malivoire, I signed on as the first marketing manager. Little did I know that I was hitching my wagon to a star. (OK, I did strongly suspect!) Ann and Malivoire were to change my life.

"Working in the adrenalin-pumping environment of a start-up, job descriptions are fluid. Every day, our tiny team needed to adapt with alacrity while still keeping our "eye on the prize." Ann excels at both and is a wonderful teacher. While I had marketing skills, the wine world was new to me. Ann was patient and generous. She answered every question I had and even the ones I didn't know to ask. In all the years I've known her, her style has always been low key but also thoughtful, thorough, and precise. I'm desperately searching for another word to use for Ann rather than the hackneyed "passionate," but before it became highly overused and lost its true meaning, I suspect Ann's picture was next to the word in the dictionary. She breathed a rare quality into the Ontario wine industry.

"We spent a lot of time together over our six years working together at Malivoire. I have her to thank for introducing me to so many people who are still important in my life and for exposing me to so many chances to learn and grow.

"I was by her side the night she was named Winemaker of the Year at the Ontario Wine Awards. A more surprised winner I have never seen.

Despite all her qualifications and awards, Ann is essentially humble and not a seeker of the limelight for herself. That doesn't mean she doesn't have an honest and objective understanding of her wines' greatness! She's proud—proud of her children and her wines.

"When Ann left Malivoire in 2005, she was missed, although she had wisely nurtured her talented assistant winemaker, Shiraz Mottiar, to be promoted from within.

"We'd only been apart workwise for a year when the opportunity presented itself to work with Ann again at Southbrook Vineyards. Another exciting start-up—for all intents and purposes, despite their history in Richmond Hill—with a landmark building on the drawing board and an organic and biodynamic estate vineyard underway. It would be a complete rebrand. Pretty hard to say no to that! I would be Ann's counterpart this time, with customer experience and hospitality my bailiwick, and winemaking and viticulture hers. In the archetypal parlance we used at the time to define Southbrook's essence, she would lead the "creators," and I would lead the "lovers."

"And lead, she did! Always by example. Ann was taking her place at the forefront of organic and biodynamic viticulture in Canada, generously sharing her knowledge and nurturing those who sought to learn from her. She's assisted countless aspiring winemaking talents with advice, connections, and encouragement. Yes, she's cultivated a lot more than just vines! But I'll leave others to address that in their tributes.

"Later, after I moved on from Southbrook and was establishing myself as a marketing consultant, Ann gave me one of my earliest assignments by asking me to help her and Peter [Gamble] create a presence in Ontario for their new Versado wines from Argentina. Another start-up! This time, I would be working with Ann on something that was her very own (with Peter, of course), and her generosity rose to an even higher level. That largesse extended to a visit to their beautiful Villa Viamonte in Mendoza and some of my favourite lifetime memories.

"Ann's other assignments for me included some early work with Sperling Vineyards in BC. I love how she gives guidance and then lets me do my thing. We continue to work together today, but our friendship leads the way. It's been an honour to watch Ann's children, Juliet and

Lauren, grow up in front of my eyes. I hosted many a "birthday party" for Lauren as a child as her birthday fell on our traditional Boxing Day party day. I watched Juliet traverse her tweens and teens, go to university, work as Southbrook's shepherd, and marry Martin. She's now a little further away, running a unique farming business in Nova Scotia. And now, Ann and Peter, and my husband Stan and I even share a wedding anniversary! And we've shared many a fantastic bottle in celebration and friendship. Their generosity definitely extends to their legendary cellar!

"What an honour to be asked to write about Ann! Jenn Wilhelm gave a gift to so many in our industry when she offered us the opportunity to share our thanks and praise to these women who changed both the Ontario wine world and our own lives. Thank you."

Ann Sperling by Jill Richardson Branby
General Manager, Sperling Vineyards

"I started in the wine industry with a part-time summer job at CedarCreek Estate Winery in 1994. Ann Sperling, a renowned BC and Ontario winemaker (and my aunt), arranged an interview for me for a position to clean the wine shop after hours and nanny her three-year-old daughter Juliet (my cousin) during the day. Okanagan summers are the best as a teen, and being around the burgeoning BC wine industry at the same time was such a privilege. I assisted with bottling, adding BCVQA stickers to bottles (new at the time) and helped wherever needed.

"We'd always spent summers in Kelowna at my grandparents' property, and everyone was required to help prepare for the upcoming grape harvest. The season would start with Sovereign Coronation table grapes, harvested in late August. Little kids and big kids, all the cousins, aunts and uncles worked together to put handles on baskets or build masters (the main boxes that hold the individual baskets.) It didn't matter if you were a beginner or a pro; everyone worked together. I can still smell the warm hay from the box shed and hear the music on the old boombox, with us all piled in there, dusty and hot.

"During the summer of 2003, conversations had started about possibly creating a family winery. Ann and Peter, and my parents Susan and Paul, reached out to family members to see if they were interested in collaborating. I was a single mom of an adorable 2.5-year-old, working in reforestation and attending university. Having watched Ann trailblazing over the years, I jumped at the opportunity to work with her. She connected me with Elena Galey-Pride at Malivoire Wine Company for an interview, and we picked up and moved to Niagara so I could hone my skills in the wine industry.

"Ann gave me the opportunity to learn about the wine industry—and wine—in a way that few people do. Living with Ann and Peter, there were nightly discussions over bottles of incredible wines. I assisted at their exclusive winemaker tastings, took courses at Brock with Linda Bramble, and worked closely with the team at Malivoire in retail and marketing. I earned my stripes. I learned the ins and outs of wine tasting, luxury wine marketing, organic viticulture and agriculture, biodynamics, regenerative agriculture, and so much more. The trajectory of my life truly changed forever.

"That same wine year, I met my husband-to-be in the tasting room at Malivoire. Rickard came in for a wine tasting with friends from Sweden and later said he "knew" as soon as he saw me. We married less than a year later and are celebrating our nineteenth year together this summer, with our four children.

"Sperling Vineyards Winery became real in 2008. We harvested our first crop, made 600 cases of wine, and started the adventure. My husband took on the vineyard manager and assistant winemaker roles that same year, working beside Ann, learning from the best.

"Ann has always been an incredible teacher. Generous, thoughtful, incredibly hard-working, tenacious, and genuinely brilliant. She has pushed and inspired me to be better every day. I am indebted to her for so much of what I've learned in the wine industry over the past twenty years, particularly the past fifteen at Sperling Vineyards. I am always incredibly proud to say that she's my boss, colleague, aunt, and even more so, my friend.

"As a family, we completed our last harvest in 2022 at Sperling Vineyards. It's been an emotional time for all of us, and the transition to new ownership hasn't been without its ups and downs, but one of the things I'll miss the most is working with our incredible team, particularly with Ann. She's a legend, and I've been so lucky."

Barbara Leslie

"How did I end up here, my nose poised dreamily over a glass, inhaling mouth-watering suggestions of fruit and cream, apples, and caramel? I have no idea. What I do know, as I look back on my life, is that at just about every turn there was somebody there to open a door."

Barbara Leslie was born in Montreal in 1948. She says was a serious and quiet child, having had what she refers to as a Victorian upbringing, "where children were left pretty well to their own devices." For the first four years of her life, Barbara had nannies and rarely saw her parents or other children. She recalls a memory in which she had just begun school and was given crayons and paper. She confesses "I didn't know what to do with them."

When asked about her aspirations as a child, Barbara states that the environment in which she was raised didn't encourage girls to think about careers but to focus instead on marriage and motherhood. Her father believed that women shouldn't be permitted to drive a car, claiming that "Women are too easily distracted and therefore make unsafe drivers." Consequently, Barbara's mother never pursued obtaining a driver's licence.

Attaining a university education certainly wasn't an expectation for young women either. Though an anomaly at the time, Barb's Aunt Betty (her mother's sister) was a graduate of Oxford University and insisted that her niece also attend a well-regarded university. Barb remembers being enthralled by her Aunt Betty and following her life with slack-jawed awe. Betty had hobbies and interests and held fascinating conversations in which she wasn't averse to sharing her strong opinions. So, off to McGill University young Barbara went, where she majored in Italian, adding a third language to her repertoire.

She spent the summer of 1969 studying in Perugia, Italy, at l'Università di Perugia per gli Stranieri. Although she had moved away from her constrained family environment, she found herself with other female students in a home overseen by a stern woman with strict rules and curfews. However, this was her first taste of freedom and teenage Barbara found inventive ways around these restrictions. Barbara was a good student and enjoyed her studies but her thirst for adventure soon had her skipping classes and hitchhiking through Italy with friends. She had been sent to Italy to master the language and learn the culture, both of which she did successfully, and in her own way!

Following graduation, Barb took a job at the Montreal General Hospital typing addresses on envelopes meant for invitations to the hospital's 150th anniversary celebration. Looking back, she says these envelopes were her introduction to coordinating large events. While this position wasn't permanent, Barbara demonstrated such efficiency, attention to detail, and aptitude that the hospital wanted to keep her on.

After the event, Barbara began editing the hospital's newsletter and contributing to its magazine. She names her boss there as one of her early career role models, saying she was "a multitalented woman with a talent for getting things done. She was inspirational and a great guide. She told me what she wanted done, how to do it if she needed to, and then she'd let me do my stuff. But she was always there to back me up." Under this mentorship Barbara says she learned a great deal and enjoyed the role, though it was short-lived. She was newly married, and her husband had accepted a job in Toronto. Unfortunately, the marriage was also short-lived and upon its demise Barb returned to Montreal, now a single mother in need of work. She recalls this time in her life as terrifying and overwhelming.

As fate would have it, she happened to come across a man with whom she had crossed paths before, and they recognized one another.

He offered Barb a job with the Opimian Society, then Canada's premier wine club. Barb shares that the name Opimian has its roots in ancient history, relating to a spectacular vintage in 121 BC collected by a Roman consul, Lucius Opimius. Opimian was founded to circumvent the poor and often undrinkable selection of wines available at the provincial monopolies in early 1970s. This was a revolutionary association at the time. There was nothing else like it; it was the only way to get access to many of these premium wines. Members could order cases of wine from several offerings circulated to them throughout the year. The society coordinated the importing and delivery to a monopoly outlet close to the member's residence through the private order department. Along with the wine offerings, members received a newsletter, providing wine education, tasting tips, and articles about international wineries. Moreover, there were knowledgeably led seminars and guided tours through some of the world's principal wine regions. The newsletter eventually evolved into a full, four-colour magazine called *Winetidings*, the first of its kind in Canada to fill the nation's burgeoning wine interest. The articles were written by premier wine writers like Linda Bramble, Tony Aspler, David Lawrason, and Konrad Ejbich.

Barb says, "I got to know these talented contributors as I progressed through the ranks to assistant editor, editor, to publisher, and immersive travel coordinator and guide." Although she was initially hired for her exceptional editing skills, Barb, with her curious mind, absorbed and amassed so much wine knowledge along the way that she, too, was considered an expert within these circles. It's important to note that Barb was the first female editor and publisher of a Canadian wine magazine and her meticulous attention to detail was one of the reasons why the magazine was so respected.

Fondly, she remembers meeting and working with Thomas Bachelder. She tells, "Thomas was destined for greatness in the wine industry. He joined the staff of *Winetidings* in 1987." Thomas, along with his wife Mary Delaney, became close friends of Barb. Thomas and Barb collaborated on a book published in 1990 entitled *For the Love of Wine*.

During this time, Barb found another mentor in Judy Rochester, the woman to whom she reported at the Opimian Society. Barb notes, "She was brilliant. She supported me, she taught me, she encouraged me. She was a fantastic lady." Barbara looks back on her time with *Winetidings* and says she learned so much, not only about wine but also of the technique of preparing and editing each edition, which she found enjoyable and rewarding. "I learned a lot about design as well as writing, fitting things in, and how printing works. I found the technical part of it and the production a lot of fun, and I liked reading everything."

Barbara worked with the Opimian Society from 1982 to 1999. She appreciated the travel and opportunities to meet national and international winemakers whom she says were so open and eager to share their passion. She maintains some of these relationships today. Barb has always enjoyed the people behind the craft, relishing occasions to connect with winemakers at events and tradeshows where her love of wine and fluent French and Italian allowed her to move with ease. Often, these were opportunities to meet the people and taste the wines featured in the articles she poured over in her role with the magazine.

On one such introduction, Barbara recalls a sales rep, new to Canada, whom she says was really missing authentic Italian food. Montreal is known for its exceptional restaurants and Barb told him about one nearby, to which he then insisted she and her date accompany him and his sales partner. She remembers the pair being so exuberantly taken with the place that they asserted all four must partake in the chef's multi-course menu with wine pairings. Another chance introduction bonded over love of wine, languages, and fine cuisine resulting in an immensely enjoyable, albeit very late night of merriment. Barbara laughingly recounts the tale, ending by saying that her career has led her to meet "really super-duper people" from all aspects of the industry.

Her journey has not been without challenges. When asked to identify a particular one, she notes, "Being laid off during an economic downturn in the 1980s. That was really difficult as a single mom. There were no jobs available, and I didn't have the personal confidence to sell myself then. I don't know that I could do it now even but at least I know it's needed. I was terrified. And felt put down and rejected; there is all kinds of emotional stuff that comes with being laid off." Despite knowing that the job loss was due to elements outside of her control, Barb struggled with these difficult feelings.

In 1998, Barb says she moved to Niagara on a whim after visiting the area. She had been thinking of moving out of Montreal, possibly to British Columbia. But she recalls standing on the deck of the very first winery she visited, Vineland Estates Winery, looking out over the rolling vineyards and seeing the lake in the distance, and reminisces with wonder, "There was such a great sense of openness. And I thought, 'This is what I need. This is the place I need.'"

Admittedly, Barb wasn't sure at the time what she would do when she got to Niagara. Once here, however, she was approached by Maleta Estate Winery, asking her to come and work in their retail store, educating customers on the nuances of wine tasting.

Barb's keen tasting skills and knowledge of the world's wine regions quickly made her an invaluable asset to the local industry. She soon found herself happily immersed in assisting with events such as the Toronto Wine and Cheese Show and The Ontario Wine Awards. The industry at that time was small and tight knit, and it wasn't unusual to find her pouring wines at local events, sharing her knowledge and love of wine with both residents and visitors and to the Niagara region.

Barb began teaching wine appreciation classes part-time, and in 2001 she officially joined the faculty team of the Winery and Viticulture Technician program at Niagara College, teaching sensory evaluation of wines and mentoring the students throughout their practicum internships. Barb accepted this role enthusiastically and devotedly set about getting to know the people behind each of the Ontario wineries so as to match the students with wineries and people aligned to their personalities, unique skills, and end goals. She was genuinely invested in the success of both the student and the winery itself.

In addition to helping to match students and placement wineries, Barbara's role entailed visiting students onsite and meeting with them and their supervisors to ensure that the placement was rewarding for both parties. She was supportive and encouraging of the students but also firm in that this was a learning experience that they needed to embrace with openness and positivity. She was a valued and knowledgeable liaison between current and future generations of industry professionals.

Barb's dedication to wine, writing, and education continued to weave together when she worked with Tony Aspler to write *Canadian Wines for Dummies*, published in 2009. Barb credits Tony as influential in her career. "He knew so much about wine, and he was such a gentleman. He was a joy to work with. When he asked me to write with him that was really something special." Barb recalls the struggle of trying to fit their writing into the style that the Dummies series required, with a compulsory ratio of text to images meant to make the reader comfortable with the pace and content. The publisher had a system and template that sold and had to be adhered to. She said of the process, "We just put our heads together and went back and forth with each other until it was complete." Although she enjoyed working with Tony, Barb confides that the book wasn't as successful as they had hoped. "At the time, even at that time, there was such a negativity about Canadian wine. People didn't think it was worth anything. Despite the fact that when you put BC together with Ontario, there was quite a lot to write about."

Barb spent twelve years with Niagara College and was instrumental in launching and facilitating the Wine Sales and Profitability Symposium, fellow Wine Educator Workshops, and the inaugural Lieutenant Governor' Awards for Excellence in Ontario Wines. She coordinated practicums and student research projects as an instructor in Niagara College's Winery and Viticulture program. She mentored students in wine and wine business education, used her skills in liaising with winemakers and winery principals, and coordinating conferences, trade shows and wine judging sessions. Her experience in planning and executing major wine events was critical in the success of each of these endeavours, many of them the first of their kind in Ontario. She has an ability to look at a project and see each of the steps that need to be laid out and followed. The physical time flow seems to come naturally to her. These strong project management skills have made Barb an invaluable asset to countless endeavours. She can visualize the big picture and pull each of the pieces in to bring ideas to fruition.

"To get something done you have to start at X and work towards Y and you have to have A, B, C and L, M in there, too." Of this process she says that while not all elements of a project are always enjoyable, there is a sense of satisfaction in getting it done. She concedes that many of the projects were enjoyable simply because of the people who pitched in to make them a success. It is with this understanding that Barbara has approached so many aspects of her career and has joined in and added her humour and elbow grease to many situations. By creating a genuine sense of comradery and purpose, she can find pleasure and laughter in the most mundane tasks, even the endless washing and polishing of wine glasses!

Barb worked tirelessly to promote the Canadian and Ontario wine industry: leading seminars for the Ontario Wine Society; using her connections to bring visitors from Assiniboine and other colleges to Niagara for wine education; organizing and often leading tours to nearby wineries to showcase some of the spectacular talent and wines. She notes that helping visitors to discover some of the smaller craft wineries was so rewarding. She was thrilled to send people back with a greater understanding of the Niagara wine industry; the wines themselves but also the people and the visions and goals that they were setting. In 2014, Barb was the recipient of a special Lieutenant Governor's Community Volunteer Award for her contributions to the Ontario wine industry and community.

In her role with the Opimian Society, Barbara had been in a unique position of having to master the behind-the-scenes skills of organizing people, tours, itineraries, meals, accommodations, and more. Drawing on what she had learned, she brought her valuable global expertise to Niagara, to create an elevated experience for visitors of all kinds. She was keenly able to understand and anticipate what they would want to know, as well as to exceed their expectations by incorporating encounters that lead to lasting relationships. She was a connector. She knew the right people to bring together. She presented a fulsome experience of Niagara's wine industry, from small independent growers to large conglomerations, formed through international mergers. For the educators she toured, this was critical in the knowledge they gained, took away and consequently shared with their students about who and what the Niagara wine industry truly was. By giving them the experiences, paired with personal stories from growers, winemakers, and businesspeople, she made it as easy as possible. Barb astutely recognized the value of story telling and how much easier and more genuine it would be from firsthand learning and genuine face to face connections.

Aside from the wines, she believes that our strength as an industry lies in the people and the developments that they have forged, the education and technology that they have embraced. The people drive the success. Through dedication and perseverance. Despite the early naysayers who vowed that they wouldn't pour Ontario wines in their restaurants. "These passionate people built acceptance, through perseverance and belief in themselves as an industry and belief in their product. We are now at a stage where there is far more acceptance of Ontario wines than there is rejection."

If she were writing a letter to her twenty-year-old self, Barbara would say "Be more curious. Be more observant. Be less complacent." Barb is grateful for the doors that have opened for her but says thoughtfully that "life might have been more interesting if that hadn't been the case. I was raised as a child to be complacent, to believe that someone would always be looking after me. Like I'd be the little wife. And yet I knew that wasn't really reality, that couldn't really be reality."

She feels that her career in wine, writing, travel, and education unfolded almost of its own accord, with each role leading naturally into the next. Barbara recalls that she got a lot of enjoyment out of learning how things worked when she began at the magazine; she found the typesetting and mechanics of the process so interesting. When asked what she thinks she might have done had she not entered the wine industry Barb says she may have gone into computer sciences. She mentions the female mathematicians in the film *Hidden Figures* and thinks such a career would have been stimulating for her curious mind.

Barb notes, "It's important to have mutual respect for the people that I'm with, professionally and personally, and to help out when I can. To open a door for somebody or to reach out, to support people. That to me is very important." After retirement, Barb began volunteering with Canadian Federation of University Women (CFUW) and acting as communications chair. CFUW is a non-profit, local, provincial, national, and international organization of women committed to the pursuit of knowledge, promotion of education and improvement of the status of women, children, and their human rights and well being.

When asked which part of her career she feels most proud of Barb says, "Just survival. That I made it through. That I did the things that I was asked to do, and fairly successfully, so that people would ask me to do other things. That seems to me to be a success. I didn't make the newspapers, but it made me feel good to do it and to have someone ask me to do it again." Each position she took on was new and hadn't been held by anyone else previously. She shaped the roles personally and brought her unique skills and approach to each.

When asked what we can do to build on the industry's success, without hesitation Barb says, "Keep learning. Be determined. Look at technological advances and how we can use them and when not to use them. Move out of the sphere of creation. Everyone must think about marketing as well. Keep researching. Find new grape types. Find new grape clones, new yeasts, ways to work with the climate; just keep digging and researching all the time. And be daring as well. Try to do something different."

If she could give advice to those considering a career in Ontario's grape and wine industry Barb says adamantly, "It's not what you think it is. If you're going to do this business, you have to be ready to get dirty. You must be a businessperson and be creative. And it's not easy! You've got to work very, very hard." Having said that, she also feels that people will continue to be drawn to the industry, not just for the wine but for the lifestyle. "From the outside, it doesn't look like a hard slog, whereas if you're working in the city everything is a hard slog. The rewards of this industry are different than those of living in the city, making a lot of money, or having a fancy car. If you want to make wine, there is a whole other set of rewards. This industry is about community and conviviality. Those are the rewards. And sharing the wine with friends at the end of the day."

If she isn't travelling or helping friends, you will likely find Barb in her garden or planning her next gathering of friends and neighbours, new and old. Barb loves entertaining friends and family and enthusiastically pours Ontario wine, almost always presenting the bottle with a story about the winemaker, grape grower, or salesperson whom she spent time getting to know during her visit. She makes a point in keeping in touch with graduates, following their success, and supporting their growth in the grape and wine industry. She adds that being able to visit the wineries, connect with the people behind the wines and discover the nuances of each vintage is exciting year after year. She is a connector, a creator of community wherever she is, both professionally and personally. For Barb, a stranger is simply a friend she hasn't yet met. Having met her once, you will be forever greeted and welcomed as a friend.

For each of us in this industry there is something that holds us here, that binds us to the community with passion and dedication. For Barbara it has been the people themselves, and the conviviality that comes with sharing wine, which she feels often brings out the best in people, bonding over the shared quest of growing, making, and promoting wine. The sense of comradery and the relationships built along the way are the most valuable take aways from our journey.

Post-Chapter Note

On April 13, 2023, Barb Leslie passed away after suffering a brain aneurysm. Her family, friends, colleagues, and students gathered to mourn and celebrate an extraordinary woman, mother, grandmother, mentor, friend, and trailblazer.

She was honoured at the 2023 Ontario Wine Awards, and it was announced that a scholarship had been formed in remembrance of her impact on the Canadian wine industry and dedication to students and education. The award, founded by George Brown College, will go to a deserving student in wine studies. Barb would be humbled by this scholarship in her name but also thrilled that it would help to support and grow another ambassador for the Ontario wine industry.

SHARING A GLASS

Tributes to Barbara Leslie

Barbara Leslie by Thomas Bachelder
Co-owner and winemaker, Bachelder

"I was mentored by Barbara Leslie, and she became a friend.

"In the late 1980s, I was an aspiring musician, wine journalist, and home winemaker. The Opimian Society was a driving force in the Canadian wine industry, so I joined. I had no money to speak of, but I somehow bought a few good bottles. Judy Rochester, the Montréal-area secretary of the Opimian Society and also the publisher of *Winetidings* magazine, became aware of my keen interest and got me onto the *Winetidings* tasting panel as a guest. I showed so much enthusiasm that I became a regular member. I learned from the other experienced tasters—at the time, arguably the best in the country—as we wound our way through all the world's wine regions over the next few years.

"Barbara Leslie (*Winetidings* editor), who organized the tastings, took me under her wing, and soon I was contributing articles to the magazine. Soon enough, I was working for Judy and Barbara at Kylix—the company that produced *Winetidings* (now *Quench Magazine*) and La Barrique (later Vins et Vignobles), rising to assistant editor at the magazines, while also helping to write wine catalogues for the AmexVin Wine Society and, sometimes, the Opimian Society.

During this time, Barbara made sure I went to every professional tasting that went on in Montréal, and this was where I really started to learn how to taste. Barbara encouraged and mentored me in all of this, to the point where we eventually collaborated on writing a book. '*For the Love of Wine* was a book meant to inspire burgeoning wine lovers and was offered to all new Opimian members. After this, she encouraged me to write a "Home Wine" column in *Winetidings*, and then this grew into a book, which Barbara patiently edited, entitled, 'You MADE this?!' It was quite a success and sold by mail order and in-home winemaking shops for quite a few years!

"Of course, although I loved the purity of home winemaking (no commercial pressures, I thought at the time), it was time to take the jump and dare to go to wine school in Burgundy!

We were as poor as church mice in Burgundy, but Barbara ensured we stayed in baguettes, cheese, and wine by offering me a monthly column entitled, "A Year in Burgundy." What a thrill! She even used one of my photographs of harvest as a cover shot for the magazine (now that bought us a nice bottle or two of Burgundy!). While in Burgundy, we met Barb in London (over with the Opimian Society on a wine trip) and went to museums. Once again, she took us under her wing and bought us a great meal at Fortnum & Mason.

"After school in Burgundy, we kept in touch with Barb and then-boyfriend Gord Clarke while we were back in Montréal. An especially fond memory is when we met Barb and Gord in Boston for a weekend of wine shopping and wine bars. They then kindly drove us and our bicycles back to Montréal in Gord's old van, talking and laughing all the way! What a time!

"We lost touch for a bit when in 1999, we threw ourselves into the organic sixty-hectare Pinot Noir start-up Lemelson Vineyards in Oregon. When we ended up coming to Canada for Boisset to talk about Le Clos Jordanne, we found upon arrival, to our delight, that Barbara had already moved to Niagara from Montreal the year before.

"I will never forget the scene: there she stood in the doorway of her Port Dalhousie house—arms open—welcoming us and our young daughters (Esmée, 6, and Violette, 3). We stayed with Barb and her son Michael while we interviewed for the Le Clos job and visited Niagara, our new viticultural region. Never missing an opportunity to serve Niagara wine, Barb gave me my first taste of the new Pinots—2001 and 2002 13th Street at the time. She was our little family's only Niagara friend—now so far from our home in Québec and far from good friends in Oregon and France—but what a friend Barbara was!

"Once the Clos Jordanne was a little more established, we continued to see Barb socially, by then with partner Michael East. But we also worked with her as the practicum coordinator for Niagara College—she placed the appropriate Niagara College Winery and Viticulture Technician co-op students with our team—and then steadfastly followed them all as they helped us make wine!

How did Bachelder find our "Bat Cave" in 2013–2014? We connected with the owners through Barbara and Michael East, of course! That contact was the gift, the game-changer that enabled us to get our own cellar space and our retail licence.

"Barbara Leslie—always passionate about wine, helping others, and never in the spotlight. Barbara has never looked for thanks—she has always believed in us, as we did in her—she is a true mentor, and our friendship was 'meant to be!'"

Barb Leslie by Yvonne Irvine
Winemaker & Founder, Maenad Wine Co
Assistant Winemaker, Creekside, Queenston Mile

"I began Niagara College's Winery and Viticulture Technician program in 2006 and graduated in 2008. Barb was there from the beginning of my studies. Her official role was to help students coordinate their practicum placements (co-ops). But she was so much more. She was our support system, our unofficial guidance counsellor, and she had an open-door policy and let us know that we could talk to her about anything. Whether it was related to school, or work, or how we were feeling, or what we hoped our career trajectory would look like… she was there for us.

"In what was at that time a very male-dominated industry, it was very important to her that female students did their placement at wineries who would value them, treat them well, and give them the same opportunities that the male students were given. It may sound like a given today, but in 2007 that wasn't necessarily the case. Granted, the hours are long, and it is hard physical work, but being female doesn't mean that we aren't strong and capable of the lifting or the hours of manual labour in the vineyards and cellars. Still, there were places who only wanted to hire males, or places who didn't treat young women well or equally. Barb would flat out tell us, "No, you aren't going there for your placement."

"This first position was meant to be a positive learning experience, during which we were mentored by a winemaker and exposed to the various aspects of winery work. If it was a negative experience, in which a student was made to feel shamed, incapable, or harassed, they would often leave the industry before really getting started. Barb steered us away from places like that and towards wineries and winemakers who were invested in mentoring the next generation, regardless of gender. She made it a point to be aware of what was happening in the industry; she was always looking out for us and had our best interests at heart. When she visited students at placements, she asked real questions. She asked if we were happy, and feeling good about the experience we were having, and what we were learning. She genuinely wanted to know that we were okay, mentally, emotionally, physically, and having the best possible experience. It wasn't just a show or a posed photo opportunity. We felt cared about and supported by her. Her role was one of the most important parts of our college experience, but she went above and beyond for all of us. She was our core support.

"As a winemaker now, I have mentored co-op students, kept in touch with a few, and have taught a course at Niagara College. This has all given me even greater appreciation for what Barb did in her role because it's a lot to care enough to guide each of these people, year after year. To be genuinely invested in each and every one of them, to sincerely want them to do them well in their future, to give them the information and the guidance they need to succeed; it's a lot of effort. Barb would have seen so many students go through the winery and viticulture program each year, for the many years she was there. She not only guided them through their education years, but she continued to communicate with them after their graduation, and in some cases, even if they chose to leave the wine industry. She would reach out to see that you were okay, that you were doing well, she always let her past students know that she was there for them, if they need someone to talk to, or lean on if you needed to.

"As you are growing in this industry, you are trying to find your way and how you fit, and which winery is most aligned with what you are looking for. She was invaluable in providing guidance, and even after graduation she would email out opportunities she heard about to alumni.

It's a special role she played in so many lives. She had an incredible impact on people. She put so much time and care into each student and the next generation of winemakers and wine industry professionals. Both male and female.

"I think we sometimes forget about what the industry used to be and how hard it was, especially for women. We see an industry today in which women hold many positions, but most of those are still assistant winemakers or junior roles of some sort. We are in the growth phase of seeing more women in head winemaker positions and senior roles and we still have a long way to go to see equality but, it is progress from where the wine industry was fifteen to twenty years ago, where there were very few women working in the production side of making wine. I feel that there has been significant change over the last decade. I am one of the younger women in the industry so I can only imagine how challenging it was for women before me.

"It was one of my reasons for starting Maenad Wine Co in 2020. Maenads were the followers of the Greek God of wine, Dionysus. They were known for unconventional and wild behaviour, for practising ecstatic dance, and performing feats of strength in the forest. I thought, these are often not the women we have celebrated historically. Traditionally, women were expected to be polite, soft spoken, pleasant, dressed appropriately. I really wanted to celebrate the women who are living their lives according to them, to the beat of their own drum, who do speak up, who act and dress on their own terms and who celebrate and support one another. This brand is meant to create wines that push boundaries, and to celebrate women of all kinds, with all lifestyles. I always appreciated that Barb modelled that, that she spoke up and advocated for us and told and showed us that we deserved to be treated well, as equals, not less than because we were women. She was educated and strong and she encouraged us to be as well.

"Barb would often come to events and tastings at Creekside and always asked to see me. When I had my first public tasting of Maenad Wines, Barb came out to celebrate and support me, thirteen years after I had graduated! She told me how thrilled she was to be there, how happy she was for me, and how proud she was of me. She wanted to talk with me, to see how I was doing, to taste the wines I had made. She has supported me throughout my career, has watched me grow, and cheered me on. That's Barb. She celebrates you, your growth, and encourages you to find your unique place in the world. She is a very special person and has had a significant impact on so many of us working in the wine industry today. I don't think she realizes just how impactful she has been."

Barbara Leslie by Sara d'Amato
Writer, Critic, Sommelier, Educator, Consultant
Partner/Principal Critic
WineAlign.com

"For lovers of Canadian wine and for those of you who made their start in the Ontario wine industry, Barbara Leslie is a name to be remembered. Since some of you did not have the opportunity to meet this sincere, intuitive, and articulate woman, I would like to tell you a little bit about her from my perspective as of one of the many students who benefitted from her patience, enthusiasm, and generosity.

"In 2003, I was a fresh-faced student at the newly created Niagara College Wine and Viticulture Technician program, and my very first class afforded me a front row seat in Barbara Leslie's Intro to Sensory Analysis. Students came to know her as "Barb"; she didn't stand on ceremony or formality, but there was nothing casual or unprepared about her lectures. She had an incredibly careful, metered way of speaking, a thoughtful tone where every word was meaningful—surely a sign of her editorial background. Always poised, patient and respectful, she led her students on a well-researched exploration of our own undiscovered potential and taught us to hone our sense of smell and taste to better appreciate the world around us.

"Barb was an early riser in the age of women in wine here in Canada. In the '80s and early '90s, Barb became involved with the Opimian Society and was appointed the first female editor and publisher of the *Winetidings* magazine. Barb was already the editor when Tony Aspler began writing for the publication. Tony found that Barb had a tactful way of nudging her writers in the right direction as well as a keen eye for the right turn of phrase. Quick to develop an ardent interest in the rapidly changing face of the Ontario wine industry, she made Niagara wine a focus of her writing. Barb's insight and editing prowess proved valuable when she co-authored *For the Love of Wine* with Thomas Bachelder in 1990, as well as the ever-popular *Canadian Wine for Dummies with Tony Aspler* in 2000.

"Respectful critical thinking was a most valuable trait that Barb conveyed to her students, and as a wine writer, I now see that her teachings were foundational. An apt criticism demands an understanding and respect for the people, circumstances, and place. Misunderstanding can lead to misjudgement. Criticism was always constructive with Barb, a trait I endeavour to take with me whenever I critique wine. Classes with Barb taught me respect for all wine, those that I didn't understand as much as those that I revered. Barb taught me to see beyond biases and understand the intention of the winemaker. Whether the wine was correct or flawed, she gave me the language to describe its intricacies and the depth of knowledge to understand the place from which it came.

"Barb was fair, impartial, and always an excellent judge of both wine and character. A little enthusiasm on the part of the student was all Barb needed to help them excel.

"It pains me to write this post-mortem as I began writing this tribute before her quick and untimely passing. Barb, a toast to you and to many happy and long-lasting memories!"

Barb Leslie by Liina Veer
A friend

"Barb was my friend. She was kind and generous as I acclimatized to my new life in Niagara, arriving six years ago. We met at the St. Catharine's chapter of the Canadian Federation of University Women. Barb was a key member of the executive over many years. Serving as newsletter editor, communications chair, photographer, and doer of all the other tasks that needed execution to ensure a successful event.

"There are little gems hidden throughout Niagara that only a guide can help you find. My guide was Barb. She introduced me to the Avondale

Dairy on Stewart Road. Ice cream cones, sundaes, banana splits, and milkshakes. All the things that let you live in the moment on a sunny day.

"Then there were the wineries and the wine. I continue to be a novice when it comes to wine. Still missing the descriptors that others speak of during tastings: grass, flint, chocolate, clove. But I now recognize the "cat box" aroma of my favourite varietal. Thanks to Barb. Between sips of wine, we shared stories about our lives.

"Barb introduced me to the little specialty shops, the Rodman Hall Art Book Club and we attended various one-off gatherings, like an evening with a psychic medium. Frequently, a drive home together meant a short stop, selecting items in a store for drop off at a women's shelter or a children's community Christmas party.

"Our first Christmas party invitation in our new community was from Barb. An evening of old and new friends where conversation and laughter came easily. And yes, it was a full house: lots of people appreciating the warm hospitality with the start of new friendships.

"Barb was also a most significant part my life in the fall of 2021. I was undergoing treatment at the Walker Family Cancer Centre daily for six weeks. Barb took me every Friday.

Barb was gracious and fun. And a deep well of knowledge on many things.

"It was easy to love Barb."

Nicolette Novak

"Life changes in a heartbeat. Nothing lasts forever. That in and of itself is frightening, but it also offers opportunities if we can see them. That's what life has shown me. Be flexible. Dig deep. Be strong. Control what you can and remain focused on the key things; good friends, family, and good health–physical of course, but also emotional and spiritual, whatever that may mean to you. We each need to feed our spiritual soul as much as we feed our body. These are the things that will sustain us."

On July 29, 2021, an email simply entitled, "Moving On" was sent by Nicolette to subscribers of The Good Earth Food and Wine Co's aptly named newsletter, "the good dirt."

"Time to say goodbye," recipients read upon opening the message. My hand was already on my heart, and I was holding my breath as I read on.

"Just over two decades ago, a simple idea to showcase the best of Niagara food and wine gave birth to The Good Earth. It has grown from those early culinary experiences in my cottage kitchen, into this magical destination that celebrates good food, good wine, and good friends. The Good Earth is my life's work, my family, and my home. Like everything in life, the time has come to step back and hand over the reins to a new generation. This will be my last summer at the helm of the business."

Tears welled in my eyes. I continued reading as Nicolette graciously and favourably introduced the new owners, heaping on praise, accolades, and assurances that the new owner "Christine has the passion and the skills needed to steer The Good Earth into the future. It will be in good hands! I can't wait to see the next chapter unfold. The success of The Good Earth is its people—the talented chefs, our dedicated wine making team, the men and women who work the land, our wonderful service staff and the myriad of loyal clients and friends. Thank you all for contributing to the success of The Good Earth!"

Seven months after publicly breaking that news, now sitting in the corner of a local bakery, Nicolette Novak opens up about what her life was like as the self-titled "Proprietor and Facilitator of Fun" at The Good Earth. She starts with some background on the original concept she had for her family property, and how she coaxed and nurtured that idea to fruition.

"It wasn't a farm; it wasn't a winery… it was agritourism. It was something unique at the time. No one really understood what I was trying to create. It grew from a tiny seed, an idea." While agritourism and urban escapism might be well known buzzwords today, twenty-five years ago in Niagara this was a nascent concept. Enticing folks from the bright lights and alluring glamour of the city to spend a day cooking in a family cottage was not so trendy. It was considered much more chic by most to dine and be seen in fashionable restaurants, with meals prepared by acclaimed chefs and European wine poured by trained sommeliers. Nicolette had had the unique perspective of living both lives. She had travelled the world, eaten in elegant restaurants, drunk fabulous wine, and enjoyed the charms of many of the world's most sought out metropolitan destinations. She wisely sensed that there were people with a hunger to know where their food came from, to meet the chefs behind the white curtain, to experience the rewarding joy that comes from preparing and enjoying a meal with loved ones. She knew that people wanted and needed to connect back to the land and the good earth.

"My parents met in Canada but were both born in Europe. Although they each had privileged and interesting backgrounds, they came here with nothing. My mother Betty was born in Budapest (one of nine children) and emigrated to Ireland (the birthplace of her mother, my granny,) as a twelve-year-old during the war after her father died as a prisoner of war. My father Karel was an only child born in Prague. He thought of [the move to Canada] as an adventure and relished not having to take on the mantle of responsibility with his family's business, the Staropramen brewery. It was founded by my ancestors in 1869 and nationalized by the communists during World War II. My paternal grandparents Milos and Hana came to Canada two years after my father established roots here.

"I was an only child, and that was lonely in many ways." She laughs a bit ruefully here. "I could never learn to skip double Dutch. It was my mom and the telephone pole trying to help me learn to skip double Dutch. Still, I had a happy childhood. I loved being on the farm. My father worked the farm full-time and after many years he had built it into something quite substantial." With obvious pride, and a sense of awe, she says, "He started it when he was twenty-five years old and within thirty-one years, he had expanded to 250 acres." With a sorrowful voice, she reveals, "He died in 1987. He was only fifty-six years old.

"The farm was a classic fruit farm of that time in Niagara, comprising primarily of fresh market peaches, cherries both sweet and tart, blue plums, along with Bartlett, Bosc, and Anjou pears. Some years we grew field tomatoes.

"The house I grew up in was a charming white clapboard, green shuttered farmhouse with imposing maple trees (unfortunately long gone now due to old age). There was the red packing barn and then my grandmother's cedar shake cottage, which is where The Good Earth started and where I lived until this year. There is a huge pond that is home to great horned owls and blue herons and other wildlife."

Nicolette recounts without apology that her mother was never the typical farm wife. Betty always worked off the farm. First as a secretary (so was the term then) for Olivetti Underwood Typewriters in Hamilton. Following that role, she taught elementary school, which in and of itself was quite extraordinary. The Teachers University in Ontario wouldn't recognize Betty's credentials from her boarding school in Ireland. Not to be deterred, Betty persisted in the merit of her qualifications and did indeed begin teaching at St. Martin's School in Smithville.

Betty enjoyed her professional career independent of the farm and her husband was happy that she didn't have to be packing peaches. The two supported one another and had a very good relationship. Betty was a source of pride and a welcome respite from the farm life when Karel needed. She was his oasis and Betty adored him. They cherished their time together and often travelled as both a couple and family. Although Betty wasn't always part of the farm crew (there were days that it was all hands needed), Nicolette remembers that her mother did bear many of the worries of the farm and was well informed of the finances and mortgage payments. Since Betty was congenial and charming, she was the person meeting with the bank, and smoothing over documents with lenders.

Nicolette's paternal grandmother, Hana, on the other hand, did work alongside her son. He was an only child and Nicolette remembers her grandmother as overbearing. She worked hard on the farm, kept a sharp on eye on things, and took pride in her role. Nicolette admits that her grandmother often drove Karel nuts, but they valued and respected one another and had a good working relationship. She was a "tough character" and her relationship with her daughter-in-law was strained at best. Hana was a survivor, Nicolette says, a strong woman, cutting her lawn with a push lawn mower at the age of eighty and living well into her nineties.

Nicolette herself worked on the farm since the age of twelve, even confidently driving tractor. After graduating from university in 1981, and enduring a futile job search, she returned to the farm to work for a year. Laughingly, she reminisces, "My dad used to say that I was the best tractor driver of the bunch!" She felt that as the farmer's daughter, not only did she have to pick and pack peaches and cherries and learn to drive a tractor, but she also had to do it better than everyone else because she was family.

She recalls that the year she returned home to the farm to work. She didn't want her watch to be ruined but also recognized the importance of time management. So, she went down to the local drugstore and bought an inexpensive Timex watch just for this purpose. "It was $9.95. It had a Snoopy character on the face, with a little tennis racket counting the minutes. I kept that watch in the pocket of my jeans all the time. It even survived being laundered and put through a dryer cycle. It wasn't even waterproof! When I pulled it out, it was still ticking. I remember being so amazed at the resilience of that watch." With a touch of nostalgia she says,

"You know, when I was moving recently, I came across that old watch. The strap was broken so I got myself a new strap and it's still working perfectly! Just an old-school wind up watch but a relic of the time." She shakes her head with a wry smile.

Nicolette reveals that she never foresaw herself staying on the farm. "We had strong ties to Europe, and we travelled a great deal. I studied international relations and wanted to go into the foreign service. I certainly did not intend to live in Beamsville my entire life. I really thought I would eventually get married and have a gaggle of kids." With pressed lips and a far-off look, she shrugs, "But life throws curves at you."

She returns to her childhood here and tells that her parents had an interesting and diverse mix of friends and family, many of whom had a significant impact on young Nicolette. "As an only child, I was comfortable in adult environments. I really adored my uncle, my mother's eldest sibling. He worked for the foreign service [Secret Intelligence Service, MI6]. His name was Hubert, lovingly referred to as 007 1/2 by all of us. His work was always shrouded in the deepest secrecy. The scope of his work only became known to us after his death. He received the Order of the British Empire for his services to the Crown. He lived in London, England so when he visited, he would come for six weeks and stay with us on the farm in Beamsville. He loved that no one knew him. He could relax, go bird watching, and read. He would spend the holidays with us and that was so special. I really just adored him. I loved when he visited, and it was also the biggest treat to go and visit him in London. He was magical.

"There were other colourful characters as well. In particular, I remember Peter Menzel, a fascinating man and a good friend of my parents. He also came to Canada with nothing at all and built himself a very successful car dealership business. He was an avid sailor and in my twenties he would invite me to join him on sailing journeys in the Med with his family. He was a real renaissance man. Very inspiring. He was very well read, had so many interests and was very, very clever and capable. He was an art lover and an historian, loved music, and supported the early days of Tafelmusik in Toronto. [Exciting, cross-cultural orchestral music played on period instruments. The organization believed in the value of music and the arts and supported the education and training of future musicians.]

"I loved his eclectic mix of being so testosterone driven on one level and on the other, so warm and lovely and artsy. Despite having made it big and being so wealthy, he was humble. When he threw a party, for instance, he invited all his friends from all walks of life. If you were his friend, you were invited and genuinely welcome. It didn't matter if you had zero or plenty. And he always entertained with style. For his sixty-fifth birthday, he threw a spectacular party in his huge car dealership. It was excellently catered by North 44 with Russian service, sixty guests, black tie, trapeze artists, and all the stops pulled out. That's just who he was. He lived large. I just loved him. The last chunk of time I spent with him was in in 2000 when I went on a safari with him and his wife. That was really special.

"He died shortly after, and suddenly, of cancer. That was really tragic and surprising to me. I always thought he would either topple off of his boat into the ocean, or be eaten by a lion on safari, or something… not felled by cancer and dying in a hospital within two weeks. He was very special to me. He and my Uncle Hubert, and of course my parents, were the main influences on me in my youth."

Nicolette pauses here, and as the listener, I can't help but consider the impact these special people had on her. Perhaps the title she created for herself at The Good Earth was chosen as a nod of admiration to them. Listening to her reminisce about her beloved uncle and larger-than-life friend, Peter Menzel… She noticeably admired their ability to pull people together, from all classes, and create a special experience for them, a memorable experience during which everyone present felt significant and warmly welcomed. That is truly what Nicolette herself went on to cultivate at The Good Earth. A place where diverse people from all walks of life, were genuinely welcomed around the table, encouraged to share, and participate and, when they bid farewell, they felt connected and pulled to return to that warmth. That magic was Nicolette.

Prior to embracing this title and her role at the farm, Nicolette had other plans for her life and career. Plans that she admits were derailed in her twenties when her father died.

"Looking back, I've come to think of it as a gift in some ways. I mean, it was awful, it was so awful on so many levels. It was very hard on my mother—she was only fifty-two—and on my grandmother to lose her son." Her brow wrinkles and her shoulders tense in remembering. She sighs deeply and pulls herself back. "I think it some ways, although it didn't seem like it at the time, taking over the farm actually gave me freedom. I would never have come to back to the farm otherwise, and therefore would never have contemplated doing what I did."

Nicolette shrugs and shakes her head in hindsight. "Sure, I could have practised law or something more mainstream. I probably wouldn't have happy doing that for long. Who knows were I would have ended up? Somewhere boring, probably." She finishes with a laugh. (Somewhere boring, I highly doubt!)

"I came back to the farm on July 22, 1987. That was the day my Dad died, and I came back the same day. It was the start of our peach harvest so, honestly, I couldn't do much more than react and hold shit together as best I could. That's all I could do." Her gaze shifts to the window, and she stares outside, memories seem to tug her back in time to that fateful summer. There's a faraway look in her eyes before she takes a deep breath and continues. "When the season was over, I had had some time to think. The truth was, I had always loved the farm. It was my home. I loved the seasonality of farming. I loved the fact that we were reacting along with nature to the seasons. The planning was sometimes difficult but once the season was underway, there wasn't really time to think. Mother Nature was driving the bus and you just had to hop on and go for the ride.

She admits, "Prior to returning, I had been working in Toronto and it had gotten to the stage where I wasn't terrifically thrilled with what I was doing anymore. I was struggling with the question of what next. I think the timing was right in that allowed me to rethink what I wanted to do with my life. I saw this as an opportunity and a challenge. It was only after that first winter that I saw the farm as something that I might do full-time.

"It's crazy really. I was twenty-eight years old, and I marched into the bank and announced that I was going to continue with the farm." She laughs, remembering her young, naive, but confident self. "It's a wonder the bank gave me a dime! I was very lucky. I had a lot of mentors to help me. I didn't have an agriculture degree. Everything I knew about farming I had absorbed by living on the farm, working with my dad, and watching it all happen. It was challenging but I thought, *What the hell, I'm gonna do this!*"

Nicolette names the Ministry of Agriculture, Vineland Research, the entomologists, and Kevin Ker as extremely helpful. Philip Andrewes, a local MPP, became a trusted advisor to her at this time. Coincidentally, they had worked together in Toronto at Queen's Park, but his property also abutted her family farm. Seventeen years her senior, Nicolette had known him since she was a child. "My dad had always said to me that if anything were to happen to him, Philip was the person I could trust. He was incredibly helpful and a wonderful mentor. We ended up going into a partnership together. Still to this day, he is a good friend, and we get together often."

In 1996, after almost ten years of running the farm, Nicolette took a step back. She was coming up to her fortieth birthday and half jokingly says she had what she describes as a mid-life crisis. She reveals that she was, and had been, physically and emotionally exhausted for years. The all-consuming work of running the farm and business left her wholly depleted at the of each day, with little time to focus on her own life outside of the property. A decade after the death of her father, Nicolette finally gave herself space and time to grieve.

She sold half of the farm, leased the balance of the land to Andrewes Farms Ltd., and moved back to Toronto. During everything she had on her plate in that time, Nicolette had also returned to school and had recently completed the Canadian Securities Course (CSC). Shortly after moving back to Toronto, she says she happened to quite literally bump into a previous colleague on the corner of Bay and King Streets. They began to chat and catch up, and the following Monday she began working with a small public relations firm handling investor relations. She enjoyed this two-year time out, as she calls it, and divulges that this time away from the farm made space for her to meet and fall in love with a man, what she refers to in retrospect as "The Big Romance of My Life."

"We plan, God laughs" as the saying goes, and once again, Nicolette's plans were derailed. Her paternal grandmother had lived for years in the little cottage on the Lincoln Avenue family farm. In the summer of 1998, she broke her hip in a fall and had to move into a nursing home. Nicolette reveals that simultaneously, "The big romance went south, and it was time to re-evaluate my life."

During her earlier travels through Europe, Nicolette had visited a unique cooking school in Naarden, in North Holland, in the Netherlands. It left a lasting impression. She remembers pondering the thought of developing something similar in Niagara but tucked the idea away for years. It was during this personal re-evaluation that the idea resurfaced, and the concept of The Good Earth Cooking School began to grow. She returned home energized with new plans. She immediately got to work renovating the little cottage and opened the school in October 1998. Her goal was for it to be a small, intimate place for guests to experience the bounty of Niagara, from her own and other small-scale farms, while learning from and cooking with talented local chefs.

While she loved the family farm, she was also keenly aware firsthand of the monumental amount of work required in running it as a successful, self-sustaining agricultural business each season. Selling so much of it to the neighbouring Andrewes Farms Ltd. freed Nicolette up to develop the Good Earth Cooking School & Food Co., while still living on and celebrating the property she loved. She felt strongly that it was time for her to incorporate some fun into her life, and into the lives of others. With this in mind, she purposely titled herself proprietor and facilitator of fun.

"I wanted to express to people that what we were doing here was fun. That they were going to have fun. That the experience waiting for them wasn't going to be stuffy. People noticed it; it was catchy and fun."

"When I started from my kitchen table, I remember getting people's phone numbers, creating schedules, typing up labels, stuffing, addressing and stamping envelopes, sending out mail... so by the time you came to the cooking school for your first class, I already felt like I knew you, and you me, because we had already had so much correspondence. That truly made each person special to me.

"It was challenging. It was crazy, I didn't have a business plan, and everyone thought I was nuts. But you know, I just had this idea and I needed to do it."

Ever humble, her personal intention was always to celebrate others and the gifts that Niagara had to offer. She provides insight by sharing, "I like to think that I was the porthole into the area. I didn't have any vested interest in any of the other businesses in the area, I just knew that I loved Niagara, it had so much to offer, and it was just starting. You could feel it. It was fun to be a part of that."

Smiling, she continues, "I still remember some of our first guests, and I keep in touch with many of them. Margo Glick, for instance, came out with her friend Janice Okun, the food editor for the *Buffalo News*. They came out on a FAM tour (a familiarization tour designed to build brand awareness for promotional purposes) in 1998 and I have been in touch with and friends with Margo ever since.

Nicolette feels that it's important to remember that this was prior to The Food Network before people were able to see everything that went on in professional kitchens. Chefs simply were not accessible to the average person. Open kitchens weren't yet popular; chefs performed culinary magic behind the dining room walls. She believes that this is one of the reasons that her cooking school was so intriguing to visitors. Introducing grapeseed oil, learning how to deglaze a pan, char and peel a red pepper, or use a rasp. Never mind using copious amounts of 35 per cent cream! These just weren't things that were available to view on YouTube back then.

She wanted to connect people with their food and with the chefs who created these gastronomical masterpieces. It was fascinating for guests to gather around the communal prep table, to listen to the chefs tell stories of the ingredients, their travels, mentors, and culinary journeys. They laughed together, experimented, and were able to ask questions about the hows and whys and various techniques used. Food unites people. Guests went away having learned through a unique experience. They were proud to share what they had mastered afterwards with friends and family and often returned, excited to introduce their own guests to future classes.

It was also novel to showcase the few female chefs in Niagara at that time. There were a few exceptional pastry chefs but very few executive chefs. One of the first to lead classes was talented Virginia Marr, a Certified Chef de Cuisine (CCC), successfully leading the large culinary brigade as the executive chef at the Pillar and Post Inn. She was brilliant and passionate while also putting guests at ease with her approachable manner. The CCC professional designation was the top designation cooks in Canada could aspire to, only achieved after passing the rigorous training and exams required by the Canadian Culinary Federation.

In addition to well-known chefs, Nicolette also made sure to spotlight new and young talent. "Don't get me wrong" she declares adamantly, "I knew there was a need to draw attention to these women excelling in what was then a male-dominated industry, and I wanted to do that, and I made sure to do that, but I wanted to showcase good people, gender aside. The cooking school required something more than just talent or big names. The chefs needed to be engaging, passionate, knowledgeable, and willing to share that knowledge with our guests. I had no room or patience for egos."

There were remarkable pastry chefs, whom, as a profession, back then, were largely uncelebrated, presented almost as an afterthought, along with the dessert menu at the end of a meal. Their delectable creations often regrettably brushed aside with the proclamation, "Oh I really couldn't! I just don't have the room for another bite!" Nicolette believes that one should be presented with the entire menu, desserts included, in order to determine for oneself how limited stomach space or budget room will be allotted.

Therefore, desserts, both sweet and savoury, were always a part of the menu at The Good Earth Cooking School. They were seasonally driven, focused on what was being harvested at the moment, early summer berries, cherries at their July best, juicy August peaches, and crisp autumn apples. Jams, jellies, pickles, sauces, and compotes were often featured throughout the class to showcase the art of preserving nature's bounty and, of course, were available for guests to purchase to enjoy a taste of Niagara no matter the season.

Her keen mind always tuned to ways to celebrate her beloved property and region, a new idea was born. The Blossom Brunch was a perfect way for Nicolette to combine the beauty of spring with a farm-to-table menu prepared by a talented team of passionate female chefs. The fragrant pink and white blossoms promised more good things to come and the VQA wines poured proudly by area winemakers, including Icewine, brought the idea of celebrating seasonality full circle.

It was meant to be a feel-good day all around, planned and orchestrated by Nicolette to showcase the people and produce of Niagara. She wanted to share this magical, beautiful corner of the world with everyone. Those who lived nearby and those who travelled the busy QEW highway each day, never knowing of the wondrous gifts Mother Nature had bestowed here. Nicolette loved watching the enchantment on their faces as guests arrived and exclaimed over the stunning backdrop of blossoms. Signs and sounds of spring were everywhere on the farm, and folks were so ready for the warm sun, bright colours, and fresh flowers. At that time, in 1999, many people were just realizing that there were world-class wineries dotting the Niagara region. Nicolette wanted people to recognize that they didn't need to travel to Europe or California to visit fabulous wineries and restaurants, with picturesque landscapes. Ontario already had all of these within driving distance.

Not a detail was overlooked by Nicolette that day or on any day that followed. As she had when Nicolette's father was alive, Betty was warm and welcoming and happily played the role of proud mother and glamorous hostess. She was equally supportive of Nicolette's plans for the farm as she had been of her late husband's.

When the decision came, years later, to open a winery on the property, Nicolette thoughtfully paid homage to her mother Betty with the creation of the vivacious and popular wine: Betty's Blend. Betty and Nicolette became affectionately known as the Widow Novak and Maiden Daughter.

Time passed quickly, as it does when you're busy, and soon, The Good Earth Cooking School had been open for ten years. Nicolette and her team were doing a lot of off-site catering to wineries who didn't have chefs or food programs of their own. The Good Earth team would cater barrel-cellar dinners, experiences for wine club members, and other seasonal events like harvest and holiday parties. Beyond tiny staff rooms with sputtering fridges packed full of forgotten lunches and expired cream, most of the locations lacked functioning, never mind chef-worthy, kitchens, with space or equipment to roll out five-course meals for fifty or more guests.

As a result, off-site catering was, and often still is, an exhausting circus of endless list making and checking, gathering, packing, lugging, improvising, and setting up a kitchen, and then tearing it all down and packing it up, only to return to your own site and unload and unpack it all again. At the end of these long nights, piles of dirty dishes, utensils, and endless pots and pans still needed to be washed and put away by weary staff members. Most of the time, the price paid for catering is barely break even for the reason that much of this behind-the-scenes planning, executing, and post-event work simply isn't recognized.

Nicolette decided to pull it all together in one place. She had the farm with its produce and space, she had the professional kitchen, she had the talented chefs, so why keep dragging them to other locations when they could create their magic on their own already perfect property? In fact, premium wine grapes had already been planted on the property in 2002 and were being managed by Phil Andrewes and his son Chris. It seemed an easy decision to fill in the remaining piece of the puzzle—a winery.

She did her research, and also gathered friends and colleagues, supporters of The Good Earth, all with minds and opinions she respected, for what she calls "a blue sky session." She asked them where they saw The Good Earth going and growing for success. All agreed that a small craft winery was the best way forward.

They couldn't have known it at the time, but in hindsight, Nicolette reveals that this was, in fact, "a terrible decision" for a multitude of reasons, not least of which was that the opening of The Good Earth Winery coincided with the crippling recession of 2008. Rather than celebrating and flocking to visit a new winery, folks were tightening their wallets and cutting out luxuries like dining out and purchasing wine. Coupled with the volatile political environment and an uncertain US presidential election, the timing couldn't have been worse. But Nicolette herself had already paid out hundreds of thousands of dollars for expensive tanks, barrels, winemaking equipment, staff, and the design and build of a new retail space. These were dark times for many, and she was no exception. In a sombre voice, she admits, "I was terrified. I don't think I have ever felt so close to bankruptcy as I did then. It was a disaster."

Pulling herself back to the present, she regrets that the winery itself had such negative and stressful beginnings. However, she was still passionate in her goal to bring wine and food together in its place of inception, to embrace and share the concept of terroir in such a down-to-earth and approachable manner, and to educate in an unpretentious atmosphere. She recalls an earlier wine class she took with Linda Bramble. Linda passed on her vast knowledge in such an enthusiastic way, insisting that the best wine and food experiences will elevate both the food and the wine, without needing fancy glasses and linen tablecloths.

Nicolette whole heartedly agreed and wanted to bring it back to basics for people. Good wine, good food, good company, in a restorative bucolic setting. It really doesn't get much better than that. Nicolette wanted to create these experiences and make them attainable and unintimidating for the average person. "I wanted to take away the stuffiness and, you know, I really think that helped me turn the corner in a tough market and contributed to the success of The Good Earth as a whole."

When asked who she looked to for inspiration, Nicolette is quick to name Debi Pratt, stating with admiration. "Debi took this area to a whole other level. She is amazing. She did it with class, with intelligence, with elegance. She knew her stuff, but she made people at all levels of wine knowledge feel comfortable. It was simply amazing to witness. I absolutely love her.

"Linda Bramble, too. I really learned so much from her, and not only about wine. I remember the first wine class I took with her. She asked each of us our names, and then repeated them. And that was it! She remembered them! I was astonished. I asked her what her secret was. When I worked in politics, it was really important to remember people's names, the context of their world, and why they were in that circle. You had to know a lot about them. But Linda said what mattered most was being present, in the moment, with who they were right then, with what they chose to share in that introduction. I've never forgotten that. She is an amazing human being, and she leaves an impact on people."

Nicolette is quick to express gratitude for the many people who helped her navigate the winery, from its inception, design, and support along the way. She names Ed Madronich, owner and president of nearby winery Flat Rock Cellars and at that point chair of the Wine Council of Ontario (an organization now renamed Ontario Craft Wineries, comprised of stakeholders with a focus on the development and success of Ontario's VQA wine sector, through partnerships and marketing). Ed was a great source of information, support, and even financial backing when Nicolette's investors backed out.

Len Pennachetti and Helen Young are another couple for whom Nicolette is grateful. "I met Len while I was still farming, and he was just beginning to transform Jordan Village. I remember telling him that I thought his plans were ambitious, to say the least." The Pennachetti family was one of the first to plant Vitis vinifera grapes in Niagara in the late 1970s. They went on to found Cave Spring Vineyard and opened the winery in 1986. With a strong focus on the land, they were early embracers of the farm to table restaurant concept. A like minded visionary herself, Nicolette tells, "When the restaurant first opened I used to bring fruits and vegetables to Michael Olson... I think that's really when my friendship with Len and Helen began. They have become great friends and we have shared some wonderful times together travelling and celebrating life over the years."

It really is remarkable what Nicolette created in such a short time. She recounts, "The cooking school started in the little kitchen in my cottage in 1998. The following year, the outdoor kitchen was added under a huge sail, which having been destroyed once too often by windstorms, eventually got replaced with a steel structure. The year after that, I renovated my single-car garage and added to it, creating the structure, which still houses the cooking school. In 2009, construction of the bistro took place with a pergola covered patio for alfresco dining. The following year, the pizza oven was added. The buildings were all done in board and batten and were designed to mirror the cottage garden style of the original little cedar shake cottage. The laneway was always kept as just a laneway, and the first thing to welcome guests was the impressive and majestic sycamore tree. The family home remained my mother's home until she was hospitalized in 2020."

Thoughtfully, Nicolette shares, "There were so many changes between establishing The Good Earth Cooking School in 1998 and the sale of the property in 2021. The recession of 2008, the pandemic, but mostly, for me, it was my mom getting sick. My focus had to change. She and her care had to become my complete focus. It's tough at the best of times to care for a parent, and to make that transition to caregiver, but especially challenging when you are alone. I was alone and I needed to find a good home for her. In a pandemic, no less."

Awe and gratitude slip into her voice as she adds, "You know what was really amazing in all of that? People came forward to help! Long time guests and friends of The Good Earth who knew and loved Betty. They genuinely cared about her. And about me. That to me, was a real gift. They were invaluable to me through that process. It wouldn't have happened with out them.

"Dr. Zahira Khalid for instance. A young woman, ten years my junior but very accomplished. We met through The Good Earth when she attended a few classes on her own at the cooking school. She had dined with us several times and came to our New Years Eve events on her own. I have always been exceptionally fond of and impressed by her. She is such an amazing woman on so many levels. Just a ball of positivity, radiating incredible energy. I always looked forward to seeing her. Because she was there so often, as part of our Good Earth Family, she had met my mother and had seen some of her decline.

"Zahira came for New Years Day brunch 2020. We started chatting, and she asked intently how I was doing. I just told her the truth. I said, 'Oh my god, Zahira, I really don't know what to do. My mom is in such terrible shape, and I just don't know what to do.' From that moment on, she stepped in. She said, 'Nicolette, this is what I do. I will come on Saturday to assess her, and we will get the ball rolling.' THAT was a game changer. SHE was a game changer. I was at my wits end and really didn't know what to do next. I had been struggling with the system and it was all getting more and more difficult. I had to schedule someone to visit Mom at lunch time while I was working. Her world had shrunk so much as she became more immobile, and the dementia progressed. I could be with her in the morning and the evenings, but I had a business to run. My mom had a good circle of friends herself, all women, who thankfully came to the fore to help and would come and stay with her in the daytime, but it was becoming apparent that this wasn't really working.

"The first week of February 2020, we admitted her to the hospital and Zahira completely took over her file at that time. Mom couldn't walk anymore; she lay in bed in a fetal position and completely fell apart. It was just terrible. She had just begun to adjust when COVID-19 hit and hospitals and went into crisis mode. They were urging me to take my mother home, but I knew I could not provide the level of care she needed. I was feeling really torn. Fortunately, I had a lot of friends who were doctors who told me to stand my ground and keep saying no. I was really coached and supported by them in that decision, and I was so grateful for that. They kept warning me about what a disaster it would be and that convinced me that I was making the right choice for Mom, and also for me. Because I know that there's no way I could have done it all. I had hit rock bottom and I knew it." Her shoulders are tense, and she exhales deeply before continuing.

"I remember one day, in the midst of the pandemic, I was standing in the retail store, alone, because why have staff? Let's face it—no one was coming up the drive, the bistro was closed. I would bring two newspapers to read and hope that I had some wine orders to pack up for delivery or curbside pick up. I remember just slumping over the cash register and thinking, *My God, is this it? How will I ever retire? Will they just find me here dead one day?* Really! This is what I was thinking. The only way out was to sell. I wasn't building a legacy for my family. There was no next generation eagerly waiting to inherit the business.

"My mom and I had been the Widow Novak and Maiden Daughter for so long. With the Widow down for the count it was just the Maiden, and I was tired. Tired on every level. I'm a great believer in that there is a season for everything and everyone, and my season had come to an end. I knew it was time.

"When my mom moved into the nursing home, I was organizing the sale of the Good Earth, and looking for a new home, as mine had always been on the farm property. It was busy and stressful, and difficult for me to get there to see Mom everyday. I told her, 'Mom, you have lots of visitors. People come to see you everyday.' She replied, 'I know. I worked at it my whole life, I worked at making friends.' And you know what? She was right. She had friends in every age group. She loved people, and people loved her. That was her particular gift.

"For me, I think my gift was building. I loved the creativity of it. Everything from designing what it looked like, to creating the feel, getting the sense of atmosphere just right. The farm was my canvas. It was all very satisfying. Challenging but satisfying. It was certainly never boring! It was always changing and growing, never static. Until those last years, I saw opportunities everywhere and I was always excited. I never a shortage of ideas, just a shortage of time and money." She laughs out loud here. "That hasn't changed! I have so many ideas everyday. I could do a million things but… I'm tired. That is what's great about the new gang at The Good Earth. They have ideas and energy. I think that they recognize that were given something special that has an established following and incredible potential, and they can take it to the next level with renewed energy and fresh ideas. All I can say now is, 'Don't fuck it up.'"

Admittedly, the biggest sacrifices Nicolette feels she had to make as the proprietor of a multi-faceted business were her time and her relationships. The regret in her voice is evident as she confides, "I just didn't have any time to invest in friendships outside of the business. Friendships need work, friends need you to be available, to be present, and I just couldn't be. With a restaurant, my work time was everyone else's play time. I missed weddings, holidays, and so many events. I also felt that as a leader, I needed to work as hard as my team. I didn't feel right taking off for the weekend and I lived on property. I ate, slept, and breathed The Good Earth. Don't get me wrong, I loved it, but I don't think I truly knew how much I was missing at the time."

She shrugs and smiles ruefully, "Maybe that was a blessing. I was fortunate in that I did have a few friends who stuck beside me through thick and thin but romantically… I don't think I'm single by choice." She shakes her head and frowns reflectively. "I really just never had the chance, never gave myself the time to go down that road. In fact, I made my real estate lawyer laugh recently when I told them, I may be old, but that doesn't mean I may not find somebody. For the first time in my life, I'm relaxed; I may be able to meet someone and take the time to explore the possibility of companionship. Also, I just didn't want to complicate shit before either. I didn't have the energy for more complications."

Ironically, the connections and relationships that she made with guests top Nicolette's list of rewarding experiences from her time at The Good Earth. She lights up with pride and pleasure as she recalls the people, the laughter, and the stories that were shared over the table at the cooking classes.

"I truly believe that everyone has a story to tell. There was something about the cooking classes that led people to open up, to share things about themselves. For some guests, it was pretty organic, and for others, I had to work a bit. In the end, I think they opened up because they sensed that I genuinely wanted to know them as a person. Which I did. I absolutely love people and love getting to know them. I wanted to connect with them, and I wanted them to connect with one another. There are lifelong friendships that started at some of those cooking classes. People bonding over their mutual love of food and wine, and other things that were shared and discovered in those hours together. Many of those people have stayed in touch with me and tell me that they have travelled with other people they met in those classes. It was just so gratifying and it's truly what kept me going day in and day out. The people." Thoughtfully she adds, "I think sometimes we underestimate the impact we can have on the people around us in small ways.

"I felt good about what we were doing. We didn't overcharge and I believe that guests left feeling that every penny spent was worth it. Smiling faces, meaningful experiences from simple lunches to weddings, helping to make these times special for people. A lot of people ultimately felt part of the family, like coming to The Good Earth was like coming home. That is priceless and so rewarding. That made me feel special to be able to share what was truly my home. From start to finish, The Good Earth was a labour of love and I'm very proud of what we were able to do there.

"I also loved being a part of the greater community, other visionaries, and like-minded people. We were an eclectic bunch. To be successful back then, we had to think outside of the box, be creative, refuse take no for answer, and always continue to push back and question the bureaucratic and political bullshit. I absolutely loved working with and getting to know the chefs and winemakers. I loved their creativity and talent. I loved being a part of all of it. I felt so fortunate to be doing what I was doing with this group."

For Nicolette, one of the hardest things about the sale of The Good Earth was the timing. In the middle of the pandemic, while gatherings were banned, there could be no last soiree, no great celebration of what they had created, no grand finale. She wishes she could have pulled her cherished people close to her, on the land she loved, for a final thank you to both the people and the magical place she feels they created together, for a proper goodbye and a passing over of the stewardship to the new owners. Sadly, she says, "It was very anti-climatic. I just packed up and drove away. That was all I could do." She shakes her head, shrugs her shoulders, and lets out a deep sigh.

"I grew up on that farm. I lived on Lincoln Avenue from the age of four, and I'm now sixty-three. That's a long time to live in one place, almost sixty years. The only time I lived away from that land was my few years in Toronto."

During her time in Toronto Nicolette had loved to entertain. She would often invite friends over and throw dinner parties. She says, "From the day I opened The Good Earth Bistro, I don't think I threw one dinner party. I just didn't have the time to plan and orchestrate that."

One of the plus sides of selling The Good Earth is that Nicolette now has time for the things and people she loves, on her own terms. One of her favourite things to do is still to share good food and good wine with good company. She sometimes has two or three dinner parties a week in her new home. She loves thoughtfully planning and cooking the meals and choosing the wine. Not surprisingly, her main passion remains the people whom she draws together over the meal.

The consummate hostess, her notebook of scribbled ideas and recipes to try also contains thoughtful Venn diagrams with overlapping circles of people and groups she would like to connect with, and to connect with one another for mutual enjoyment and benefit. She reveals that this notebook is comprised of three columns of names. When making a guest list, she takes care to never group people with others they know. Instead, she groups them based on things they have in common, hence the Venn diagram. Many of the names are folks she met through The Good Earth who have since become friends that she now has time to invest in. "It's an art to put the right people together," she says.

Always the connector, Nicolette's goal is building relationships. As she did decades ago when planning The Good Earth, she views herself and her home as the portal for bringing people together. She may feel that food and wine are the glue, but we all know that the real glue, the real draw, is Nicolette herself. Warm, welcoming, generous to a fault, Nicolette continues to greet her guests with the same genuine smile as she has since 1998 when The Good Earth was an extension of her home.

"I'm having fun and it's great. Sure, I'm filling other people's plates and cups but, really, in the process, I'm filling mine again. I'm in a new place, a new town, a new home, I have no connections to any of these things. I need connections with good people as I figure out how I want to move forward with my next chapter. I'm just getting my footing."

At the end of the day, getting together with loved ones, the unwinding, the unburdening of one's worries and fears, the lightening of one's load through sharing, is really where much of life's magic can be found. She has once again created a place where people are genuinely welcomed around the table, encouraged to share, feel connected, and pulled to return to the warmth and the magic that is Nicolette.

She's become involved with Bravo Niagara. Co-founded by a mother and daughter team in 2014, the not-for profit organization brings together world-class musical artists. The website reads: "Take the beauty and cultural heritage of the Niagara Region. Mix in musical excellence, social activism, education, and a love for the arts. What do you get? A one-of-a-kind festival that you won't soon forget." It sounds to me like Nicolette is finding her circle of eclectic, creative, visionaries, a circle whose goal is also to bring people together, to celebrate one another and the beauty of Niagara.

All that being said, Nicolette admits that she really doesn't know what life after The Good Earth will hold. As we talk and I write, we are still in a pandemic, life remains limited and small in many ways. She is looking forward to putting down some roots and planting gardens. She misses her gardens and her soil, lush with decades of nutrient rich diversity. "I realize they will never be the same because that takes time, and I probably don't have another twenty years, but I have today."

She reminds us: "Life changes in a heartbeat. Nothing lasts forever. Sometimes we don't realize this until later in life when we lose someone close to us. But it's true. That in and of itself is frightening, but it also offers opportunities if we can see them. That's what life has shown me. In the tough times, just get through it. One day at a time. They will pass. Be flexible. Dig deep. Be strong. Control what you can and remain focused on the key things; good friends, family, and good health—physical, of course, but also emotional and spiritual, whatever that may mean to you. We each need to feed our spiritual soul as much as we feed our body. These are the things that will sustain us."

Reflectively, she shares, "I remember when I got the news that my dad had died. I was in my twenties, living in Toronto, I had a cool job, a great apartment, nice clothes. And then the call came. It was shocking to all of us. I remember driving back to Beamsville. A few days later, all of my mom's family had flown in from Europe. The house was full of people; it was noisy and roasting hot. I couldn't sleep. So, at four in the morning, I was sitting on the front stoop of our kitchen steps, in the cool air, and I said to myself, *This is it. You've got a choice to make. You can either crumble or you can pick yourself up, face the next day, and see where it takes you. You either move forward or you fall apart.*

She lifts her shoulders. "I thought then, and I still believe now, that moving forward makes the most sense. But let's not kid ourselves. It's hard and there is no guarantee things will work out. Focus on what matters, good friends, good family, good health, in all ways."

"You know," she notes now, "it's ironic that I didn't want to farm anymore because it was all encompassing." She laughs and shakes her head. "I had no idea that what I was starting was going to grow into what it did, and demand just as much of my time and energy.

"I seldom took the time to think about what I had created or what it was like for people to arrive at the property for the first time because I never sat in my garden, you know, just sat, and looked around and thought, *Wow, this is really beautiful,* because honestly, I didn't have the time. I was so busy building and assembling all the puzzle pieces. I ran like a lunatic. All the time. But you know what?" She smiles widely, leans forward, and reveals in a gleeful stage whisper, "It was fun. It was a great journey, and I would do again."

SHARING A GLASS

Tributes to Nicolette Novak

Nicolette Novak by Chef Virginia Marr

To preface this tribute, I connected with Chef Virginia Marr via video call. She made it abundantly clear that The Good Earth was truly a magical place. Over the course of our conversation, she let me know that it wasn't just fruit and vegetables Nicolette grew on the farm; it was also people.

The word terroir is derived from the word "terra," meaning earth. In the wine world, terroir refers to the unique characteristics of a specific place: the environmental factors, the soil, the sunlight, the quenching rain, strengthening breezes, the climate, the nutrients in the soil, and the growing conditions and atmosphere around each vine. Terroir is thought to contribute to the characteristics of the grapes, and the finished wine itself.

In our conversation about Nicolette, Chef Virginia Marr likens Nicolette to terroir and the people she mentored to the vines. "She gave us a place to grow. She nurtured our soil and impacted so much of who we each became because of her. Yes, we chefs came to the cooking school to share our love of food, but we stayed because of Nicolette. The food became secondary. The community that she created was what was so important to all of us. And Nicolette herself. Just being around her elevated us all.

"I remember the early Blossom Brunches. They were wonderful experiences. We were all up and coming at that time. Without Nicolette's help I don't think that we would have blossomed like we were able to at that time. Everyone who ever came to a Blossom Brunch loved it. They touched each of us personally because guests could talk with the chefs, they could talk with the winemakers, and they could talk with Nicolette, who really was the hostess with the mostess. Betty, Nicolette's mother, would circulate through the guests and make a point to connect with all of them. She was truly extraordinary, and the only person who could pull off leopard print and costume jewelry and look fabulous!"

"Nicolette was very grounded. We could all talk to her. She listened and she cared about each of us. She was very knowledgeable about who was who in the area and she always managed to find the right fit for everybody. Like, 'Oh, you want to do this? This is who you should work with. Let me connect you.' A few years after the first Blossom Brunch, all of us girls were together at The Good Earth celebrating because Anna [Olson] was getting her own show. We were all so thrilled for her. It was a sisterhood.

"You know that song, by the Eurythmics? 'Sisters are Doing It for Themselves.' Well, we used to sing it: 'We're coming out of the kitchen, 'cause there's something we forgot to say to you. Woman to woman, we're singin' with you.' We had so much fun, and Nicolette was the facilitator. None of it would have happened without her." Virginia is laughing here, remembering, but there is an emotional catch in her voice before she continues.

"Years later, Nicolette helped us out with Women in Gastronomy (WIG). She was quintessential to organizing that and she was the master of ceremonies. It was still a pretty novel concept. We worked with and celebrated female winemakers and chefs. We held the event at the Pillar and Post where I was the executive chef. We secured great sponsors and included a competition with awards for the female culinary students at Niagara College."

The culinary and winemaking industry was, and still is, notoriously difficult for females to work their way up in. For anyone with children or family members to care for, it poses real challenges of long hours, evenings and weekends, physically demanding work, very little recognition, and very little monetary remuneration. A supportive community was and is invaluable. Women in gastronomy sought to create and provide that community by showcasing successful women in their respective fields and bringing them together with the next generation.

"Where you've been doesn't matter to Nicolette. Where you're going matters to her. She accepts all parts of you, quirks, and all, and she wants you to be successful. I think she saw something special in each of us whom she invited to The Good Earth, into her own kitchen at the beginning. That's where it all started. Nicolette would set up a few stools around her breakfast nook and couple high tops. It wasn't an era where chefs cooked in front of the guests. That was Nicolette's vision."

Fondly Virginia recalls, "We were allowed to be awkward as we built up our confidence. It was a safe space. I remember one of the first times I was cooking there. I was making a smoked bacon cornbread and I totally forgot to put the bacon in." She shakes her head with a smile "After I put the cornbread in the oven, one of the guests says, 'Hey, weren't you supposed to put the bacon in there?' I said, 'Oh yeah! Well, we'll use it somewhere else!' And it was okay! Nicolette poured more wine, we all laughed, and it was okay.

"I believe, looking back, that this was the launching pad where I began to gain the in-person confidence I would need to later become a chef professor. In the meantime, it certainly gave me the confidence to venture out of my own kitchen into the dining room at The Pillar and Post. I became comfortable speaking with guests, answering their questions, bantering, joking. That took some bravado that I didn't always have."

"The Good Earth was a place, but Nicolette was the terroir we were able to grow from."

Nicolette Novak by Elisabetta (Isa) Mottiar
Celebrated Niagara Chef

"When Jennifer asked me to compose some thoughts about Nicolette, I thought, "Where do I even begin?" How to express the impact this remarkable woman has had on my life and the community of Lincoln?

"I have known Nicolette and her family forever, literally. My mother had worked on the family farm with other Italian immigrants since their arrival to this country, and I spent my youth by her side there. Eventually Nicolette's farm is where I spent some of my best teenage years toiling away at her small fruit stand. Although she was the boss, she would become a good friend and mentor.

"Nicolette is the definition of motivation and courage. She will keep you on your toes when manners and etiquette are questioned; it is a joke around the house that we will send my daughter to Nicolette's for a week to learn proper etiquette... Or is it? She has allowed many of the female chefs in Niagara and abroad to be celebrated for their talent and has always been an advocate for all chefs, as her love for good food and wine shines through each plate and glass of vino that she shares with her friends. Did I mention her friends were also all the customers she welcomed to Good Earth? They kept her going through the roughest of times, and she allowed moments of respite and self-indulgence for them when needed. She also gives great hugs. The BEST!

"Nicolette is someone whom you can trust to give you her most honest opinion when needed. I have benefitted from countless conversations that have helped me through life. There are too many good laughs, excellent dinners, moments of heartache, and honest and provoking conversations to mention here. Nicolette, the resilient and wonderful woman I call a friend, mentor, and visionary."

Nicolette Novak by Chef Ross Midgely

"I remember my very first experience at The Good Earth, in 1999, when Nicolette was still running intimate cooking classes out of her small cottage home, tucked neatly in behind the old schoolhouse which would eventually become TGE (and then the bistro, the outside wood oven, the winery, the gardens... My God, what a powerhouse of vision, determination, and follow-through she is!). I was cooking under Stephen Treadwell at Queens Landing Inn, who had been invited to be a guest chef for the day's class. Needing a pair of hands to do the "heavy lifting," Stephen asked me to come along as "apprentice."

"I will never forget coming into the kitchen where Nicolette was setting up for the guests and being embraced by Nicolette's mother, Betty, resplendent in leopard-print blouse and leather pants. In her aristocratic Hungarian-English accent, she asked me if I was "passionate." The Earth tilted a bit on its axis; where, exactly, was I?

"Nicolette seemed to like my chutzpah and I began to be invited as "guest chef" going forward. Since that day, Nicolette has been a support of every sort to me: a mentor, a therapist, a co-conspirator in the world that is Niagara hospitality. I ended up conducting more than seventy classes over more than twenty years with Nicolette at TGE, and even spent a season "over-summering" as a cook in her exquisite bistro.

"Nicolette's approach to hospitality is the most authentic I've seen in anyone over my career; it's in her bones! Well raised, she has poise, intelligence, passion, intensity, understanding, compassion, and tenacity. She is mirthful, mischievous, and happy to throw F-bombs with all the pirate chefs she allows to co-host with her. Driving into every class all those years, I knew I would be passionately embraced (like mother, like daughter!), get a big kiss and, then, as I was about to begin my class, she would say something like: "Doesn't Ross have such a deep radio voice, the frequency that make your ovaries tingle…" Red faced and flustered, I would begin, knowing it was a truly friendly tousle and that she was firmly "in my corner." And she was, every single time we got to do the "Ross and Nicolette show."

"Finally, and I am stretching no truth here, the entirety of my cuisine, my menus, my approach, have been moulded by Nicolette's hand and baked in TGE oven. I am not alone—Nicolette has grown so much of Niagara's culinary talent. I made a pact with myself that every time I was invited to submit menus to Nicolette for our upcoming classes that I would always put at least one dish on the menu that I had never tried. Some were winners, some were losers, and many stuck around to be my voice through food—it was Nicolette who supported that. I will never forget it and the bravery it took for Nicolette to allow up-start cooks all over Niagara to paint freely on the canvas that bore her name. Unprecedented support and conviction, not only for what she was accomplishing for her business, but for every cook that she allowed!

"I am thrilled to say that Nicolette is still very much in my life (mostly therapist these days!). She is a treasure and a rock for me. I love her. And I bet if you've had the pleasure, you do, too."

Nicolette Novak by Leonard Pennachetti and Helen Young
Leonard Pennachetti, founder of Cave Spring Vineyards
Helen Young, founder of Inn on the Twenty

"Nicolette has been a vibrant and engaging friend to us, to our businesses (Inn on the Twenty and Cave Spring) since our inception here in Lincoln. At the beginning, Inn on the Twenty was started with the objective of expressing the abundance and joy of Niagara to folks who perhaps viewed It as merely the route to Niagara Falls... We knew it was so much more. Nicolette assisted us by literally heaving great bushels of tree fruit to our kitchen back door that we incorporated into our menu—a distinctly new concept in the early '90s. We used to put our kitchen inventory out front in our dining room in the bushel baskets it came in and guests would wonder at it: "Where is this from?" and "How do you get such beautiful fruit?" were common questions. To us, it was hard to credit, but folks just flew past Lincoln's farms and orchards without much more than a glance in order to see [Niagara] Falls. Nicolette engaged with us in the ambition to make people stop and smell, not the roses, but the apricots, cherries, plums, and peaches of Niagara.

"The inception of Nicolette's cooking school, The Good Earth, was a further step in embedding in customers' minds that we had a glorious region right here in Ontario. To cook amid an orchard: what could better convey the message we sought to spread? And, of course, for it to be done in style and in her inimitable good humour made it an instant success.

"And then finally, to start a farm winery at Good Earth brought Nicolette into our peer group as a winery owner. Again, her wit and intelligence benefitted our joint interests as she acted as an articulate and passionate spokesperson for our industry.

"But most of all, our greatest benefit from knowing Nicolette is her personal friendship. Her generosity and hospitality is so widely recognized that we need hardly say much on this score, except that an invitation to her home is jumped at without delay!

"Finally, Nicolette is an inheritor of a family tradition of entrepreneurship, kindness, and joie de vivre from her family. Karel and Betty, her parents, and her whole clan of cousins have had the great good fortune of seeing their history played out in a way that extends all that they have prized over the decades. They and us have been enormously enriched by her passionate hard work."

Madame Andrée Bosc
(1935– 2021)

A book about Niagara wine history, or Canadian wine history, for that matter, would not be complete without mentioning le grande dame of the industry, Madame Andrée Bosc.

Mother, wife, grandmother, teacher, winery matriarch, and Niagara ambassador extraordinaire, Andrée was full of life and full of passion.

Regrettably, I wasn't able to interview Madame Bosc for this book, to ask her the same questions as the other women or hear her stories firsthand. What is shared below is only a small portion of her incredible life and impact.

What I remember about her and hear consistently from all who knew her or had the pleasure to make her acquaintance in any way, was that she lived life to the fullest, that she embraced every day as an opportunity to make an impact on the people around her. And make an impact she most certainly did, on her students, on visitors to Château des Charmes, and on her colleagues, friends, and family.

She was born in extremely humble circumstances in French Algeria, North Africa. She was the third generation of her family born there, a family who went from Spain to Algeria to work for the French. She was a young wife and mother in her twenties when she came to Canada with her husband Paul and their young son Paul-André. As the family's first language was French, they settled in Montreal where Paul Sr. begin working at the SAQ, the Quebec liquor board. When Paul was offered a winemaking position with Château Gai in Ontario, he asked his wife what she wanted to do. They had arrived in Montreal only ten months prior, she was pregnant with their second child, she didn't speak English, and she was tired from being on the move. But Paul was a winemaker, that's what he wanted to do and Andrée believed in him. She wanted him to have this opportunity and she was willing to sacrifice for him.

In that moment, Andrée made a decision that impacted not just their small family, but also the Ontario wine industry. Without her approval, the young couple would have stayed in Quebec. Instead, they packed up and headed to Ontario, eventually opening their own winery. Paul Sr. grew the grapes and made the highly reputed wine. Andrée, in addition to running the winery's finances, working full-time as a teacher, and raising their family, became the heart of its infamous hospitality, setting a standard of excellence for the region.

She innately understood that relationship building was key. She didn't just pour wine for visitors, she poured herself into every experience they had, by sharing stories, recipes, her hand knitted blankets, laughter, and friendship. It has been said many times that people visited Château des Charmes for the first time to try the wine, but they returned to experience the level of hospitality and genuine connection that was Madame Andrée Bosc.

The winery website lists the Bosc family team members and includes this about their matriarch:

> Madame, as she was affectionately called, was a former French teacher who loved welcoming her former students to the winery. She was a tremendous ambassador for the winery. In 2006 she, along with her husband, were named Niagara-on-the-Lake's Citizens of the Year and presented with the Lord Mayor's Award of Excellence. Madame Andrée passed away March 6th, 2021. Madame wore many hats (and scarves!) during her remarkable life

including a legacy as a great ambassador for Château des Charmes and the Niagara wine community.

That year, Château des Charmes made a vibrant rosé wine in her honour, the 2021 Rosé, Cuvée D'Andrée, with the following note:

"We dedicate this delightful Rosé to Madame Andrée Bosc—wife, mother, and winery matriarch. We wanted to make a wine with as much joie de vivre as Madame."

JENNIFER WILHELM

Tributes to Madame Bosc

Madame Bosc by Suzanne Janke
Estate Director
Stratus Vineyards

"I joined Château des Charmes as hospitality director days after returning to Niagara from a three-year stint teaching in Kyoto, Japan, and Seoul, South Korea. The events coordinator position was posted in the local paper the day my flight arrived. As I had worked in agritourism throughout my youth and for the best caterer in the region before my stint in Asia, the wine industry's evolution was of great interest to me.

"As a young twenty-something, I imagined this post would last a year or two. Paul Bosc Jr. hired me. During the final interview, his father, Paul Sr.'s first words to me were, "Teaching... teaching... what the hell does that have to do with anything?" Taken aback by the abrupt and strong tone of his voice, I became keenly aware that I was joining a family business of strong, no-nonsense characters, and that I was going to have to prove myself in short order. Soon after, I met the winery matriarch—Madame. Like many, I was already perplexed at the "personality imagined" behind someone simply named Madame. Minimally coiffed, in kaftan and clogs, she appeared simple and unassuming. Yet her pace, strength of character, and almost brash confidence contradicted any perception of simplicity. This force never diminished throughout my near-decade of employment there. Her hands were always full of the day's cargo—papers, files, books, groceries, supplies for the winery, knitting needles and yarn and, of course, her Bichon Frise.

"At first, she paid little attention to me, referred to me as Susan instead of Suzanne, and carried on about her business as though I was not even there. My first major task was to host a New Year's Eve gala, and with a full house, I was able to first witness her Madame persona in full force. The new Château building had only opened a year before, and the guest list included well-heeled and passionate boomers from across Southern Ontario, many of whom had been Charmes' fans since the early days. While now in a grand foyer with spiral staircase and chandelier, many guests happily recounted stories of washing their own wine glasses alongside Madame at the Creek Road estate vineyard kitchen at events held there.

"As I witnessed for the next nine years, this interaction between guests and the winery remained steadfast. She entertained everyone with dynamism, humour, and stories. She was a "star"! Customers adored and were intrigued by her strong, magnetic character. She'd entertain all week long and several evenings into the wee hours. During private events that had rented the tent-covered terrace, she could be found sitting at a corner white wrought-iron patio table overlooking the splendour of the event with a glass of wine, sometimes confused as a guest; other times well known as "Madame." And after the attendees had all gone home, she would spend time sipping and chatting with the catering team, chefs and servers alike. And while one might think she'd take the following day easy, I can't remember a single one where she wasn't hustling around the Château, overseeing the cash transactions, handling the mail, banking, and admin. She was a "tough" cookie… There was no time off, no vacations, and no excess.

"In my early days, I didn't appreciate the tremendous stress she must have been under. I didn't understand the historical context and inherent challenges of leaving French Algeria and being forced to restart a home and life in a new country. I underestimated the fear and financial burden incumbent with a new multimillion-dollar investment that relied on agriculture, the continued resistance of the Ontario wine marketplace, and never mind the responsibility and exhaustion of being the sole female amidst a diverse and powerful family trio of men. There were often tense and opposing views on operational items, but she rarely relented. She simply did not waiver. This was sometimes hard for employees. It was sometimes hard for me. I remember little details we would argue over—white lights versus coloured lights, real plants versus artificial ones, and the types of cheeses served to guests during a tasting. I learned over time to approach our differences with facts and objectivity instead of emotion and deferred to her "proprietorship" as much as possible without compromising my own beliefs or integrity. And over time, she and I became quite close, and I believe she trusted me and my commitment to the business and industry. She appreciated my hard work and long hours, and I appreciated her ability to seduce guests and hospitality professionals, administer a good part of the business, and maintain her role of motherhood and wife all the while. She had a distinctive "joie de vivre," which seemed best expressed when she was host to the joy and appreciation of the wines, the atmosphere and the "fruits of her family's labour."

"An avid reader and knitter, Madame loved children and long hoped to be a grandmother. Baby blanket after baby blanket was knit, often while entertaining winery visitors. Many of these were offered to customers, staff, or friends who had little ones arriving in their lives. I was lucky enough to receive two of these blankets that I continue to treasure despite my sons having well grown out of their use.

"She was an undeniable force in the early days of Ontario's wine industry. Anyone who knew her will acknowledge all she did to pave the way for today's modern experience of wine and wine culture. She painted it with her own unique brushstroke, infinite energy, and commitment. A very special person indeed, her boundless energy and pride in her family conveyed in every glass poured and shared.

Madame Bosc by Debi Pratt

"Andrée Bosc (Madame) and I first met through our full-time teaching careers and we both found ourselves drawn part-time into the wine world. Whenever we were not in the classroom, we were expanding our love of wine. As time went on our paths crossed more in the wine world with Madame's involvement in her family business, Château des Charmes, and me with Inniskillin.

"She always greeted everyone with her infectious smile and genuine welcoming nature. She was such a vibrant person embracing all that she did whether as a teacher or in the wine business or her love for her family.

"I shall treasure my memories of my time with her over the years and I will always picture her with a smile on her face. We laughed at us finishing our teaching day and driving to Toronto to work at our winery tables at the different wine shows. We would wave across the room at each other, laugh, shake our heads, and continue to pour wine. When the evening was over, we would chat about how crazy we were to drive an hour and a half to continue our night duties after a full day in a classroom. Exhausted but happy, we both loved what we did. We each understood the hectic pace but still needed to laugh about it together. We did it because we knew we had to for the success of our wineries, but we genuinely wanted to as well.

"She and I were doing similar things early on. I would have guests visit Inniskillin in those early years and I would ask them where else they had been. If they said Château des Charmes, I always asked if they had been lucky enough to meet Madame. If they had, they would rave about her and their experience: "Oh yes, she took us into the cellar, and we tried this amazing wine that isn't even out yet!"

"Madame built an incredible and loyal clientele base. She knew how to make people feel special and also to sell wine. I would then call her up and say, "Andrée, I hosted the same people as you did today. They told me all about their visit with you." And we would laugh and share stories. Really, I just used it as an excuse to call her, to laugh together. She was a very strong woman and an early mentor.

"She was the master at garnering loyal customers with her personal touch. She shared stories, special wines, and always welcomed everyone to Château des Charmes on behalf of the Bosc family. Château des Charmes's customers loved the wine, but they also really loved Madame. Madame's strength, enthusiasm, and tireless energy was present in all she did—through tastings, tours, launches, special events, wine dinners, trade and consumer shows, or "hosting the world."

We looked to each other for advice or simply to share thoughts that were good for Niagara-on-the-Lake and our entire wine industry especially regarding tourism. She was very vocal on what she believed in and shared her many messages about our quality wines and tourism wherever she could. She spoke with conviction and confidence with her passion showing through at all times. It's hard to believe that her voice has now been silenced but her years of contributions will always be remembered by those of us that were lucky to know her, work with her or simply call her our friend.

"Along with her husband, Paul, and two sons, Paul Jr. and Stefan, the Bosc family were all involved and recognized as an amazing pioneering family building a strong reputation with their premium, quality wines and their many efforts to keep building our wine industry. She was so important to this groundbreaking era.

"She was simply the best!!! What a legacy she has left for her family, Château des Charmes, and the Canadian wine industry. She will continue to be an inspiration and role model for women in the wine world as well as women in the business world.

Afterword

Sue-Ann Staff has the rare and enviable position of being personally impacted by *all nine* of the extraordinary women featured in this book. She may not be the only one, but I sought out her perspective as Sue-Ann fills a unique position between the Ontario wine industry's founding generation and those just beginning to shape its future.

Sue-Ann's roots run deep in Niagara's grape and wine industry. Her family has lived on their Jordan, Ontario, farm for 200 years. She is the seventh generation to reside and work on the property, the fifth generation of grape growers, and the first generation to combine grape growing and winemaking on the ancestral site.

Sue-Ann has been immersed in Niagara's tight-knit grape and wine industry since birth. Some of her earliest memories are centred around harvest celebrations and wine festival parades. She is the descendant of two early Grape Kings, her grandfather Lavelle Staff, in 1967, and her father Howard Staff, in 1996. This prestigious recognition drew likeminded folks to the family farm. Young Sue-Ann trailed along on countless vineyard walks, assessing soil health, sun exposure, Brix levels, phenolic ripeness, and potential harvest dates. She was privy to many kitchen table discussions about grape growing, politics, and early winemaking in Niagara. Long before she could imagine the impact each would personally have on her, the names of Donna Lailey, Debi Pratt, Helen Fisher, and Debbie Zimmerman were part of daily discussions. She remembers that her father had immense respect for these women, the valuable work they were doing, and the significant contributions each was making in the grape and wine industry.

She shares a few memories of each of them here.

Debi Pratt

"I remember hearing Debi's name in our household from the 1970s onward. Inniskillin was gaining traction, and it seemed in the news every third day. The spotlight was on Donald and Karl, but Debi connected the dots, took pictures, contacted the press, and cut out newspaper articles to chronicle their success. She executed the public relations campaign. It was spectacular the way she pulled everything together. I don't think anyone else could have done it as successfully as Debi did. She was able to blend the skills of hospitality, education, communication, public relations—not to mention planning and execution because those are very different skills. But Debi did it. It was and is impressive to this day. There was no one else she could have looked to as a role model at that time. There wasn't anyone else doing this. She created the role. She somehow could see everything that needed to come together and worked tirelessly to make it all happen.

"Debi herself was always quick to give credit to Donald and Karl, but the truth is, Debi made so much of what they accomplished possible. She pulled in the public relations piece. She connected with the royal family to arrange Donald's seating with Charles and Diana. Or Pierre Trudeau's visit or that of the Queen of Bhutan. It was Debi behind the scenes with her eye on the details.

"I tell you, no one can take charge of a microphone better than Debi. She commands attention, and people listen. I remember when she was the keynote speaker at Wine, Women, and Style, a fundraising event that took place at a luncheon. People were talking, and Debi said, "I will stop until I have all your attention. Yes, I was a teacher, and I'm using those skills now." The room was silenced. It was incredible to witness. And she would do the same if anyone else was presenting and the audience was talking. She demanded respect, and she did it with such poise. And style. Damn, she is stylish! Always dressed to the nines. That is relevant because her professional attire adds to her striking appearance and commanding personality. She understood effective presentation on all levels.

"I will never forget when Debi got the Women in Business Lifetime Achievement Award. It was so well deserved. Her speech was sensational! I was the stand-in emcee. Each speech was time-limited, and part of my role was to keep the recipients on track. As the Lifetime Achievement

Award recipient, Debi knew in advance, and if you know Deb, you know that she is always prepared. She is so well-spoken. So, I was watching the time and realized that she would go over in time. But what she was sharing was fabulous! It was fascinating history and great stories, so interesting, and everyone there wanted to hear it. She has always had such a great sense of adventure.

"I was lucky to be a part of a cool tight-knit group of women that created a tasting group. It began in 1999. We each had our roles in this group. We were all focused on the same goal: moving our industry forward and supporting each other as we grew. Debi was foundational in this group. There was an exchange of information and camaraderie. We could have called another member for help or advice or to lend an ear. In any situation, the members would have come through in a heartbeat. It was extraordinary."

Helen Fisher

"Helen. My gosh. Helen is an institute in herself. She was the first woman in so many of her chosen fields. One of a kind, without doubt. She is absolutely brilliant. Helen is a woman who knows her audience, the people she is talking to, and the language to use to speak to them. She knows her stuff and will not let anyone make her feel inferior. I've seen it firsthand. Whether she is presenting at an academic conference or standing in a field.

"I once heard her tell an under-drainer, "Listen, I know you know your stuff, but I'm still going to tell you exactly how to lay this tile the way I want it done." Then there's her no-nonsense tone and all the expletives used! But she is an academic, too. I have seen her present her published scientific papers on stage at prestigious conferences worldwide—pick a country—Australia, France, anywhere! She had all the research… data… data… click… next slide. She was direct and succinct and read the crowd. She was the last speaker on the last day of the 1996 International Cool Climate Conference in Rochester, NY. She got up and said, "Okay folks, we've been through so many seminars over the last three days. The last person you want to listen to is me, but guess what? You will all pay attention, and then we are going for beers! So, dig a little deeper, sit up, and pay attention!"

"There are so many sides and strengths to Helen. There is a time to work and a time to play, and Helen excels at each. I am proud of her for the way she does both! At times, the industry changed, but what Helen had to work with didn't. What I mean by that is that grape growing takes time. Years. You can't just plant a new vineyard and instantly have grapes to study. Helen's research material was already dated by the nature of the product. Yet she still made the data relevant and useful. She was sometimes given lemons to work with, but she could always make lemonade.

"She is and has always been, thoroughly committed and thoroughly passionate. I remember meeting up with her in my second year of university. We were supposed to meet on the patio at The Jordan House. She was late and profusely apologized, "It's such a beautiful day! How could I not prune the apricots on such a beautiful day!" She showed up in dirty jeans and boots with pruners in her pocket and ordered a beer!

"We did a research project together in my third year of university. It got published by the *Canadian Journal of Plant Science*. She is named on that paper, along with two other academics. When I re-read that paper, it was written in a language that I couldn't have achieved as a student without her guidance and mentorship. She and the others made it suitable for publication in a scientific journal.

"I honestly can't imagine how many papers, journals, and abstracts she has written! It's astronomical. Whatever huge number I guess at, I'm sure I am still underestimating. She is a force. On top of that, she would have done much of this work when it wasn't funded. She did it out of her love, passion for, and commitment to grape growing."

Donna Lailey

"Donna was very intimidating. She would call it like it is, and she wasn't about to be pushed around or guilted into anything that she didn't think was a good use of her time.

"I first met Donna in 1991. I was the Grape and Wine Festival Queen, and Donna was the Grape King. There were many firsts that year. Traditionally, the parade float held a "Royal Family" comprising the crowned Grape King and a Grape Queen. There had also been a 4H Grape Princess in previous years. This very traditional trio all rode on the royal float together and had a lot of joint industry appearances over the festival season. 1991 was the first time a woman had been crowned Grape King in recognition of her contributions as a grape grower. It shook things up on many levels and prompted my title to be changed from Grape Queen to Festival Queen.

"Donna made an impression. There was no question that she deserved that recognition and honour. She was a proud grape grower through and through, from her knowledge and passion to her capable hands—grape grower's hands. This is hard work, and it shows in your physique.

"Regardless, everywhere we went that year, Donna had to constantly explain to people that she was, in fact, the Grape King. She was a farmer and grape grower, and her husband was a teacher; she wasn't there representing him. She had to prove herself repeatedly. The doubt and skeptical questioning lacked much sensitivity. She was just so matter-of-fact in responding, even if internally, she was frustrated by the same questions over and over. It was 1991, and she was a new phenomenon. I remember being so impressed by her. We spent so much time together that year travelling, making appearances, and eating chicken dinners. The schedule, at times, was demanding. On that note, she further impressed me with her boundaries and pragmatism. We were expected to attend many events and parades throughout the year, and she simply said no. She was a farmer; she had work to do in her vineyards and her successful grapes-for-home-winemaking business. By the end of our "season together," I missed being around her. With me in Jordan and Donna in Niagara-on-the-Lake, our paths didn't cross that often afterwards. When they did cross, though, it was an instant connection and friendship."

Linda Bramble

"Linda took our industry to the next level. We grew grapes well and made wine from them, but one of the things we lacked in the industry was someone to write about us, promote us, and educate us and others, not just about wine but about wine and food, tourism, customer service and its importance. Linda recognized all of that and took us to the next level. Linda was at the forefront of Niagara's shifting focus from quantity wines to quality wines. She reported about it, wrote about it, and educated us about how to serve it and what to pair it with. There were growers, and there were winemakers, and now there was Linda, a certified sommelier and an educator. It was a turning point, and Linda carried us along with her enthusiasm and passion; she made everyone see what we could be.

"I was very young at this point, but I remember my parents talking about her and knowing their admiration for her was exceedingly high. She made enjoying wine—and visiting Niagara's wine regions—a lifestyle choice. And not just for the elite but for everyday folks. She completely removed the intimidation from wine. I don't think she had anyone blazing a path to show her how to do this. She cared so much, and she made everyone else care too. She was so knowledgeable about wine, food, and how the two come together, but beyond that, even, she is so damn smart!

"She coached and mentored us. She put together a session I held here in my dining room one night. It was for women with leading roles in the wine industry. Linda put together this seminar in such an incredible way. It was so engaging, but at the same time, we learned so much from the way she created the experience and shared her knowledge and enthusiasm. She is highly talented; she made it all seem effortless.

Debbie Zimmerman

"My father thought the world of Debbie, so I've always known who she was and have followed her career all the way through. I admired her from the start. When she became Regional Chair for the Regional Municipality of Niagara, in 1997, she was so young but so devoted and focused. When Paul Martin retired as prime minster in 2006, he said on national radio that people were waiting in the wings to take up the reins. He mentioned that there was one woman in particular who was at that time in the private sector (which Debbie was), and he said that he was fervently hoping that this woman would come back into politics to lead this country. I remember thinking, "He's talking about Debbie Zimmerman!" I even asked her, and though she denied it, I still think it was she whom he was talking about. I certainly could see Debbie being our first female elected prime minister. Wouldn't this be an even better country if this were true.

"I always admire Debbie's tenacity and ability to cut through the bullshit and keep discussions focused. She is also a great listener. I'm pretty sure my dad had her on speed dial and called her at least once a month. He had enormous respect for Debbie. Sometimes when people get older, they lose their feistiness and get complacent, but not Debbie. She went to China and Vietnam with Kathleen Wynn, and at every opportunity, she advocated for the Grape Growers of Ontario. "On the bus, Debbie was continually questioning the Wynn team: "How do we get down to FOB pricing? What's the best way to speak to this audience? We have great wines in Ontario, and we want them to buy them! We are here to sell, and how can we best do that?" She has always been so committed to the people and products of this industry. She is also incredibly informed. She is always updated with new developments, from sustainability to the viruses in the vines and plant materials being brought in. Her job requires her to be multi-skilled, and she does it all spectacularly."

Ann Sperling

"The first time I met Ann, we were having our picture taken for a newspaper article about women in wine. I think it was about 1997. She was so friendly and knowledgeable.

"I have followed her career as she promoted organic winemaking and have admired her certainty in this path. She's done all the research and is so informed. She pushed the boundaries. She is synonymous with organic and biodynamic winemaking—not just in Ontario but in British Columbia, Argentina, and Nova Scotia. Her passion, dedication and work ethic are impressive. She also embodies the continuous lifetime learning piece that we all strive for. She is curious.

"As boots-on-the-ground winemakers, Ann and I have traded many stories about chauvinism in the wine industry. There was one instance when a man commented on the plaid work shirt she was wearing the same day another man remarked on the fact that I was wearing a dress while driving a tow motor. I was heading out to an event and realized as I passed by the barn that I wanted to move something. There have been so many ill-considered comments people have said to us along the way, through the 1990s in particular."

Barbara Leslie

"Of each of these women, I knew Barb the least. Our paths didn't cross as often as they did with the others.

"Barb was at Niagara College when I taught in the wine programs there. I admired her teaching style and how she could relate to the students. Wine can get so technical sometimes, and she cut out the fluff and brought it back to what the students needed to know.

"There was also a nurturing side to Barb. Later, she joined our Women Uncorked wine club and was always enthusiastic about everything happening in the wine industry."

Nicolette Novak

"When I was so stressed out and burning the candle at both ends in the first few years of opening the winery, Nicolette's words of wisdom got me through. She told me, "When you get to the end of the day, you just have to go to bed and say, 'Okay, that's all we can do today.'" So, often then, and even now, I hear her in my head, and I say to myself, *Yep, that's it; that's all we can do today.* There is only so much time in a day; we must know when to draw that line in the sand and go home. Pour a glass of wine. Go to bed. When we wake up in the morning, we return to that line we drew the day before and get back to work where we left off.

"Nicolette genuinely led by example. She had an incredible range of skills; she understood and pulled together many aspects of agritourism, from culinary to wine and hospitality. She put it all on the line and took all the risks to bring her vision to life. Nicolette is brilliant. She could have done anything with her life and been successful at whatever she chose. For all of her international travel experience, exposure to culture, and knowledge of politics, she decided to bring it all back to Niagara to pour it into her family farm. She was a visionary. She knew what she wanted to create and worked hard to bring that to fruition. What she created was truly remarkable. She was so ahead of the times. And she was hands-on through all of it. She had her finger on every pulse of that business, from how the till closed at night right through to branding.

"I don't know of a harder worker. She gave her all. And she was wise enough to know when it was time to look at what was next. I don't think she can say that she left anything behind."

Madame Bosc

"The first time I met Madame Bosc was in 1987. I was the 4H Grape Princess that year and Paul Bosc Sr. was the Grape King in 1988. There was an overlap of about a week before the new Grape Princess was announced. His coronation occurred at their original winery on Creek Road in St. David's as their new winery was still being built.

"At seventeen years old, I wasn't quite old enough to drink legally, but that didn't seem to matter to the European Bosc family. They knew I wanted to be a winemaker, and Madame proudly poured their wines and encouraged me to taste them with the group. The following year, I did my high school co-op in the lab at Brights Wines. I turned nineteen during the placement, and as soon as I did, my co-workers made a point of showing me how to taste wine. I told them that Madame Bosc had already taught me how to taste Riesling, Chardonnay, and Cabernet Franc.

"The pride Madame had for her husband, her sons, the grape and wine industry, and what they were doing as a family was so apparent. She just beamed with pride when she spoke about them and their winery. And her dogs. She loved her dogs. I always made it a point to ask about her dogs."

"In conclusion, I think it's important to note that their work isn't just their job for each of these women. These are their passions, lifestyles, and part of who they are."

Sue-Ann, thank you for sharing these memories. You are personally connected to each of these women. They are embedded in your DNA. You carry pieces of them forward with you, their wisdom, passion, and care for others. They will continue to impact others through you and through the many torchbearers who carry their flames onward to light sparks within the rest of us.

PostScript by Author

It's important, and frankly serendipitous, that when I began chronicling the stories and memoirs of these women, in hopes that others would celebrate them, remember them, learn, and draw strength from them – my own life began to unravel, in ways I couldn't have imagined. And, ironically, it was I who drew strength from these women. As I penned their words, I heard their voices and words of wisdom. As I reread their stories, I walked alongside them and was inspired by their journeys until I too, was able to keep putting one foot in front of the other, to forge my own authentic path with faith and integrity.

The process of interviewing these incredible women, and of learning about their impact on others through the tributes generously shared, has been a privilege and an honour. It has also been a gift, one that I couldn't know when I began, just how much I would need.

Our mentors and our role models never really leave us. They become embedded in our minds and hearts, as we stretch ourselves and build our courage muscles. What they pass down to us, we can then pass along to others. The ripple effect is endless when each of us chooses to pass along strength, wisdom, and inspiration.

So, fill your glass, and when it is full, lean over to the person beside you and tip some of yours into their glass. Let's keep filling each others' cups and sharing a glass.